POLITICAL PARTICIPATION
IN A
DEVELOPING NATION: INDIA

Political Participation
in a
Developing Nation: India

MADAN LAL GOEL
University of West Florida

ASIA PUBLISHING HOUSE
BOMBAY · CALCUTTA · NEW DELHI : MADRAS
LUCKNOW · BANGALORE · LONDON · NEW YORK

Madan Lal Goel (1936-   )

ISBN 0.210.22354.5

PRINTED IN INDIA

AT ANANDA PRESS, LUCKNOW AND PUBLISHED BY
P.S. JAYASINGHE, ASIA PUBLISHING HOUSE, BOMBAY 400 038

TO
MY FATHER

Preface

WHAT KIND of people are likely to participate in politics in India? How does political participation vary over major socio-economic and psychological groups? What kind of factors influence such political behaviour as voting, discussing politics, attending political rallies, and contacting public officials? These and other related questions are the topics discussed in this book.

The study is based on analysis of data originally gathered by the Indian Institute of Public Opinion, New Delhi. Important work on Indian political behaviour is currently being done at such places as the University of Michigan, University of California, University of Chicago, and the Centre for the Study of Developing Societies in New Delhi. These data, and those resulting from future relevant studies, may well lead to the revision of some of the tentative conclusions reached at this point or to the statement of others with greater confidence.

The foot-notes in the text will reveal the extent to which I have utilized insights and interpretations of many writers in social sciences. Here I would like to select for special mention the works of Lester Milbrath, Myron Weiner, and Rajni Kothari.

I am grateful to those who read all or parts of the manuscript and offered helpful suggestions: Dr. Lester W. Milbrath, Dr. Donald B. Rosenthal, Dr. Donald M. Freeman, and Dr. George John Miller.

Parts of this book originally appeared as articles in these journals : *Comparative Political Studies*, *Social Science Quarterly*, *Political Science Review*, and *Political Scientist*; acknowledgements are extended for reproducing these materials in this book.

I also wish to acknowledge aid from the Roper Public Opinion Center at Williams College in Massachusetts, which supplied to me the I.I.P.O. materials. Computer time was generously granted by the Computing Center of the State University of New York, Buffalo, where most of the data were analysed. The University of West Florida Research Council provided small, but crucial, funding support for supplemental data analysis.

I am deeply indebted to Mrs. Nancy Whitelaw, who spared time from her busy schedule to go over the first draft of this manuscript. Her skills in locating grammatical, stylistic, and spelling mistakes are indeed remarkable.

Finally, I have no words to record the many contributions of my wife in the completion of this book. She did all the computer programming, performed much of the typing, and helped in proofreading the drafts and in improving the language. But more than all this, she was a constant inspiration and sympathetic critic.

M. LAL GOEL

Pensacola, Florida
October 1973

Introduction

POPULAR POLITICAL participation has been a topic of increased emphasis in recent years. However, political participation in India, which differs somewhat from that in the United States and in the Western European countries, has received relatively little attention in the past. The study reported in the following pages is a beginning effort in the process of identification and analysis of salient trends in attitudes and behaviour in the politics of modern India.

In the literature on political development and modernization it is commonplace to speak of changing participatory patterns in the new nations. Indeed, some scholars suggest that these patterns are the very core of the process of political development. Note, for example, the works of Karl Deutsch, Daniel Lerner, Almond and Verba, and Myron Weiner, among others. Myron Weiner states that "the process of modernization itself creates conditions for increased political participation; and if modernization continues to take place in the developing areas, we can expect both authoritarian regimes and representative governments to be challenged by new participants who want to share power."[1] Daniel Lerner distinguishes traditional societies from modern societies on the basis of participation.[2] Almond and Verba declare that "the new world political culture will be a political culture of participation."[3] And finally, Karl Deutsch speaks of "social mobilization" as affecting "the politically relevant strata of population."[4]

It is true that a participation explosion is occurring in the developing societies of the world. The belief that the ordinary man has political rights and that he ought to exercise them is widespread. Large groups of people who only recently stood outside politics are demanding entry into the political system. In India an increasingly large proportion of the population has come to participate in politics over the past twenty years. Voter participation in the national elections has steadily risen, from 45.7 per cent in 1952 to 47.7 per cent in 1957, to 55.4 per cent in 1962, and to 61.3 per cent in 1967. It declined somewhat in the 1971 parliamentary elections to 55.2 per cent. These turnout levels are in marked contrast to developments in many new nations, and some older ones as well, where governments have sought to restrain participation through military oligarchies or one-party regimes. Elections in India are highly competitive, and on the average four or five candidates contest each legislative seat. The number of parties and groups is substantial. Citizen participation is high not only in elections but also in other political activities. In 1961, 40 per cent of the urban and 34 per cent of the rural population admitted being interested in political matters. In 1964, 40 per cent of the Delhi respondents said that they sometimes discussed political matters with neighbours, relatives, or friends. One out of six persons interviewed in 1967 indicated that he had participated in some activity seeking to influence the governmental decision-making process.

In this study we describe causes and correlates of these various acts in India. The major concern is the determination of social and psychological bases of political activity. How does participation vary over major social groups? Does the level of education, income, and media exposure tell us anything about whether an individual will probably participate in a given political act? Does the age, the sex, or the religion of respondents make a difference? Does political information, party identification, or a sense of political efficacy lead to heightened involvement in politics? Do participants belong disproportionately to rural and traditional or to urban and modern sectors of society? It is to these kinds of questions that this study is primarily addressed.

The purpose of this study, in brief, is to explain political participation. Till recently, very little research has been done on this subject in any major Asian country. Great as is our knowledge about political participation, it is unfortunately restricted to the Western nations. The greatest amount of knowledge is based on evidence collected in the United States; much of the remaining information comes from the European nations; and only scatterings appear from the Afro-Asian world. For instance, not a single work regarding Indian political participation is contained in the 24-pages bibliography of Lester Milbrath's book on this subject published in 1965.[5] The paucity of research in the new nations does not, however, mean that scholars do not make assumptions about political behaviour patterns in the new nations. In fact there is a tendency to presume that the generalizations derived from political research in the Western countries hold equally true for the new nations. Consistent with this belief, it is presumed that men participate more than women, the highly educated more than the less educated, the urban more than the rural, the upper social class more than the lower class, and so on. This study seeks to ascertain whether these assumptions are valid for India and, in turn, to shed light on whether some of the accepted generalizations about political participation are *truly general*.

As a preview, it may be noted that the study reported in the following pages negates some of the popular notions about political participation. The evidence indicates that, at least as regards India, "modernization" has a varying impact on different political activities; it lowers voting turnout while at the same time it enhances participation in other political activities. For instance, greater educational attainment, urban living, and greater exposure to mass media do not lead to higher turnout rates. But these attributes of individuals are associated with greater interest in politics, higher frequency of engaging in political conversations, and participation in citizen-initiated acts to influence government and politics. Our study will show that there are different "modes" of political participation. Different classes of citizens differ in terms of the types of activities in which they choose to engage. If this research is valid, then political participation ought not to be perceived as unidimensional, as it has been done in most of the literature on this subject. Different political acts cannot be neatly arranged on a hierarchical scale, where the basis of hierarchical arrangement is the difficulty of the act. Data will show that in India citizens may participate in more difficult acts (e.g. citizen-initiated activities), but at the same time not participate in the least difficult act (e.g. voting).[6]

Our study is based on analysis of data collected by the Indian Institute of Public Opinion, New Delhi. Some of the surveys analysed are national polls, based on urban and rural samples spread over all India, while others are regional or local studies. Even though the samples are not fully representative of the Indian society, they are useful for the limited purposes for which they are employed, namely, a search for correlations among different phenomena. In Chapter One we discuss the nature of these data in greater detail.

Since this study is exploratory in nature, it emphasizes the acquisition of new knowledge even though this procedure involves a sacrifice in regard to statistical refinements. Many of our hypotheses were suggested by the data themselves. Statistical tests were not used, especially inasmuch as tests for significance on limited data can at best show merely that the hypotheses reached are strongly enough related to justify their testing on new bodies of data.

Parenthetically, we should point out that this study is concerned only with the *level* of political participation and not with the *direction* of political participation. It deals only with the question of who participates in political activities and who does not; the question of why some people prefer one political party over another political party is left for further study.

In Part One we discuss data sources, nature of the samples, utility of secondary analysis for political behaviour research, and our independent and dependent variables. Part Two examines the relationship between socio-economic variables and political participation, while Part Three examines the relationship between psychological variables and political participation. In Part Four, we tie many of these variables together and examine their joint impact on political participation. The final chapter is a summary of major propositions that can be derived from this research.

NOTES

[1] Myron Weiner, "Political Participation and Political Developments", in M. Weiner, ed., *Modernization* (New York : Basic Books, 1966), p. 212.

[2] Daniel Lerner, *The Passing of Traditional Society* (New York: The Free Press, 1958), pp. 50-51.

[3] Gabriel Almond and Sidney Verba, *The Civic Culture : Political Attitudes and Democracy in Five Nations* (Boston : Little, Brown and Company, 1965), p. 2.

[4] Karl Deutsch, "Social Mobilization and Political Development", *American Political Science Review*, 55:3 (September 1961), p. 493. The literature on political modernization is vast and growing. For a useful guide to this literature, see Claude Welch, ed., *Political Modernization* (Belmont, Calif. : Wadsworth, 1967).

[5] Lester Milbrath, *Political Participation* (Chicago : Rand McNally, 1965).

[6] The term "modes" of political participation is taken from Sidney Verba, Norman Nie and Jae-on Kim, *The Modes of Democratic Participation : A Cross-National Comparison*, Sage, 1971.

Contents

Part IV

CONCLUSION AND SUMMARY

List of Tables

ILLUSTRATIONS

PART I

DATA AND METHODOLOGY

CHAPTER ONE

Data Sources

THE DATA which constitute the basis of this study were gathered by the Indian Institute of Public Opinion, New Delhi. The Indian Institute of Public Opinion (IIPO), an associate of the American Gallup Polls, has conducted a number of national, state and regional studies, and several of these are primarily political polls. The first political study, done in June 1955 in the State of West Bengal, was exploratory in nature. Though this was not a national study, the questions tested in this poll proved the utility of survey research methods in India. National studies of public opinion were made in 1957, 1959, 1961, 1962, 1964, 1967 and 1971. These All-India polls, based on urban and rural samples, varying from 2,000 to 10,000 respondents, used many of the same questions as well as similar survey techniques. Constant attention has been given to the level of political awareness, record of the past vote, political communications, and the extent of political participation in several activities.[1] The Indian Gallup polls thus provide a rich store of data which are deserving of thorough analysis.

Unhappily, a couple of the earlier polls are not available at the present time: both the 1957 and the 1959 national polls are no longer in existence. But all the major studies since 1960 were available to this writer through the Roper Public Opinion Research Center in the United States. In the following pages, we shall briefly outline each of the opinion polls which has been analysed for the purpose of studying political participation in this book. In a subsequent section, we will also discuss the sources of bias in the Indian Institute polls, and the extent to which such a bias limits the validity of findings in this study. Finally, in a concluding section we shall discuss the utility of secondary analysis as a technique of political behaviour research. The reader who does not wish to be bothered by methodological problems may want to skip this chapter.

IIPO POLLS ANALYSED IN THIS BOOK

The following discussion will include a description of the nature of each poll analysed here, the size of its sample, the places where the interviews were conducted, and any characteristics peculiar to the poll. Only the polls containing items on political participation were analysed. Several otherwise excellent polls, a few among these with large national samples, were not considered because items dealing with political participation were not available in these surveys.

1961 All-India Poll: This was the earliest study available to us. The sample used in this poll was drawn from both the rural and the urban parts of India. Altogether, 3,540 interviews—2,460 in the villages and 1,080 in the cities—were conducted. The interviews were taken in the months of September and October of 1961. This poll has added significance because it was conducted just before the general elections, held in February 1962. The poll provided us data for two of our dependent variables: the voter turnout and interest in political matters.[2]

Delhi Area Study (1964): This study was the first real political poll conducted by the Indian Institute of Public Opinion. The Institute described this poll as "a pilot study" of motivations that affect political behaviour in the Delhi area. A number of topics were investigated in respect to the last election campaign: meetings organized, the manner in which the respondent heard of these meetings, the newspapers read, the effect of mass media on opinions, and attitudes toward political recruitment. There were also a number of questions regarding partisan attachment of the respondents—which party he preferred, whether he considered himself a loyal member of the party or not, which party would he join if he were to leave his present party, etc.

This poll also provided the largest number of dependent variables explored in this study. In addition to voter turnout, items were available on the following: attendance at public meetings, political discussions with friends, neighbours and co-workers, and monetary contributions to political parties.

The sample was confined to the Delhi Corporation area from which 15 constituencies were chosen on the basis of their being representative of the whole area; a sample proportionate to the population of each of these constituencies was taken randomly to obtain 500 interviews. The Institute could not complete eight of the interviews, and therefore the final count of the poll is 492. The questionnaire of this poll was designed in consultation with Samuel J. Eldersveld of the University of Michigan, and is similar to the one used in Eldersveld's Detroit Area Study.[3] The limitation of the poll was its small sample and its restriction to one city. Its usefulness lay in its having raised more questions than any other IIPO poll concerning political attitudes of the Indian people.[4]

Public Attitudes to Law and Order Poll (1964): This is a study of the attitudes of the Indian people toward the most familiar instruments of law and order, namely the police. The survey is based on two random probability samples of 300 each. One sample was drawn from a major industrial city in north India, Dehra Dun. The second sample was drawn from a rural area in the same geographical location but thirty miles distant from the city. The questionnaire of the study was designed by David H. Bayley of the University of Denver.[5]

This study proved to be of limited usefulness for present purposes. It did contain a large number of questions concerning peoples' attitudes toward the police, but there were few questions which dealt directly with the subject matter under investigation here. In the text, this poll has been referred to as the "Law and Order" or "L & O" study.

1964 All-India Poll: This survey is the first national poll which went beyond the usual IIPO preoccupation with measuring voting intentions of the Indian electorate. The specified aim of the poll was "to find new associations between personal attributes and social attitudes—particularly those connected with economic development and political participation—on an all-India urban and rural sample." The sample consisted of 2,014 respondents, 1,039 urban and 975 rural. Interviewing was done in early 1964.[6]

The whole study owes its origin to Karl Deutsch and Bruce Russett, then of the Political Data Program at Yale University. So far at least one article[7] has been published on the basis of this study. Next to the 1967 All-India poll, this was the most useful study.

1966 Urban Poll: This poll was conducted in May 1966, with a total sample of 2,000. Of these, 1,000 interviews were undertaken in the four Indian metropolitan cities of Bombay, Calcutta, Delhi, and Madras with 250 interviews in each. The remaining 1,000 interviews were taken in ten large Indian cities—with 100 interviews in each city. These cities were: Bangalore, Hyderabad, Trivandrum, Patna, Lucknow, Bhopal, Chandigarh, Ahmedabad, Cuttack and Jaipur.[8]

The poll was limited to the educated cross-section of the universe, i.e. no illiterates were included in the sample. The sample therefore is not representative of all the people in urban India but only of its literate section. The poll was of limited usefulness for present study. Its results have been reported only if they were supported by other more representative polls. Furthermore, only one dependent variable could be explored with the aid of this poll: voter turnout.

1966 Metropolitan Poll: This poll is identical to the 1966 Urban poll, except that its sample of 1,000 was restricted to the four metropolitan cities of Bombay, Calcutta, Delhi and Madras. Like the Urban poll, its sample bypassed the illiterates. The interviewing was done in the months of August and September of 1966.[9]

1967 All-India Poll: In terms of its sample size and representativeness, the 1967 national poll has the most significance for our purposes. The poll was taken just before the Fourth Indian General Elections, and the Institute was staking its reputation on correctly predicting the outcome of the elections. The Institute sought this prediction not only with respect to the party positions in the Lok Sabha but also with respect to their strength in the various state assemblies. For this reason, the sample chosen was rather large: 10,000 persons were interviewed in 15 different states. It may be noted parenthetically that some 843 respondents in the States of Gujarat and Uttar Pradesh were asked questions concerning only their voting record. The effective sample on many measures, therefore, is only 9,157. The sample was half urban and half rural; the interviewing was done over four months, November 1966 to February 1967.[10]

It is fitting to mention that an Institute calculation of the 1967 poll data indicated a 38 per cent support level for the Congress party in the Lok Sabha elections. The Congress party actually received 40 per cent of the popular vote in the 1967 election. In view of the fact that the 1967 poll is the most representative poll available, this writer has placed more confidence in the results from this survey than from others, particularly in those cases where different surveys show conflicting results.

1970 U.P.-Bihar Poll: This was the latest poll analysed for this research.   The poll was conducted in early 1970 following the major split in the Congress party in November 1969.   Students who are interested in public reactions to this split should consult the poll as it contains useful data on this subject.   The sample for the U. P.-Bihar survey is 1,350, divided as follows—Uttar Pradesh: 750 and Bihar: 600.[11]

BIASES IN THE IIPO SAMPLES

No sample is ever fully representative of the universe it stands for. But some samples have greater precision than others.   One factor on which precision depends is the sample size: larger samples yield greater precision by reducing chance errors due to sampling.   An informed estimate is that 1,500 respondents is about the minimum sample size required for a national study.[12]

The Indian Institute of Public Opinion has employed adequate samples for its national polls, varying from 2,000 to about 10,000. However, merely having large samples does not guarantee representativeness.   A rigorous procedure has to be followed to assure that the people selected to be interviewed reflect fully the characteristics of the population.   This can be assured by randomly selecting the respondents, i. e. by making certain that every adult person in the population has an equal chance of being selected.

In this sense, the Indian Gallup samples are not fully random. As it will be immediately apparent from TABLE 1.1, the structure of Gallup samples does not correspond to that of the Indian population as a whole.   Women are grossly under-represented, constituting only about 20 per cent of the samples.   The samples have also a distinct upward bias in the sense that the highly educated and the more affluent are over-represented, and the samples are about half rural even though three-fourths of the Indian population lives in the villages.

One reason for the unrepresentativeness of the IIPO samples is that they are drawn from electoral rolls prepared by government agencies.   These electoral lists are themselves somewhat

TABLE 1.1

STRUCTURE OF INDIAN GALLUP POLLS

	1967 Poll		1964 Poll		Delhi Area Study		1961 Poll	
	No.	%	No.	%	No.	%	No.	%
Sex								
Male	7802	78	1721	85	452	92	2833	80
Female	2191	22	292	15	40	8	698	20
Education								
None	2740	27	465	23	143	30	1234	41
Primary	3955	40	540	27	216	44	1184	39
Secondary	1549	16	668	33	95	19	385	13
College	1705	17	322	16	37	8	197	7
Income per Month								
V. Low (about Rs. 100)	4939	52	486	24	180	36	1547	51
Low (about Rs. 200)	2390	25	820	41	211	43	905	30
Medium (about Rs. 350)	1442	15	411	20	78	16	380	13
High (500 & above)	707	7	81	4	22	4	168	6
Residence								
Urban	5000	50	1039	52	—	—	1080	30
Rural	5000	50	975	48	—	—	2460	70

unrepresentative since they do not include all eligible voters.[13] Second, the task of administering a representative sample in an underdeveloped and polyglot country like India is trying, as any experienced researcher can testify. The reasons for this are the social customs and communication difficulties characteristic of Indian society. Women are not easily accessible to an outside interviewer, for social convention and caste restrictions prevent their being interviewed by an outsider, especially if the outsider is a male. The more traditional and rural the family, the stronger these restrictions. Lack of adequate communication facilities further compounds the problem. Some rural or hilly areas lie in remote regions, making even physical access difficult. And then, of course, there is the problem of great language diversity of the Indian people. To take a national survey, interviews must be successfully conducted in several dozen different languages and dialects.

It might be suggested that one possible way to avoid under-representation of rural residents or of women is to increase their number in proportion to their percentage in the population. However justifiable for a particular investigation, this procedure does not compensate for all the biases. It might compensate for the under-representation of rural dwellers or of women, but it does nothing to compensate for other imbalances in the samples.

In any case, considering the purposes for which these materials are used, the biases present in the IIPO samples do not altogether negate their value. Samples would need to be perfect if we were concerned with determining the frequency of a particular attitude at the all-India level. But at no point do we mean to imply that if a certain percentage of IIPO sample provides a given answer, the same percentage of the Indian people would give that answer. We confine ourselves to an examination of the correlates of certain political attitudes and behavioural patterns. Our purpose is not to determine political participation levels for the whole of India but to see how political participation may be associated with certain socio-economic, attitudinal and political variables. For these purposes, the IIPO data are not without value. Furthermore, the social groups under-represented are themselves a basic unit of analysis, so that their under-representation does not have the same significance. But most important, this study relies upon a number of surveys, spread over a period of time as well as over different geographical locations. This further helps to overcome the inadequacies of the samples.[14]

Even though this writer is confident about the validity of the findings reported in this book, a few qualifications should be kept in mind. Most of the data analysed here were gathered in 1967 and earlier. Knowing the fluid political and social conditions in India, we cannot presume that all the patterns discovered here necessarily hold true today or will hold true in the future. Second, because the samples are not as random as one would like them to be, the generalizations discussed in this book should be taken to apply more to the male, urban and literate sections of the Indian population rather than the country as a whole. Third, our research negates some of the generalizations accepted in Western literature. This should make our study very interesting to students of political behaviour and comparative politics. At the same time, before our findings are fully accepted in political science literature, they need to be tested on new bodies of data. Social scientists working in this area of research would perform a useful service by further examining the hypotheses presented in our study.

SECONDARY ANALYSIS—ADVANTAGES AND DISADVANTAGES

Disadvantages: In comparison with original data analysis, secondary analysis poses certain distinct disadvantages. In a secondary analysis, we are limited to the questions originally asked. Some of the questions which are of prime interest to us may have been only tangentially touched in the original poll. Also, except where personal contact with the authors of the original study is possible, it is difficult to know what the intended purpose of certain questions actually was, and how they were understood by the respondents. Examination of completed interview schedules can remedy some of these difficulties, but these are not always available, as they were not available to this researcher. The second distinct drawback of secondary analysis is that we are limited to the coding originally done. This creates the difficulty that we are not sure how certain categories were actually defined or what the exact meaning of certain codes was.

If more than one study is analysed, we can also run into the difficulty of non-uniformity in coding. Thus, age in one poll may have been broken down as 21-35, 36 and above, and in another study as 21-30, 31-40, 41-50, 51 and above. If this is the case, comparison of different polls is hazardous.[15]

Still another problem, and this was especially true of Indian Gallup polls, has to do with multiple punches. Before the age of high speed computers, the counter-sorter was the work-horse of social scientists, and it used to be a common practice then to squeeze as much data as possible on one card. This sometimes gave rise to multiple punches, but they offered no difficulty if data were to be analysed on the counter-sorter. These multiple punches, however, can produce combinations of holes that are meaningless to the computer. In general, computing equipment and programming languages are designed to handle numerical or alphabetical data only; multiple punches are not always acceptable to the digital computers, and they are in fact rejected as "invalid" information. Unfortunately, almost all of the Gallup polls analysed in this study had multiple punches in their card decks, and many late hours had to be spent in "cleaning" these data.

Advantages: In comparison with the disadvantages, the advantages of secondary analysis are many. The researcher is spared the cost and trouble of designing the study, setting up a questionnaire, pre-testing it, drawing the sample, carrying out the interviewing, coding the responses and finally getting the IBM cards ready for analysis. For a study involving over a few hundred interviews, these operations are massive. Survey research requires the expertise of more than one social scientist, and that is why conducting a large survey is often team work. Collecting quality data is also expensive in terms of money, and a survey study can rarely be conducted without financial support. In contrast to the high cost of original data collection, most Gallup polls can be purchased at a small price. In this sense, secondary analysis fills the research needs of an individual with *micro* resources but *macro* interests.[16]

Another distinct advantage of secondary analysis is that it offers opportunities for "developmental" or "trend" analysis. Unfortunately, most research on the so-called developing societies is not developmental. That is, if there is empirical research at all, it consists of research at one point in time. Gallup polls remedy this situation at least partly. In the Indian case, from the early 1960s onwards, for example, data are available on the political behaviour patterns of the Indian populace—data, which can be usefully exploited by social scientists.

Two recent developments are very promising for secondary

analysis.   One is the development of high speed computers which can store, retrieve and process large amounts of information at relatively little cost.   The second is the establishment of several data archives which store original data from past studies and make them readily available for scholarly use.   Among the leading data banks in the United States are: Roper Public Opinion Research Center at the Williams College in Massachusetts, Inter-University Consortium for Political Research at the University of Michigan, International Data Library and Reference Service at the University of California, Berkeley. In India, the recently established Council for Social Science Research is looking into the matter of establishing a similar data library.[17]

NOTES

[1] Students who are interested in learning the nature and content of these polls should consult the monthly publication of the Indian Institute of Public Opinion appropriately entitled *Monthly Public Opinion Surveys*. Information in the following pages is derived largely from the pages of this journal.   Henceforth the name of this journal will be abbreviated as *MPOS*.

[2] See *MPOS*, 7: 2,3,4 (Nov.-Dec. 1961).

[3] S. J. Eldersveld, *Political Parties*: *A Behavioral Analysis* (Chicago: Rand McNally, 1964).

[4] *MPOS*, 10: 3 (Dec. 1964).

[5] *MPOS*, 9: 8,9 (May, June 1964).

[6] *MPOS*, 10: 4,5 (Jan., Feb. 1965).

[7] See Bruce M. Russett, "Social Change and Attitudes on Development and the Political System in India," *The Journal of Politics*, vol. 29 (1967), pp. 483-504.

[8] *MPOS*, 11: 8 (May 1966).

[9] *MPOS*, 12: 4 (Jan. 1967).

[10] *MPOS*, 12: 7,8,9 (April, May, June 1967).

[11] *MPOS*, 15: 8 (May 1970).

[12] An excellent discussion of sampling procedures is available in Charles H. Backstrom and Gerald D. Hursh, *Survey Research* (Evanston, Ill., Northwestern University Press, 1963), Ch. 2. Also see Morris H. Hansen, *et al.*, *Sample Survey Methods and Theory*, *1* (N. Y.: John Wiley, 1953).

[13] Western readers will be interested in learning that electoral rolls comprise the most extensive lists of people available to the survey researcher in India.   In this connection, Samuel J. Eldersveld, *et al.*, who directed the 1964 Delhi Area Study, comments: "The procedure for selecting respondents in villages and mohallas was random selection from the electoral lists. These lists, up to date for

the previous local elections, were the best available. They were not completely accurate as we subsequently discovered, but no feasible alternative was open to us without the expenditure of tremendous amounts of time and money. Block listings and house listings, particularly in the high density sections of the city, would be misleading because large numbers have no house address. Our experi - ence indicates that electoral rolls are a fairly reliable list of adults. A more serious problem is the mobility and transiency of the population, both urban and rural, which makes the discovery of the whereabouts of respondents often impossible." See *The Citizen and the Administrator in a Developing Democracy* (Glenview, Ill. : Scott, Foresman and Co., 1968), pp. 145-46. Readers may also wish to refer to "Appendix A" on survey methodology in David H. Bayley, *The Police and Political Development in India* (Princeton: Princeton University Press, 1969).

[14] It may be useful to identify here several important studies which are based, wholly or in part, on data gathered by the Indian Institute of Public Opinion. See Hadley Cantril, *The Pattern of Human Concerns* (New Brunswick: Rutgers University Press, 1965); Albert Cantril, *The Indian Perceptions of the Sino-Indian Border Clash: An Inquiry in Political Psychology* (Princeton: The Institute for International Social Research, 1963, Mimeographed); Samuel J. Eldersveld, "The Political Behavior of the Indian Public," *MPOS*, 9: 4 (Jan. 1964), 3-13; Samuel J. Eldersveld, V. Jagannadham, and A. P. Barnabas, *The Citizen and the Administrator. . ., Ibid.*; Bruce M. Russett, "Social Change and Attitudes on Development and the Political System in India," *Journal of Politics*, 29 (1967), 483-504; Donald S. Zagoria, "Kerala and West Bengal," *Problems of Communism*, 22: 1 (Jan. Feb., 1973), 16-27; and David H. Bayley, *op. cit.*

[15] Some very useful suggestions on how uniform coding categories can facilitate analysis of data are discussed by Kenneth Janda, *Data Processing: Applications to Political Research* (Evanston, Ill.: Northwestern University Press, 1965), Ch. V.

[16] Secondary analysis is especially useful to a Ph.D. student aspiring to finish his dissertation. It is one of the inexpensive methods of solving the so-called ABD (All But Dissertation) problem at most American universities. Students interested in this aspect may wish to refer to Barney Glaser, "The Use of Secondary Analysis by the Independent Researcher," *American Behavioral Scientist*, 6: 10 (June 1963).

[17] Many data archives, some small and some large, have sprung up in recent years. See Stein Rokkan, "Archives for Secondary Analysis," *International Social Science Journal*, 1 (1964), and Rokkan, ed., *Data Archives for the Social Sciences* (Paris: Mouton, 1966). For a list of major data archives in the United States, see Herbert Hyman, *Secondary Analysis of Sample Surveys* (New York: John Wiley, 1972), Ch. 9. This book contains convenient lists of research designs, problems amenable to study, archives, and other sources of data.

CHAPTER TWO

The Dependent and the Independent Variables

THE PURPOSE of this study is to describe and explain political participation in India. Or, in the language of social science, political participation is the *dependent variable*, and our effort is to find *independent variables* that are correlated and associated with it. But what is political participation? What kind of political activities are included in our concept of political participation?

In the West, the conventional concept of political participation has been a narrow one. It has included campaign and partisan activities during election time—activities like discussing politics, convincing another person to vote a particular way, distributing party literature, attending political meetings, contributing money to campaigns and other activities of this nature.[1] Recently, the concept has been broadened somewhat. Matthews and Prothro define political participation as "all behavior through which people directly express their political opinions."[2] This definition is broad enough to cover such conventional activities as voting and discussing politics as well as such unconventional acts as demonstrations, sit-ins, and marches. Consistent with this broader concept of political participation, a 1968 study conceives political participation as made up of three major dimensions: (*a*) Conventional Political Participation: such activities as talking politics, joining a political party, taking active part in a campaign, being a candidate for public office, etc.; (*b*) Communications of Protest and Support: sending support or protest messages to political leaders; (*c*) Unconventional Political Participation: rioting and demonstrating.[3] Unfortunately, the Indian Gallup materials, following the Western tradition, pertain mostly to conventional political activities, and little information is available on participation in riots and demonstrations.   Our discussion in this book, therefore, will be limited to the following political actions: voting, attending public meetings, political interest, discussing politics, attempting to influence political decisions, and making a monetary contribution.   Since subsequent chapters focus on independent variables, in this chapter, then, we will discuss briefly each one of these dependent variables.

Voting Turnout

In the literature on political participation, voting is about the most thoroughly researched political act. It is common for political surveys and opinion polls to ask a question on the past voting record of the respondent. The Gallup polls follow this tradition, and we have data on voter turnout from all the IIPO surveys analysed in this book.

The questions that provided data on turnout read: "Did you vote in the last elections to the Lok Sabha?" (If yes), "would you mind telling me which party you voted for?" Only those persons were classified as having voted in the last election who replied "yes" to the first question, and in addition were able to identify the party in answer to the second question. Those who indicated that they had voted for an "independent" candidate were included in the voter group. It may be argued that this interpretation introduces a slight bias in the results. This may be so, but the number of persons affected by this procedure was small, so that the results were not significantly altered. The two-stage question employed by Gallup would produce effects similar to the screening questions used in American voting studies, and thus help in reducing from analysis those persons who might have bluffed about their voting.[4]

Attending Public Meetings

The process of electioneering varies from one culture to another. Though radio and television play a prominent role in the United States and the United Kingdom, they are of minimal importance in India. Public meetings, on the other hand, which have almost disappeared from the American scene, are a significant component of Indian political campaigns. Almost all political parties organize public meetings, and party notables are brought to address the masses. During the Nehru and Shastri administrations such mass rallies were very popular, but evidence indicates that such mass gatherings were on the decline in 1967.[5]

Two IIPO studies contain questions which permit us to explore attendance at public meetings and rallies: the Delhi Area Study (1964), and the Law and Order Study (1964). The question asked in the Delhi Study was: "One of the things we are interested in is just how much attention you paid to the last election campaign. For example, almost all the political parties organized public meetings. Did you attend any meetings? (If yes), how many such meetings did you attend?" The breakdown of answers to this question was as follows:

Attended None	311 (63%)
Attended One to Three	108 (22%)
Attended Four or More	73 (15%)
TOTAL SAMPLE	492 (100%)

The Law and Order Study used a rather different format for a related question: "Do you ever participate in public meetings, processions or demonstrations?" Out of 600 persons interviewed for this study, 137 (or 23 per cent) replied that they did. When further queried as to what kind of "meetings, processions or demonstrations" they participated in, only two persons indicated that they took part in demonstrations. The rest indicated that they attended some kind of public or election meetings. Because of the insignificant number of respondents who took part in demonstrations, the whole group of 137 is considered as having attended public meetings, and it is presumed that the political behaviour tapped here is similar to that tapped in the Delhi Area Study.

POLITICAL INTEREST

The question on political interest comes from the 1961 All-India poll. It read: "Do you take interest in political matters?" Of the total sample, 36 per cent replied "yes," 52 per cent replied "no" and 12 per cent had "no opinion" (total sample: 3,540).

It may be argued that the question on political interest does not measure political participation since no outward political behaviour is involved. A person may be interested in politics and yet be inactive as far as expressing this interest is concerned. Logically, this is possible, but a large body of research indicates that the two concepts (political interest and political participation) are closely related. Most empirical studies, where political interest is usually treated as an independent or an intervening variable, have found that a person who is deeply interested and involved in politics rarely fails to participate in politics. Because this is so, political interest has been included in our list of the dependent variables. It would have been simpler to exclude this variable but by doing so we would have ignored some very interesting data.

DISCUSSING POLITICS

The most ubiquitous form of political participation is "discussing politics." Some time or another, nearly everyone gets caught in a discussion or a political debate, be it with friends, colleagues or relatives. The Delhi Area Study, alone among the surveys analys- ed for this book, explores this dimension of political involvement.

	Discuss	Don't Discuss or No Answer
Neighbours	159 (32%)	333 (68%)
Relatives	74 (15%)	418 (85%)
Fellow Workers	103 (21%)	389 (79%)

Three questions relating to talking politics were asked in this survey: "Do you sometimes discuss politics with your neighbours?" "Do you sometimes discuss politics with your relatives?" and "Do you sometimes discuss politics with the people you work with (or with the people your husband works with)?" The overall break-down of answers to these questions was as shown in the table on the preceding page.

The answers to these three questions were merged, and an index of political discussion was built. The number and percentage in each category emerged as follows:

Do not discuss *at all*	296 (60%)
Discuss with *one* group	82 (17%)
Discuss with *two* groups	114 (23%)
TOTAL SAMPLE	492 (100%)

ATTEMPTING TO INFLUENCE POLITICAL DECISIONS

Voting certainly is the ultimate method by which the citizenry controls what the political leaders do, but there are many other methods through which it attempts to influence politics. Among such methods are working with neighbours and friends to get them to write letters or sign petitions, working through an organized group or a party, taking the matter to the court, personally contacting a high official, and so on. Undoubtedly, these activities require a higher degree of political sophistication and a deeper involvement than does the mere act of voting. It is for this reason that not many people can be expected to be active in the things listed above.

Two items in the 1967 and the 1964 surveys, one with respect to local decision-making and the other with respect to national decision-making, help us to explore this dimension of political participation. The questions read: "Have you ever done anything to try to influence a *local* decision?" and "Have you ever done anything to try to influence a *national* decision?" Responses to these two questions measure claims about whether the respondent actually did something to attempt to change a policy or a law, and they constitute the basis for our index of "participation in political influence activities."[6] In most cases, persons who were active at one level were also found to be active at the other level. We, therefore, decided to merge the two groups. The frequency of responses was:

	1967 Poll	1964 Poll
Participants in (Local or National) Influence Activities	1560 (17%)	346 (17%)
Non-Participants	7594 (83%)	1668 (83%)
Total sample	9154 (100%)	2014 (100%)

An important distinction should be made here. Although in referring to the persons who say they have attempted to influence local/national decisions we use such short terms as "participants in political influence activities," we say nothing about whether they actually wielded any influence. Thinking that one can influence the government or even attempting to influence the government is not the same thing as actually influencing it. A citizen may try to exert influence over political leaders, but they may or may not be moved under his influence. This distinction should be kept in mind while reading subsequent chapters.

MAKING A MONETARY CONTRIBUTION

This is the last of the dependent variables explored in this study. In the case of poor people, giving money to a political party may be an indication of deep commitment to a partisan cause, but some wealthy persons may look upon monetary contributions as substitutes for personal involvement in politics. People in the Delhi Area Study were asked: "In the last campaign, political parties asked people to contribute money. Did you or any one in your family give any money to a political party during the campaign?" A small percentage (7 per cent) of people indicated that they had made a monetary contribution—36 out of 492. This is not surprising since 80 per cent of the sample had an income of less than Rs. 250 a month—perhaps too small to spare any for campaign purposes, no matter how deep was one's involvement.

WHY NOT A POLITICAL PARTICIPATION SCALE ?

In political science research, it is a common practice to rank in order different types of political participation, i.e. from that activity engaged in by the fewest to that engaged in by most. The various types of participation are regarded as a subject of a concept we call "political participation." The unidimensionality of the various political acts can be demonstrated by Guttman scaling.[7] Lester Milbrath, for instance, speaks of political participation as being "cumulative"; this cumulative characteristic arises from the fact that "persons who engage in the topmost behaviors are very likely to perform those lower in rank also." His hierarchy of political involvement includes voting and initiating political discussions at the bottom, attending a political meeting in the middle, and holding a public office at the top of the scale.[8] Matthews and Prothro, in a 1966 study of Negroes in the United States, also used a Political Participation Scale (PPS) with the following rank order of activities: talking politics, voting, taking part in campaigns, holding public office or belonging to a political group.[9]

The justification for building a political participation scale is that different political acts are not only interrelated but are, in fact, different expressions of the same psychological predisposition. Since all political acts are but a subset of the same phenomenon, knowing about a person's participation in one activity enables us to predict that he will participate in another activity. Those persons who participate in the most demanding form of participation will also participate in the less demanding ways. For example, we would expect that a person who takes an active part in campaigning will also cast a vote.

However, this is not always empirically true. Invariably we can expect some "errors" in responses, i.e. some responses would not fit the logical hierarchy. "Errors" may occur because respondents did not correctly interpret certain questions, or because answers were incorrectly coded, or some other such reason. Since there are always bound to be "errors" in responses, it was found necessary to develop a criterion which permitted the using of scaling techniques even with the presence of these errors. This technique is called Coefficient of Reproducibility (C.R.); the C.R. is merely the proportion of responses falling into the pure scale pattern. It is generally agreed that a minimum C.R. of 0.90 constitutes an acceptable scale.

This matter of 10 per cent errors is not so serious if the errors are distributed more or less randomly over the whole universe. But if there is a clustering of errors, the unidimensionality of the scale is questionable even though it may have the required C.R. of 0.90. It is in this regard that Guttman scales are not always satisfactory in political science. For instance, the political participation scale developed by Matthews and Prothro has serious shortcomings. Their PPS makes the discussion not only somewhat cumbersome but also hides much interesting data which would have emerged if the scaled items had been kept distinct. The Matthews and Prothro data clearly indicate that the act of voting is a special act for the Southern Negro and does not fit the usual participation hierarchy applicable to middle class, white Americans. Southern Negroes are generally non-scale types, for many among them have never exercised their franchise even when they contribute money to political groups or attend political meetings.[10]

In the Indian case also (though for different reasons), voting is a special kind of political activity. Some persons take part in more demanding things but they do not vote. This pattern will emerge more clearly in subsequent chapters. Building a scale would have forced us to assign artificial ranks to these respondents and would have obscured important patterns in the Indian political behaviour. For these reasons, we have settled for a separate discussion of each political act and its correlation with independent variables. By doing so, we preserve the rich variety of our data. Our procedure conforms to the emerging view of political participation in the literature on politics. For instance, in their highly acclaimed monograph,

Verba, Nie and Kim argue that participation is "multidimensional." "Citizens differ not only in the overall amounts of participation they perform but also as to the types of acts in which they choose to engage. Furthermore, these different types of acts are quite distinctive in form and [function and can almost be thought as alternative participatory systems."[11]

THE INDEPENDENT VARIABLES

So far we have been discussing the major dimensions of political participation, or the political activities that comprise political participation in the context of this study. Now we will discuss the independent variables, how they can be classified into different groups, and interrelationships among these groups. Since our data are derived from the Gallup surveys, our choice of independent variables was limited to the items available in these polls. In this book, the effect on political participation of the following variables has been investigated: (1) place of residence, (2) education, (3) occupation, (4) income, (5) age, (6) marital status, (7) sex, (8) religion, (9) caste, (10) mass media exposure, (11) geographical mobility, (12) political information, (13) attitudes toward political recruitment, (14) party preference, (15) party evaluation, and (16) the feelings of civic competence. These sixteen characteristics have been divided into two groups: (1) Socio-economic or Demographic Variables, incorporating the first eleven characteristics listed above, and (2) Psychological or Attitudinal Variables, incor-

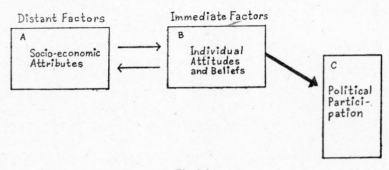

Fig 2.1
Model of Political Participation

porating the last five characteristics.

Fig. 2.1 is a diagramatic representation of the interrelationships between these two groups of variables.[12] The box on the extreme right (C) represents the dependent variable, political participation. Boxes A and B represent socio-economic and psychological variables respectively. In terms of time sequence, the set of variables at the right (B) have a more immediate impact than those toward the left (A). These two types of variables affect not only the dependent variable but also one another. This is represented by double arrows in the figure. Thus, for example, the level of an individual's political activity is a function of his political information and knowledge, which in turn are affected by the level and quality of his formal education, and which in turn are a function of the economic level of the respondent. Because these factors are interrelated, it is often essential in social science research to control the effect of these "third" and "fourth" variables.

An important point to remember is that the effect of socio-economic factors on political participation is never direct. It is always mediated by individual personality. Education, income level, and the place of residence affect political participation only because they have impact on the personality and the belief system of the political participant. Figure 2.1 therefore includes no direct causal links between socio-economic variables (A) and political participation (C); the direct causal link is only from B to C, individual belief system to political participation.

We shall begin with the variables which are less immediate in their effect on political behaviour. Part II examines participation as a function of socio-economic factors: the place of residence, education, occupation, income, age and marital status, sex, religion and caste, mass media exposure, and geographical mobility (Chapters Three to Eleven). Part III deals with participation as a function of individual attitudes and beliefs; the variables included are: political information, attitudes toward political recruitment, party preference and party evaluation, and the feelings of civic competence (Chapters Twelve to Fifteen). In Chapter Sixteen, a modest attempt is made to tie several of these variables together to examine their joint impact on participation.

NOTES

[1] Lester Milbrath, *Political Participation* (Chicago, Rand McNally, 1965) is a good guide to this view of political participation in the West.

[2] Donald R. Matthews and James W. Prothro, *Negroes and the New Southern Politics* (N. Y.: Harcourt, Brace & World, Inc., 1966), p. 37.

[3] See Everett F. Cataldo, Richard M. Johnson and Lyman A. Kellstedt, "The Urban Poor and Community Action in Buffalo," a paper prepared for delivery at the Annual Meeting of the Midwest Political Science Association, Chicago, May 2, 1968.

[4] Another student of Indian voting behaviour has followed a similar procedure. Albert Cantril, in a study of political involvement of a Rajasthani village, reports that if his respondent said that he had voted in the past election, but during another part of the interview could not identify the person or the party he had voted for, he was classified as a non-voter. See his Ph.D. dissertation, "Political Participation in Indian Villages" (Massachusetts Institute of Technology, 1965), pp. 199-200.

[5] Bimla Luthra, in a study of election campaign in the city of Delhi, notes, "The Fourth General Elections seemed to show a marked decline in the use of mass meetings and mass rallies as compared to 1957 and 1962." Some of the reasons cited for this decline were: huge expense involved in renting canopies, mats and public address systems; absence of such leaders as Nehru (in the Congress party at least) who attracted the mass of people; the atmosphere of violence and unrest that prevailed during the 1967 election and the clashes between opposing party supporters." See "Techniques of Election Campaigns in Delhi," *Indian Political Science Review*, 1: 3-4 (April-September 1967), pp. 251-72. In his 1965 study, Cantril found that 63 per cent of the villagers interviewed reported having attended mass meetings, *op. cit.*, p. 210.

[6] Among the pressure methods mentioned were: work with local groups of friends and neighbours to get them to write letters or make representation personally to leaders; take the matter to the court; do something very strong such as march in a demonstration. Social correlates of these activities are discussed in Chapter Fifteen below.

[7] The technique was initially developed by Louis Guttman in the field of attitude measurement. See Samuel A. Stouffer, *et al.*, *Measurement and Prediction* (Princeton University Press, 1950). The Scalogram Analysis is also discussed in Fred N. Kerlinger, *Foundations of Behavioral Research* (N. Y.: Holt, Rinehart and Winston, 1965), and Matilda W. Riley, *et. al.*, *Sociological Studies in Scale Analysis* (New Brunswick: Rutgers University Press, 1954).

[8] Lester Milbrath, *op. cit.*, pp. 17-18.

[9] Matthews and Prothro, *op. cit.*, pp. 52-58, 523-25.

[10] Hugh Douglas Price, in a review of the Matthews and Prothro volume, comments as follows regarding their use of the political participation scale: "This is a routine 1950's scale, developed for national samples, which hardly seems ideal for tapping the special circumstance of the Negro in the South. Indeed, for Southern Negroes the widespread denial of the vote, and related need for belonging to a political group if one is to register means that a great

many Negroes are non-scale types (as the author duly notes on pp. 524-25). It should be kept in mind that in later chapters the 'high' participants generally include many Negroes from Deep South areas who have never seen a ballot, but who may have given a dollar to the NAACP or participated in a voter registration school. More seriously, the heavy reliance on the participation 'scale' tends to substitute a methodological gimmick for the broad substantive question of how Negro interests are awakened, articulated, or aggregated." *American Political Science Review*, 61:3 (Sept. 1967), p. 779.

[11] Sidney Verba, Norman Nie and Jae-on Kim, *The Modes of Democratic Participation* (Sage, 1971), p. 8. They identify four different modes of participation: voting, campaign activity, cooperative activity, and citizen-initiated acts. Also see, Sidney Verba, Bashir Ahmad, and Anil Bhatt, *Caste, Race, and Politics* (Sage, 1971).

[12] This conceptual model is adapted from Matthews and Prothro, *op. cit.*, pp. 322-23.

PART II

SOCIO-ECONOMIC VARIABLES
AND
POLITICAL PARTICIPATION

*Social stratification and social divisions are relevant
factors for the study of political behaviour in any
society. These divisions have even greater relevance
for the study of political behaviour in India. Educational and income differences are significant, caste
and religious divisions persist, and sex and age
stratification is steep. To what extent these distinc-
tions are significant is the topic of this part of the
book. We shall try to answer a simple question:
In what social groups in India does one find the
major pockets of political involvement, political
interest and political participation?*

CHAPTER THREE

Urban-Rural Differences

THE LANGUAGE of social sciences is full of terms like "urban-rural dichotomy", "urban-rural conflict", and "urban-rural contrast". One of the major mainstays of political research in the United States has been the study of the differences in urban and rural conditions and the effect these differences have on political behaviour; it has been found in many American studies for instance that rural dwellers are less likely to become active in politics than city dwellers.[1] Current theorizing in the area of political development is also full of references to urban-rural differences. Students of social mobilization, for example, indicate that urbanization is associated with sharp increases in the level of political participation. One noted political thinker, Daniel Lerner, perceives urbanization as the key step in a society's march toward the status of modern nationhood. Lerner writes:

The secular evolution of a participant society seems to involve a regular sequence of three phases. Urbanization comes first for cities alone have developed the complex of skills and resources which characterize the modern industrial economy. Within the urban matrix develop both of the attributes which distinguish the next two phases—literacy and media growth. There is a close reciprocal relationship between these, for the literate develop the media which in turn spread literacy.... Not until the third phase, when the elaborate technology of industrial development is fairly well advanced, does a society begin to produce newspapers, radio networks, and motion pictures on a massive scale. This, in turn, accelerates the spread of literacy. Out of this interaction develop those institutions of participation (e. g., voting) which we find in all advanced modern societies.[2]

In the modernization sequence, Lerner conceives urbanization to be the first step which is closely followed by higher levels of literacy, mass media, and finally political development. The movement of people from farms to flats is said to trigger a social chain reaction which leads to increased literacy, exposure to mass media, and voting turnout. In brief, urban society as opposed to rural society is perceived as a *participant* society.

How applicable to India is Lerner's assertion that urban areas as opposed to rural areas are centres of political activity? We shall examine this question in these pages. Lerner's other hypotheses are examined in our subsequent chapters. Three of the Gallup studies analysed for this book are of all-India character, i. e. they are based on samples drawn from both urban and rural India. These three studies — 1961, 1964, and the 1967 national surveys—and a fourth one of a north Indian community entitled "The Law and Order" study constitute the sources of data for discussion in this chapter.[3]

The urban-rural differences on participation in various political activities are reported in TABLE 3.1. In examining the data on political interest we discover that residents of urban communities are somewhat more interested in political matters than are residents of rural communities. In 1961, 44 per cent of the urban and 34 per cent of the rural dwellers indicated that they "take interest in political matters"; this represents a 10 percentage point difference between the two communities.

When we examine our data on voter turnout, however, we find that the rural dwellers are slightly more active than (or at least as active as) their brothers in cities and towns. Four of the five Gallup polls from which we have reported data support this interpretation. The 1961 study indicates a slight reversal, but the difference between the turnout rates of the two communities here is not large. The largest difference between the two communities is indicated by the 1967 study, where rural residents voted by 8 percentage points more than urban residents. There is thus clear evidence that the village turnout is equal to or greater than city turnout.

When we turn to attending public meetings, we again discover that rural dwellers are slightly more active than urban dwellers; 25 per cent of the former as opposed to 20 per cent of the latter indicated that they joined public meetings and rallies. Concerning

TABLE 3.1

POLITICAL PARTICIPATION
BY URBAN-RURAL DICHOTOMY

	Urban	Rural
Percentage of Vote		
1970 UP-Bihar	88 (399)	92 (951)
1967 national poll	62 (5000)	70 (5000)
1964 national poll	69 (1039)	70 (975)
1961 national poll	54 (1080)	51 (2460)
Law & Order Poll	75 (300)	77 (300)
Percentage Attending Meetings		
Law & Order Poll	20 (300)	25 (300)
Percentage Interested in Politics		
1961 national poll	44 (1080)	34 (2460)
Percentage Participated in Activities to Affect Decisions		
1967 national poll	17 (4391)	17 (4704)
1964 national poll	19 (1039)	14 (975)

NOTE: The numbers in parentheses are the bases on which the percentages were computed. In this and the following tables, only the percentage of respondents participating in politics has been reported; to find the percentage of those not participating, subtract the percentage reported above from 100.

participation in political influence activities, the 1967 poll shows no difference between rural and urban residents, but in 1964, urban dwellers indicated a slightly higher level of activity.

It may be argued that urban-rural difference on political participation reflect variance due to such factors as education, mass media exposure and income levels. This is a valid argument, for city residents are likely to have higher educational and income levels as well as greater exposure to newspapers and other media. But this is a question which we choose to defer to in chapters on Education, Income and Media Exposure in the subsequent parts of this book. We will be content to note here that the absence of significant differences between the political participation rates of urban and rural residents persist even when camparisons are made between people of similar education, income, and exposure to mass communication. In summary then, we may state that the residents of urban communities as opposed to those of rural communities express a greater degree of interest in politics, but when it comes to implementing this interest through activities like voting and attending meetings, the rural residents are as active as or slightly more active than urban dwellers.

Supporting Research

Here, we would like to present evidence from recently published materials in support of our findings. In an extensive analysis of survey data from six political systems (the U. S., the U. K., Germany, Italy, Mexico, and India), Nie, *et al.*, found no significant correlation between urbanism and the level of political activity. The absence of significant positive correlation between urban residence and political activity existed in all the six nations; in three countries the correlation was slightly negative. In India the correlation coefficient was an insignificant .035, and when controls for social status and organizational involvement were introduced, the correlation reversed direction from positive to negative. The authors of the study concluded, "The least expected pattern is the consistent *absence* of any relationship between urban residence and political participation. Only in two nations (the U. S. and Mexico) is the relationship significant at the .05 level, and even in these nations the relationship is weak, explaining less than one per cent of the variance in participation. For nations as developed as the five reported [here], the tendency for urbanization and mass political activity to co-vary is *not* because city-dwellers are more active than country-dwellers. The absence of a relationship between urban residence and activity rates at the individual level may, thus, help to erase from the literature on political development an ecological fallacy."[4]

Another important cross-national study which supports our general pattern reports the results of an investigation in the following six countries: Argentina, Chile, India, Israel, Nigeria, and East Pakistan. In this investigation, Alex Inkeles also found that urban residence had very little effect on "participant citizenship." If there is a positive association, it is the result of such other factors as education, income, and media exposure. In the words of the author, "...Our most striking finding is precisely that urbanism, despite its high zero-order correlation, fails to meet the test of being an independent school of citizenship. Neither urban origins, nor the numbers of years of urban experience after age 15, produce significant increases in active citizenship when other variables are controlled. This is confirmed by many special matches."[5]

Cameron, Hendricks and Hofferbert came to a similar conclusion regarding the hypothesized effect of urbanization on voter turnout. Using election data at the subnational level from five nations, France, India, Mexico, Switzerland, and the United States, the authors reported, "Perhaps the most interesting finding is that urbanization, when isolated from other dimensions, is not positively associated with participation." In fact, the path coefficients of urbanization and participation were found to be negative for national elections in all five countries. This trend was general enough for the authors to say "that urbanization, distinct from its industrial and commercial aspects, does not induce participation. The effect may well be negative."[6]

Still another study which contradicts conventional wisdom about political behaviour comes from Japan. In this research, the author found that the residents of rural areas indicated a somewhat higher level of political interest than did urban residents. The differences on turnout were even steeper. For example, residents of Astugi and Nita (rural samples) turned out in heavier numbers to vote (94 per cent) than residents of urban Yokohama (78 per cent) in the 1963 House of Representatives elections.[7] These findings raise doubts about some of the accepted generalizations in political science.

These findings, however, are contrary not only to most research conducted in the Western nations, but also to conclusions based on an analysis of aggregate data available on India. For instance, using state aggregate data, Professor Myron Weiner of the Massachusetts Institute of Technology found that, in general, states with higher proportion of urban population recorded higher voter turnout. The correlation coefficient between per cent urban population and per cent voter turnout in the 1962 state assembly elections was 0.58.[8] On the basis of this finding, one should not conclude that people living in the cities necessarily have higher voting frequency than those living in rural areas; such a conclusion would be subject to criticism on the grounds of "ecological fallacy."[9] Indeed, as Weiner himself notes, "the higher voting turnout is not simply a function of urbanization since the rural areas of the highly participant states have a higher voting turnout than the rural areas of the low participant states."[10] Furthermore, even when turnout is higher in cities, the variation was found to be rather selective. For instance, in 1957, when the Indian Election Commission reported data separately for urban and rural areas as well as for men and women (practices discontinued since 1957), male turnout in the parliament elections was slightly higher in the villages (55.43 per cent in cities as against 55.76 per cent in villages), while female turnout was lower in the villages than in the cities (38 per cent as against 52 per cent). Since 1957, it is probable that rural women have caught up with their city sisters, for the spread of modernizing influences has had a greater relative impact on rural life, thus bringing parity between urban and rural turnout rates.

The Indian Gallup surveys also suggest that the rural people might be becoming more active as years pass. This is seen from the difference in figures from the 1961, 1964 and 1967 polls. In 1961, urban people turned out at the polls by 3 percentage points more than the rural people; in 1964, this difference was nearly closed, and in 1967 rural residents had higher turnout by 8 percentage points than that the urban residents. On participation in political influence activities also, the urban dwellers were ahead of the rural dwellers in 1964, but by 1967 this gap was closed. The Indian Gallup data thus offer some evidence that a shift toward rural activism is taking place in the country. We should, however, be careful not to misinterpret these data because the differences in urban and rural participation rates are rather small. We shall have to await additional evidence from more recent and more representative surveys to fully accept such trend analysis. The question of changing urban-rural gap on voter turnout can also be answered by the use of constituency data published by the Indian Election Commission. This can be done by separating urban and rural constituencies and comparing their turnout rates. However the analysis of electoral aggregate data is not part of the scope of this work; the reader interested in this type of research should consult the works cited in the notes.[11]

Parenthetically, it is interesting to note that the shift toward rural activism at the mass level as suggested by our data may also be taking place at the leadership level. Myron Weiner in his study of political leadership in West Bengal found that leadership in that state was moving from urban to rural areas. Most of the rural states in the legislative assembly were now held by rural-born members. "The trend in both the assembly and in Parliament is for more of the younger members to be rural born. While only 56 per cent of the MLA's born before 1900 came from rural areas, 79 per cent of those born after 1920 are rural."[12] In a district in Madhya Pradesh A. C. Mayer found a shift in power within the Congress party from an urban leadership to an uneasy coalition of urban and rural leaders.[13] In Orissa, F. G. Bailey has documented a gradual movement of Congress leadership from the more urbanized middle groups to a wider array of groups that include rural and princely elements from the hill districts.[14] In Madras, Andre Beteille has pointed out similar tendencies toward ruralization of political power.[15] The greater ruralization of political leadership is also evidenced in the occupational distribution of members of the Lok Sabha. A 1969 study by Ratna Dutta indicates that the percentage of lawyers declined from 35 to 17.5 from the First to the Fourth Lok Sabha, whereas agrarian interests increased from 22.4 per cent to 31.1 per cent. The latter group now constitutes the largest single occupational category in the Parliament.[16]

EXPLANATIONS

The fact that political participation among residents of urban areas is not higher than among residents of rural areas may appear surprising at first, for cities have been presumed to be the hub of political activity in the new nations. There is some justification for this view because nationalist leadership in many of the Asian and African countries grew up in cities where the Western ideas of democracy and representative government first took root and where the new universities created a class of lawyers, doctors, teachers, and journalists. Urban areas also have a higher incidence of those factors which are believed to be significantly related to political participation: factors like mass media, literacy, prevalence of civic organizations, etc.

How can we account for the fact that urban residents in India, unlike those in the Western democracies, are not particularly more active than rural residents? Several reasons may be advanced to account for this phenomenon, but all these are in the nature of speculations.

A major difference between rural and urban residents seems to us to be greater attachment to the locality, or the community among rural residents. The term community in this context may mean group, caste, faction or the whole village. This attachment in part is achieved from village residential patterns, where members of a given caste are likely to live together. Houses in much of rural India are in close vicinity to one another. Many Indian cities, in contrast, have grown very fast in recent years, and the new-comers are likely to be poorly integrated into these localities. Another reason for poorer integration in cities is the higher incidence of residence changes. A rough index of residence changes is available from the 1964 poll. In answer to "Where did you live before the age of 20?" 38 per cent of the urban respondents replied "elswhere." This contrasts with 25 per cent of the rural residents who gave the same answer.[17]

Integration into village life is also enhanced by factional rivalries present in much of rural India. Many research studies have shown that most Indian villages are divided into at least two factions. During election times these factions align themselves with competing political parties. The factions may switch their loyalty, but if one switches one way its opponent is likely to go the other way.[18] At election times, the factional leaders see that their supporters reach the polls and cast their ballots. Factions thus become the vehicle of political mobilization and voter turnout. It is also true that the social structure in most of rural India is still largely hierarchical thus making it difficult for many to avoid voting when voting may be seen as a group or factional activity. There is some supporting empirical evidence for this interpretation. In a comparative study of political participation, Verba, Ahmed and Bhatt found that electoral activity among the Harijans in India was "externally motivated." That is, voting was the result of mobilization by external groups, like the political parties or caste leadership. Such external mobilization for election purposes was steeper in rural India than in urban India.[19]

Another view is that in the recent elections the villages rather than the cities have been the targets of party propaganda. Because the bulk of the Indian vote comes from the villages (about 80 per cent of the population lives in the countryside), the parties can make bigger gains by focusing their campaign on the rural residents than on the urban residents. For this reason, parties organized more public meetings and rallies in the rural areas than in the cities. This also helps to increase rural voting rates.

Still another reason for rural political involvement may be the shift in the balance of power taking place from cities to villages. We have already shown that from 1951 to 1967, agrarian interests increased their strength from 22.4 per cent to 31.1 per cent in the national Parliament. These changes at the state capitals have been even more dramatic. These changes have begun to pay off in terms of economic benefits. Rural incomes have increased, while the urban lower middle classes (especially the salaried employees) have been caught in an economic squeeze.[20] In this context, Rosenthal's article on "Deurbanization, Elite Displacement, and Political Change in India" is very relevant. Rosenthal argues that since Independence political influence has gradually moved away from urban areas. By "deurbanization," he does not mean an actual population movement back to the countryside, but "increasing participation in political power by a greater number and variety of social segments and individuals."[21] In a rural nation, of course, this means power for a wider range of rural interests.

These changing economic and political fortunes may in turn be related to political attitudes among the citizenry. Some evidence has recently become available which suggests that urban residents, in contrast to rural residents, are somewhat more alienated from the political system in India. A 1968 study of public attitudes toward government and bureaucracy in the Delhi State, for instance, found that the rural population was more satisfied with administrative services at all levels of the government. The rural persons also indicated that they had better relations with government officials. As compared with 53 per cent of the urban populace, 39 per cent of the rural public felt that the government took more from the people than it gave back. The authors of the study concluded: "The rural public in our study was consistently more supportive than the urban public, less alienated, more confident about how to act in relationship to officials, and possessed of more 'instrumental knowledge' about administrative process."[22] Materials on urban-rural differences concerning attitudes toward the police support this pattern. David H. Bayley found that urban residents are more informed and knowledgeable about the police, but urban residents also articulate a higher level of hostility and criticism than rural people. Urban residents are also more insecure about the safety of their persons and possessions, and they show a greater desire to own a firearm.[23] It is hypothesized here that negative feelings toward the regime and greater hostility toward output structures of the political system are in part responsible for depressed voting rates among the urban dwellers.

These then may be some of the reasons why urban political participation is not higher than rural participation.

CONCLUSIONS

Although our data have limitations, nevertheless they do clearly suggest a revision of the popularly held notion that urban living is more conducive to political activism. It might be argued that voting is a poor measure of involvement. This is not denied here, but at the same time our data indicate that urban-rural parity reported here holds true with respect not only to voting turnout but also to other activities like attending meetings and taking part in activities which seek to influence the behaviour of political leaders (like writing letters, petitioning, talking to somebody, organizing groups, etc.). The evidence presented here is at best suggestive; further research may indeed refine some of the explanations advanced in these pages. But there is a strong hint in our data that the relation between urbanism and political involvement is not as direct as a previous generation of political scientists has presumed.

NOTES

[1] For a discussion of the literature which supports this finding, see Lester W. Milbrath, *Political Participation* (Chicago: Rand McNally, 1965), pp. 128-30, and Robert Lane, *Political Life* (N. Y.: The Free Press, 1959).

[2] Daniel Lerner, *The Passing of Traditional Society* (Glencoe: The Free Press, 1958), p. 60. For a modified confirmation of Lerner's causal thesis in the Western nations, see Gilbert R. Winham, "Political Development and Lerner's Theory: Further Test of a Causal Model," *American Political Science Review*, 64: 3 (Sept. 1970), pp. 810-11. Some emphasis on urbanization is also evident in the works of Gabriel Almond, and G. Bingham Powell, Jr. See their *Comparative Politics: A Developmental Approach* (Boston: Little, Brown and Co., 1966), pp. 93-94.

[3] Information on these and other opinion polls analysed in this book is available in Chap. 1 above.

[4] Norman H. Nie, G. Bingham Powell, Jr., and Kenneth Prewitt, "Social Structure and Political Participation: Developmental Relationships," Parts 1 & II, *American Political Science Review*, 63: 2-3 (1969), pp. 361-78; 808-32. The quote is at p. 365. This article presents the most thorough and most comprehensive investigation of the effect of socio-economic factors on the level of political activity. The data on the U. S., the U. K., Germany, Italy and Mexico are taken from Almond and Verba's *The Civic Culture* (Boston: Little, Brown & Co., 1965). The data on India are from Sidney Verba, Rajni Kothari and Bashir Ahmed's cross-national research programme on "Social and Political Change." Political participation in this article includes these items: talking politics, contacting local authorities, contacting national authorities, involvement in election campaigns, membership in political organizations and political parties. It does not include voting. The best predictor of political participation, according to the authors, is organizational involvement, followed by social status. This finding holds true in all the six countries.

[5] Alex Inkeles, "Participant Citizenship in Six Developing Countries," *American Political Science Review*, 63: 4 (Dec. 1969), pp. 1120-41. The quote is at p. 1140. This article is a part of the research programme of the Harvard Project on Social and Cultural Aspects of Economic Development. The "participant citizen" is a person who is informed and interested in politics, is more likely to identify with the State in competition with the primary social units, participates in civic affairs (the participation scale does not include voting), and supports the use of rational rules as a basis of government. Inkeles found that education and factory experience were very importantly related to participant citizenship.

[6] David Cameron, J. Stephen Hendricks, and Richard Hofferbert, "Urbanization, Social Structure, and Mass Politics: A Comparison Within Five

Nations," *Comparative Political Studies*, 5: 3 (Oct. 1972), pp. 259-90. The quote is at p. 273.

[7] Bradley M. Richardson, "Political Attitudes and Voting Behavior in Contemporary Japan: Rural and Urban Differences" (Ph. D. Thesis, University of California at Berkeley, 1966), p. 39. Also his, "Urbanization and Political Participation: The Case of Japan," *American Political Science Review*, 67: 2 (June 1973), 433-52.

[8] The high voting states were also found to have higher levels of literacy (correlation of 0.43), greater circulation of newspapers (correlation of 0.38), more radio receivers (correlation of 0.59), and more roads (correlation of 0.45). Myron Weiner, ed., *State Politics in India* (Princeton: Princeton University Press, 1968), pp. 32-34. This article by Weiner is also published in Iqbal Narain's ed., *State Politics in India* (Meerut: Meenakshi, 1965). R. Chandidas also reports a positive correlation between urban population and voter turnout on the basis of his analysis of state level aggregate data. See his "Poll Participation Slump," *Economic and Political Weekly*, 7: 29 (July 15, 1972), 1359-68.

[9] See Austin Ranney, "The Utility and Limitations of Aggregate Data in the Study of Electoral Behavior," in Austin Ranney, ed., *Essays on the Behavioral Study of Politics* (Urbana: University of Illinois Press, 1962).

[10] *Op. cit.*, p. 33.

[11] Among the important analyses of the electoral aggregate data are the following works: O. P. Goyal and Harlan Hahn, "The Nature of Party Competition in Five Indian States," *Asian Survey*, 6: 10 (Oct. 1966), pp. 580-88; Gopal Krishna, "One Party Dominance—Development and Trends," in Centre For the Study of Developing Societies, Occasional Papers No. 1, *Party System and Election Studies* (Bombay: Allied Publishers, 1967); and Peter McDonough, "Party Competition and Electoral Participation in India" (Ph. D. Thesis, University of Michigan, 1969). A comprehensive analysis of the Indian census and electoral data at the district level is being conducted at the Institute of Commonwealth Studies, University of London. For an interim progress report on this research, see W. H. Morris-Jones and B. Das Gupta, "India's Political Are as: Interim Report on An Ecological Electoral Investigation," *Asian Survey*, 9: 6 (June 1969), 399-424. Another study based on census and electoral data is by Roger W. Benjamin, Richard N. Blue, and Stephen Coleman, "Modernization and Political Change: A Comparative Aggregate Data Analysis of Indian Political Behavior," *Midwest Journal of Political Science*, 15:2 (May 1971), 219-61. In this research, urbanization, in the extremes, was found to be negatively associated with voter participation.

[12] Myron Weiner, "Changing Patterns of Political Leadership in West Bengal," *Political Change in South Asia* (Calcutta: F. K. L. Mukhopadhyay, 1963), p. 207.

[13] A.C. Mayer, "Rural Leaders and the Indian General Election," *Asian Survey*, 1: 8 (Oct. 1961), pp. 23-29.

[14] F. G. Bailey, *Political and Social Change* (Berkeley: University of California Press, 1963), Part III.

[15] Andre Beteille, "Politics and Social Structure in Tamilnad," *The Economic Weekly*, 15: 28-30 (July 1963), pp. 1161-67.

[16] Ratna Dutta, "The Party Representative in Fourth Lok Sabha," *Economic and Political Weekly*, 4 (Jan. 1969), p. 179. Also see George Rosen, *Democracy and*

Economic Change in India (Berkeley: University of California Press, 1966), Chap. 7; and S. P. Verma's "Changing Pattern of Parliamentary Leadership in India, 1952-1962," (Ph. D. Thesis, University of Iowa, 1965).

[17] It is important to remember that *mohallas* in some cities may be as well integrated as villages, particularly since the new-comers in many Indian cities have settled along caste and ethnic lines. On this point, see an excellent although cumbersome (in the use of terminology) article by Donald B. Rosenthal, "Deurbanization, Elite Displacement, and Political Change in India," *Comparative Politics*, 2: 2 (Jan. 1970), pp. 169-202.

[18] A large amount of information has been accumulated concerning factional politics in India. See especially, Myron Weiner and Rajni Kothari, eds., *Indian Voting Behaviour* (Calcutta: F. K. L. Mukhopadhyay, 1965); Myron Weiner, *Political Change in South Asia* (Calcutta: F. K. L. Mukhopadhyay, 1963); Baldev Raj Nayar, *Minority Politics in the Punjab* (Princeton: Princeton University Press, 1966); Paul Brass, *Factional Politics in an Indian State* (Berkeley: University of California Press, 1965), and F. G. Bailey, *op. cit.*

[19] Sidney Verba, Bashir Ahmed, and Anil Bhatt, *Caste, Race and Politics: A Comparison of India and the United States* (Sage, 1971).

[20] For information on economic gains and losses in India, see George Rosen, *op. cit.*, Chapters 8-9. He estimates that rural employment between 1951 and 1961 increased by 38 per cent, while urban employment for the same period rose by only 15 per cent, Also see Rajni Kothari, *Politics in India* (Boston: Little, Brown & Co., 1970), Chap. 9, especially pp. 360-74.

[21] *Op. cit.*, pp. 176-77.

[22] Samuel J. Eldersveld, V. Jagannadham, and A. P. Barnabas, *The Citizen and the Administrator in a Developing Democracy* (Glenview, Ill.: Scott, Foresman and Co., 1968), p. 52.

[23] The urban-rural contrast made was a south Indian one, involving two areas in the state of Mysore, urban Bangalore and rural Tumkur district. In contrast to Eldersveld, *et al.* study, in Bayley samples, social status (education and income) was not importantly related to evaluative attitudes toward the police. David H. Bayley, *The Police and Political Development in India* (Princeton: Princeton University Press, 1969), pp. 230-37.

CHAPTER FOUR

Education

ONE OF THE MOST widely documented research findings in political science is that participation in political activities increases as the educational level of respondents rises. Among the demographic variables usually investigated in social science research—age, income, sex, occupation, place of residence, etc.—education has been found to have the greatest effect on political behaviour. Clearly, the educated person is a different kind of political actor than the person who has only a little education or none at all.[1]

There are a number of reasons for this. The most important reason, of course, is that differences in educational attainment are associated with differences in other social characteristics. Persons with higher education are more likely to be males, to have higher income, to live in better localities, to occupy higher status positions, and so on. The more educated persons also possess greater information about government and politics; they are also likely to possess a higher incidence of feelings of political efficacy. All these characteristics have a significant positive relationship with political participation.

The authors of *The Civic Culture* have done the most thorough research on the relationship between education and political participation. According to their investigation the positive relationship between education and political participation holds true in all the five nations they studied. In each nation,

> the educated classes are more likely to be aware of politics (to be aware of the impact of government, to have information about government, to follow politics in the various media); to have political opinions on a wide range of subjects; and to engage in political discussions. The more highly educated are also more likely to consider themselves competent to influence

the government and free to engage in political discussions. This set of orientations, widely distributed among those with high education and much less widely distributed among those with low education, constitutes what one might consider the minimum requirements for political participation. More complex attitudes and behavior depend upon such basic orientations as awareness of the political system, information about it, and some exposure to its operations. It is just this basic set of orientations that those of limited education tend not to have.[2]

Because formal schooling is so strongly related to political attitudes, Almond and Verba believe that education provides the shortest route to the creation of a modern political culture. The greatest advantage of education is that "skills that may take years to develop for the first time can be passed on much more easily once there are some who possess them." For these reasons Almond and Verba have called education "the most obvious substitute for time."[3]

Another noted social scientist, Daniel Lerner, regards education as one of the most important steps in the political development of a nation. Using UNESCO data from 54 countries, Lerner found strong correlations between literacy and urbanization, between literacy and mass media, and between literacy and political participation. On the basis of these data, Lerner concluded that literacy was the basic personal skill that underlies the whole modernizing process. "With literacy people acquire more than the simple skill of reading.... The very act of achieving distance and control over a formal language gives people access to the world of vicarious experiences and trains them to use the complicated mechanism of empathy which is needed to cope with this world.... Literacy becomes the sociological pivot in the activation of psychic mobility, the publicly shared skill which binds modern man's varied daily round into a consistent participant lifestyle."[4]

Our purpose in this chapter is to test the universality of these generalizations. Does education determine political behaviour of the people to the extent that Almond and Verba, Lerner, and others claim it does? Unfortunately, most generalizations about political participation are derived from research conducted in the Western nations. These findings have not been adequately tested in the non-Western settings. The research reported in the follow-

Table 4.1

POLITICAL PARTICIPATION AND EDUCATION

	Illiterate	Literate, no formal Education	Some Primary	Finished Primary	Some Secondary	Finished Secondary	College, Univ.
Percentages							
1967 national poll	70	—	71	74	68	60	51
1964 national poll	64	—	69	79	75	63	64
Delhi Area Study	71	76	82	—	75	63	54
1966 urban poll	—	—	63	—	—	62	62
1966 metro poll	—	—	65	—	—	61	63
1961 national poll	38	—	—	65	—	56	45
Law & Order Poll	73	—	—	74	79	78	86
Percentage Attending Meetings							
Delhi Area Study	32	35	39	—	45	41	27
Law & Order Poll	17	—	—	31	16	34	27
Percentage Taking Interest in Politics							
1961 national poll	12	—	—	46	—	54	65

TABLE 4.1—(Contd.)

	Illiterate	Literate, no formal Education	Some Primary	Finished Primary	Some Secondary	Finished Secondary	College, Univ.
Percentage Discussing Politics							
Delhi Area Study	13	18	24	—	27	29	43
Percentage Participating in Activities to Affect Decisions							
1967 national poll	6	—	15	22	22	21	28
1964 national poll	4	—	17	15	19	20	34
Percentage Giving Money to Parties							
Delhi Area Study	4	6	7	—	17	10	0
Number of Cases							
1967 national poll	(2640)	—	(1378)	(983)	(1236)	(1221)	(1587)
1964 national poll	(466)	—	(305)	(235)	(316)	(316)	(320)
Delhi Area Study	(139)	(70)	(74)	—	(69)	(94)	(33)
1966 urban poll	—	—	(540)	—	—	(834)	(625)
1966 metro poll	—	—	(402)	—	—	(342)	(254)
1961 national poll	(1322)	—	—	(1358)	—	(529)	(330)
Law & Order Poll	(252)	—	—	(175)	(88)	(38)	(44)

ing pages does not *fully* support the existing model of political participation.   Evidence available from other Asian countries also does not support the existing model.[5]

GALLUP STUDIES

We are fortunate that all of the Indian Gallup polls analysed in this study have information on educational background of the respondents; education is one of the standard demographic variables which all the IIPO studies include in their questionnaires. There is a small difficulty, however. Different Gallup studies provide different breakdowns for education.   There are no standard coding categories for schooling.   For example, the 1961 poll has these coding categories: illiterate, under matric, matric, graduate, and above; the Delhi Area Study has the following classification: illiterate, literate but no formal education, primary pass, under matric, matric, graduate, and above; the 1964 national poll, which has the most detailed breakdown, follows this scheme: no education, some primary, finished primary, some secondary, finished secondary, intermediate college, graduate, and above.[6]

This non-uniform classification, however, may be a blessing in disguise.   If all the Indian studies point to a similar relationship between education and political participation, even when education is coded differently, our confidence in the validity of the findings increases. Such a relationship indeed must exist in the Indian society; it is not a spurious finding.

TABLES 4.1 and 4.2 report information on political participation levels of various educational groups. In TABLE 4.1 the actual coding categories for education have been preserved; in TABLE 4.2 the same information is summarized into four educational groups: no education, a little education, matric, and college. TABLE 4.1 indicates that no matter which way education was coded, some uniformities in data do appear. Thus, in general, the higher educated groups have lower turnout than illiterates or the poorly educated persons. (There are some exceptions to this general trend, which we will discuss in a moment.)   A curvilinear relationship also emerges with respect to attending public meetings and rallies. The picture is changed, however, when other measures of participation are examined—interest in politics, political discus-

TABLE 4.2

POLITICAL PARTICIPATION AND EDUCATION
(EDUCATIONAL GROUPS MERGED)

	Illiterate	Some Schooling	Matric	College
Percentages				
1967 national poll	70 (2786)	71 (3955)	60 (1548)	52 (1705)
1964 national poll	64 (466)	77 (857)	63 (350)	64 (320)
Delhi Area Study	72 (141)	78 (216)	62 (95)	53 (37)
1966 urban poll	*	63 (540)	62 (834)	62 (625)
1966 metro poll	*	65 (402)	61 (342)	63 (254)
1961 national poll	38 (1322)	65 (1358)	56 (529)	45 (330)
Law & Order Poll	73 (252)	76 (263)	78 (38)	86 (44)
Percentage Attending Meetings				
Delhi Area Study	32 (141)	40 (216)	41 (95)	27 (37)
Law & Order Poll	17 (252)	21 (263)	34 (38)	27 (44)
Percentage Interested in Politics				
1961 national poll	12 (1322)	46 (1358)	54 (529)	65 (330)
Percentage Discussing Politics				
Delhi Area Study	13 (141)	24 (216)	29 (95)	43 (37)
Percentage Participating in Activities to Affect Decisions				
1967 national poll	7 (2739)	20 (3599)	21 (1335)	28 (1462)
1964 national poll	4 (466)	18 (857)	20 (350)	34 (320)
Percentage Giving Money to Parties				
Delhi Area Study	4 (141)	10 (216)	10 (95)	0 (37)

* The 1966 urban and the 1966 metro polls did not include illiterates in the sample.

NOTE: The numbers in parentheses are the bases on which the percentages were compu t ed .

sions, and political influence activities. Using figures from TABLE 4.2, we will examine these differences in greater detail below.

In examining data on political interest in TABLE 4.2, we discover that education is very strongly related to interest in politics: the highly educated are much more likely to say that they take interest in political matters than do the illiterates. For example, only 1 out of 8 among the illiterates as opposed to 2 out of 3 among the college educated persons report having an interest in politics. This response pattern is sustained in a poll conducted in 1969 in the state of Tamil Nadu. In both urban and rural areas, the reported interest in politics increased with education (data not given in the table). Our data also indicate that, on political interest, the real break occurs between those who have no education at all and those who have at least a little education. For example, four times as many persons with a few years of schooling as those with no education are interested in political things. Political interest rises with further increase in education, but it does not increase at the same geometric rate as on the lower educational level.

A similar relationship is revealed between education and talking politics; the more educated discuss politics more often than the less educated. As in the case of political interest, the threshold of participation in political discussions appears with literacy. Obviously education equips a person with the necessary confidence and the basic information—two of the requisites for participation in political discussions.

As regards attempts to influence local and national decisions, we again find that formal schooling is positively related to political influence. Data from both the 1967 and the 1964 national studies indicate that the highly educated are more likely to have done something to try to affect government and politics. It is clear from the above that education has a positive effect on an individual's level of political interest, and his participation in political discussions and in political influence activities.

NEGATIVE CORRELATIONS

Let us now turn to those political activities where education shows a negative correlation: voting, attending public meetings, and donating money to political parties. Taking first the act of voting, we have the widest confirmation of the thesis that the high school and college graduates are less likely to exercise their franchise than the less educated (i.e. those with a few years of schooling and, in some cases, those with no schooling at all). Six out of the seven polls in TABLE 4.2 support this general interpretation. Two additional polls, the 1969 Tamil Nadu survey and the 1970 U. P.-Bihar poll (percentages not given in the table), also confirm this trend.

Most polls show a curvilinear relationship; that is, turnout rises with literacy, but decreases with a further rise in the level of education and continues to decrease with college education. (In the 1964 poll, the illiterates and the college educated had the same frequency of voting). But the 1967 national survey indicates that the highly educated are much less likely to use the ballot box than the poorly educated—70 per cent of the illiterates and 52 per cent of the college educated exercised their franchise, a difference of 18 percentage points. The evidence is therefore compelling that higher education does not lead to higher turnout rates in India.

A somewhat similar picture appears concerning the relationship between education on the one hand and attending public meetings and contributing money for campaigns on the other. The college educated are less likely to attend public meetings or give money to parties than those having lower educational attainment. In fact the evidence on financial contribution to parties is striking. Not even a single college graduate reported having given money for campaign purposes.

To sum up, we can state that the familiar relationship between education and participation holds for such activities as taking interest in political matters, discussing politics, doing something in an attempt to influence local or national decisions, but *not* for such activities as voting, attending public meetings or donating money for partisan campaigns. Unlike the case in the Western democracies, the educated of India, especially those having higher education, are less likely to vote, to attend meetings, or to support partisan campaigns through monetary contributions.[7]

URBAN-RURAL CONTROLS

Before we explain these findings, it will be worthwhile to test the relationship between education and political participation with controls for urban-rural division. It may be argued that the difference between the less and the more educated classes in India with respect to their voting frequency is a function of their place of residence. Since the educated classes are concentrated in the cities, and since we know from our previous discussion that the urban dwellers are somewhat less likely to turn out at the polls than their country brethren, it may be concluded that the educated vote less because of their place of residence.

TABLE 4.3

FREQUENCY OF VOTING,
BY PLACE OF RESIDENCE AND EDUCATION

	1967 Poll		1964 Poll		1969 Madras	
	Urban	Rural	Urban	Rural	Urban	Rural
Education			Percentages			
Illiterate	63 (754)	72 (2030)	70 (135)	62 (331)	89 (54)	82 (159)
Some Schooling	68 (1813)	74 (2141)	75 (405)	79 (451)	88 (91)	85 (132)
Matric	62 (1021)	56 (527)	62 (237)	64 (113)	71 (154)	74 (102)
College	52 (1412)	54 (293)	66 (253)	58 (67)	65 (201)	57 (107)
Total	62 (5000)	70 (5000)	69 (1039)	70 (975)	74 (500)	76 (500)

NOTE: The numbers in parentheses are the bases on which the percentages were computed. The educational categories in the 1969 Madras poll do not perfectly match those in the 1964 and 1967 polls.

TABLE 4.3, where controls for urban-rural dichotomy have been introduced, indicates that the place of residence does not change the relationship between education and voting; indeed, both education and the place of residence are independently related to frequency of voting. Thus, both in the cities and in the villages, those with higher education (high school and above) have lower turnout than those with less education (illiterates or some education)—the highest voting rate generally is recorded by those with a little education. The data are less regular with respect to urban and rural differences at all levels of education, but the general trend is that city living does not promote voter participation.

Controls for urban-rural dichotomy were also introduced to test the relationship between education on the one hand and interest in politics, participation in discussions and in influence activities on the other (tables not given here). These controls did not significantly diminish the positive relationship between education and the political activities named above. There is ample evidence for us to conclude therefore that if the IIPO samples are valid, education does not lead to higher participation in all political activities. The evidence suggests that education does prepare an individual for higher participation. The educated person is more interested in politics, he is more likely to discuss politics with his neighbours, friends and co-workers, he is also more likely to do something to try to affect decisions. Thus the more educated person does have the basic requirement for political involvement. But when it comes to participation in open activities like going to the polls or to the publicly organized political meetings, the educated person shows restraint. The question is: *why* is this so? Why, contrary to findings in other cultures, is education not positively related to all forms of participation in India? We will offer some suggestive hypotheses to account for these patterns, but scientific explanation of this phenomenon must await future research.

One reason why the more educated persons in India, although very much interested in political matters, do not vote in the same numbers as do the less educated persons may be that exercising one's franchise is rather expensive in terms of time. Voting queues are usually long; the act of voting may require several hours of a person's time in many cases. The more educated persons perhaps cannot easily spare this amount of time. The same argument, of course, applies concerning attending public meetings. For the less educated people, on the other hand, the act of voting can take on the flavour of holidays and festivity. Newspaper reports have shown how the villagers many times turn out at the polls in gaiety, as if they were attending a local fair or a religious festival.

Another reason may be that whereas the more educated individuals vote largely as a result of individual motivation, the illiterates and the less educated individuals do so as a result of group pressures—a point that we made in the last chapter in relation to urban-rural differences. Further, it is also true that the uneducated persons are more likely to be swayed by caste ties, factional loyalties, group attachments, and even the lure of money. No one knows for sure what role money plays in the Indian elections, but if it does play any, the lower and the less educated classes are more likely to succumb to its influence. At least one piece of evidence suggests that money has been instrumental in getting out the vote. In his study of the Baroda East constituency in western India, Rajni Kothari documents that votes were promised in return for money. "In some quarters the expectation to receive payment for votes was considered part of the routine. It was a sort of business opportunity that had come and would soon go away. This was the voters' attitude in poor and 'backward' areas but it was also found in more prosperous localities."[8]

EDUCATION AND POLITICAL HAPPINESS

Lower voting frequency among the educated of India may also be a consequence of their attitudes towards the act of voting. Some evidence suggests that voting is not held in high esteem in India, nor is voting regarded as a typically correct strategy in politics. For instance, in answer to a question on what citizens would do in order to affect the decision-making process, only 3 to 4 per cent of the Indian respondents mentioned voting as a proper method. Also, education had little bearing on the proportion of respondents who mentioned this strategy. In the United States in comparison, as many as 14 per cent mention voting as an appropriate method (see the chapter on Civic Competence for these data). In the Western nations, it is also true that many citizens regard voting as among the important civic duties.[9] Such civic duty feelings seem to be narrowly spread in India. This is evidenced by data in TABLE 4.4. The answers in this table are in response to the question, "People speak of the duties which they owe to their country. In your opinion, what should every citizen do for his country?"

TABLE 4.4

WHO MENTION DIFFERENT DUTIES
THAT THEY OWE TO THEIR COUNTRY, BY EDUCATION

"People speak of the duties which they owe to their country. In your opinion, what should every person do for this country?"
1967 Poll Data (Urban only).

Duties	Illiterate	Some Schooling	High School	College	Total
Vote	8	16	12	11	12
Try to understand, keep informed	1	6	11	10	7
Participate in public and political activities, express one's opinion	3	8	11	11	8
Love one's country, be loyal, respectful	20	41	52	43	40
Pay taxes	1	5	9	5	5
Defend it, serve in armed forces, if necessary	8	15	17	15	14
Obey the laws, respect authority	10	20	21	22	19
Do one's job right, raise childern properly, be upright; helpful, responsible in personal life	18	33	35	43	34
General virtues—be honest	15	26	23	22	22
Others	1	1	2	3	2
Nothing, Don't Know	40	10	4	0	11
Number of Cases	(741)	(1602)	(863)	(1201)	(4407)

Interestingly, only 12 per cent mention voting as one of the duties, but more interestingly, the college educated people accord less value to voting (11 per cent) than those with only primary education (16 per cent). Still more interesting are data in row 4, which reports percentages of people mentioning these duties: "Love one's country, be loyal, respectful." The relationship between education and this factor is curvilinear. The data in this table are marred to some extent because a large portion of the illiterates (40 per cent) gave no opinions. Yet one inference can safely be made—higher education in India is not instrumental in breeding strong love for the country, or patriotism or inculcating a belief that voting is a civic obligation.

Other recent studies point to the same conclusion. There is now growing evidence which indicates that in India higher levels of education, competence, information and knowledge do not go along, as they do in some other systems, with loyalty, patriotism or favourable opinion toward the government performance. For instance, a study of six developing nations by Alex Inkeles led him to infer that in some countries the "participant" or "good" citizens (i.e. persons who were informed, knowledgeable, participant and rational) were also more hostile and less patriotic. He found a very strong relationship between education and participant citizenship. However, the participant citizen is not necessarily more satisfied, more loyal or less hostile in each country. Rather, "it depends" on the country being studied. In India the citizenship scale is "positively correlated with hostile views of other groups and bad opinions about politicians."[10]

Another study indicates a similar pattern of attitudes among the educated elite of India. Samuel J. Eldersveld, et al., surveyed in 1964 the city of Delhi and the nearby rural areas. They found that in general the upper, more educated classes were much less supportive of public authority than were the lower classes. For instance, 56 per cent of the urban highly educated (high school and above) as opposed to 30 per cent of urban illiterates believed that public officials were doing a "poor" job. The authors of the study concluded: "The suggestion implicit in these findings is that improvement in social status is accompanied by increased hostility toward the administrative system, that there is a greater tendency to criticize public authority as a person moves from his traditional and depressed social status toward more enlightenment, higher income and more exposure to modernization influences."[11]

A negative attitude toward the political system as it is presently constituted is also suggested by an item in the IIPO materials. This item concerned whether the army rule would help or harm the country. In 1964, 7 per cent among the illiterates, 17 per cent among the matriculates, but 23 per cent among the college educated said that it "would help." In a study of Lucknow and Madurai, Joseph Elder also discounts the common presumption prevalent in some circles that increasing education is the bulwark of parliamentary institutions. He found that the highly educated persons were at least as pro-dictatorship as the uneducated persons. Elder comments, "The relative invulnerability of political authoritarianism to education might serve as a warning to any who may feel that education automatically establishes a basis for democratic form of government. Obviously there are specific attitudes that need to be generated for such a basis to be established. Literacy as such is not enough."[12]

Perhaps the unhappiness among the elite is directly related to developments which have taken place in India since Independence. The parliamentary system based on universal adult suffrage has given rise to what Weiner calls "a mass political culture"—a culture which is embedded in parochial ties of caste, language, religion and community.[13] Many ambitious politicians have discovered that appeals to caste, communal, and provincial factors pay off at the polls. Thus political parties have increasingly given preference to the ethnic and community affiliation of the candidates while nominating them for the seats. The introduction of these parochial factors, according to the elite, has had many bad consequences: villages once united have become split in opposing alliances, states quarrel over the boundaries and merit has given way to political factors for the purpose of job recruitment in the government. The party system which leads to a heightening of 'primordial' loyalties is viewed with alarm by some people. This may explain why (in TABLE 4.2) not a single college graduate reported having contributed money for partisan campaigns. This may also explain the appeal among the better educated of Jayaprakash Narayan's thesis of a party-less democracy for India.[14]

We have somewhat belaboured the point that the educated elites are not always supportive of parliamentary institutions. This belabouring has been intentional. Indeed, it is frequently asserted that education is the fastest way to create a modern democratic political culture. Our research suggests that the relationship between education and support for parliamentary institutions is context-bound as well as time-bound. Whether education leads to satisfaction and loyalty depends on the country being studied. In some countries, greater education produces a politically happy, devoted and voting citizen, while in other countries, greater education produces an alienated and non-voting citizen. India in the 1960s seems to belong to the second group of countries.

This belabouring has been intentional for another reason: the lower voting frequency among the upper status persons will appear again in several places in this book—when we are examining the effect on participation of such variables as mass media exposure, occupation, political information, citizen competence, etc. Education obviously reflects in these other variables. When this is the case, we will ask our readers to refer back to this chapter for reasons why voting turnout is low in some social groups in India.

Conclusions

In this chapter we have explored the question of education and political participation. Our research leads us to doubt the familiar relationship between education and political participation for all activities in India. We saw that as compared with the non-educated, the educated persons are more interested in politics: they are more likely to discuss politics with their neighbours, relatives and the persons they work with; they are also more likely to try to influence decision-making at the local and at the national level. But they do not implement their interest in politics by turning out at the polls or by attending public meetings to the same extent as the poorly educated. Neither do they support partisan campaign activities through monetary contributions in the same proportion. This writer has suggested that voting participation does demand a large investment in terms of time in India and this may explain the lower turnout among the educated. This writer further hypothesized that the educated elite is somewhat alienated from the present political system, and this may affect their participation in the political process. We also saw that voting obligation feelings were not importantly affected by the level of education,

further restricting voting turnout among the upper classes. Of
course, only future research could prove or disprove these hypotheses.

NOTES

[1] See Lester W. Milbrath, *Political Participation* (Chicago: Rand McNally,
1965), pp. 122-24, for research findings that support this relationship.

[2] Gabriel Almond and Sidney Verba, *The Civic Culture* (Boston: Little,
Brown and Company, 1965), pp. 318-19.

[3] *Loc. cit.*, p. 370.

[4] Daniel Lerner, *The Passing of Traditional Society* (N. Y.: The Free Press,
1958), p. 64.

[5] In Japan, voting turnout is higher in rural areas than in urban areas. The
level of education had a positive effect on interest in politics and participation
in political discussions. But higher education did not increase voting turnout in
the Japanese local elections. Bradley M. Richardson, "Political Attitudes and
Voting Behavior in Contemporary Japan: Rural and Urban Differences" (Ph. D.
Thesis, University of California, Berkeley, 1966). A negative correlation
between education and voting has also been found in urban Malaya. See Alvin
Rabushka, "A Note on Overseas Chinese Political Participation in Urban
Malaya," *American Political Science Review*, 64:1 (March, 1970), pp. 177-78.

[6] For the convenience of our Western readers, the use of various educational
terms in India may be described here. Primary pass means that the individual
has completed the first four to eight years of schooling. Matric means the
completion of high school education, which takes from ten to twelve years to
complete. The term "graduate" always refers to a college graduate, never to a
high school graduate as in the United States. Students matriculate from high
schools but graduate only from colleges.

[7] Our conclusion is generally supported in an analysis of cross-national data
by Sidney Verba, Norman Nie and Jae-on Kim. They reported that "in India,
the educated individual is no more likely (perhaps even a touch *less* likely) to
vote than the lesser-educated person." The simple correlation between education and voting in India was found to be 0.04. Education was found to be
positively related to campaign activity (.31 correlation), community activity
(.38 correlation), and personalized contacts with government (.27 correlation).
See their *The Modes of Democratic Participation: A Cross-National Comparison*
(Calif.: Sage Publications, 1971), pp. 60, 61, 76. The countries included in
this study are: Austria, India, Japan, Nigeria, and the United States. Only in
the United States was education significantly correlated with voting.

For similar conclusions, see also, Sidney Verba, Bashir Ahmed, and Anil
Bhatt, *Caste, Race and Politics: A Comparison of India and the United States* (Calif.:
Sage Publications, 1971). The voting rates among the Harijans do not vary
from those among the caste Hindus. If anything, Harijans have a slightly

higher turnout rate; 14 per cent of the Harijans and 18 per cent of the Hindus said they "never voted." The study is based on a sample of 2637 Indians, including 351 Harijans.

[8] Rajni Kothari, "Extent and Limits of Community Voting: The Case of Baroda East," in M. Weiner and Rajni Kothari, ed., *Indian Voting Behaviour* (Calcutta: F. K. L. Mukhopadhyay, 1965), p. 32. Paul Wiebe, in his study of a small town in Andhra Pradesh, also indicates that money was instrumental in getting out the vote, although other factors obviously work in conjunction with it. Lower caste groups were more likely to accept money for their votes. "... only the lower Sudras and the 'untouchable' castes of Peddur are even approached with money. Higher groups would be embarrassed by such flagrant vote-buying and take pride in not being tempted by such offers, though they do not despise the lower castes for accepting money." "Elections in Peddur: Democracy at Work in an Indian Town," *Human Organization*, 28:2 (Summer 1969), pp. 140-47, at p. 146.

[9] The duty to vote ranks high in the Western democracies, indicating effective socialization. In a survey conducted in Buffalo, N. Y., Milbrath found a high percentage of respondents mentioning voting as a duty; he reports, "Certain inputs are almost universally believed to be a citizen's responsibility: vote (93 per cent), keep informed (80 per cent), teach children good citizenship (87 per cent), pay taxes (98 per cent), have undivided loyalty to the country (93 per cent)." *American Behavioral Scientist*, 12 (1968), p. 33. Also see Jack Dennis, "Support for the Institution of Elections by the Mass Public," *American Political Science Review*, 64:3 (Sept. 1970), pp. 819-35. Dennis found 89 per cent voting duty level in the state of Wisconsin in 1966. In England, Richard Rose and Harve Mossawir report 82 per cent of respondents saying voting was a duty; see "Voting and Elections: A Functional Analysis," *Political Studies*, 15 (1967), pp. 173-201. In Germany, according to Lewis Edinger's data, voting ranks at the top of citizenship obligations; see his *Politics in Germany* (Boston: Little, Brown & Co., 1968), p. 106. Also see Gabriel Almond and Sidney Verba, *The Civic Culture* (Boston: Little, Brown & Co., 1965), Chapter V.

[10] Alex Inkeles, *op. cit.*, p. 1129. The six countries are: Argentina, Chile, India, Israel, Nigeria, and Bangladesh.

[11] Samuel J. Eldersveld, V. Jagannadham, and A. P. Barnabas, *The Citizen and the Administrator in a Developing Democracy* (Glenview, Ill.: Scott, Foresman, 1968), p. 58.

[12] Joseph Elder, "Religious Beliefs and Political Attitudes," in Donald E. Smith, ed., *South Asian Politics and Religion* (Princeton : Princeton University Press, 1966), Ch. 12, pp. 249-76, at p. 275. Myron Weiner also speculates along these same lines. Very perceptively, he states : "In the new nations it is often those who fought for freedom and created the new political order who have become most alienated from the political system. Military take-overs are almost always carried out with the blessings of many important political groups and often almost the entire intelligentsia. The shift from democratic to authoritarian political frameworks has come about not because of mass up-heavals but because of attitudes and behaviour of sections of the ruling elite—in political parties, the bureaucracy, and the military." See his "India's Two Political Cultures," in Lucian Pye and Sidney Verba, ed., *Political Culture and*

Political Development (Princeton : Princeton University Press, 1965), pp. 227-28.

[13] Ibid., p. 229.

[14] Jayaprakash Narayan, "Organic Democracy," in S. P. Aiyar, *et al.*, ed., *Studies in Indian Democracy* (Bombay : Allied Publishers, 1965), pp. 325-44.

CHAPTER FIVE

Occupation

THE OCCUPATION of a person is clearly related to the degree of his formal education. Some vocations like law, medicine, journalism and teaching require high literary skills; others like farming, manual work and retail trading do not require high educational competence. Therefore, in discussing the relationship between occupation and political participation, we are also continuing our exploration of the effect of education on political involvement. But occupational characteristics also introduce independent effects in the sense that different occupations might encourage or discourage political involvement.

Robert Lane has suggested that the following four characteristics of jobs facilitate political participation: (1) development of social and intellectual skills that might carry over to politics; (2) opportunity to interact with other individuals who are politically knowledgeable and active; (3) higher than average stakes in government policies and (4) civic or social roles which certain occupations impose on their occupants.[1] Lester Milbrath emphasizes somewhat different characteristics of jobs that are important for political participation: (1) an opportunity for political involvement in terms of blocks of time and inter-personal relations; (2) verbal skills developed or required by the job; (3) effects of government and political decisions on the job; and (4) vulnerability of the position if the employee becomes active in politics. A high score on the first three and a low score on the last criterion would mean that the job is excellent for facilitating political participation.[2]

In terms of the criteria developed by Lane and Milbrath, it can be inferred that the following classes of people in India would be politicized. The professional classes, especially lawyers, doctors, and journalists, are more likely to become active because they are engaged in pursuits where skills required to comprehend and cope with political phenomenon are most readily developed. These professional people also have blocks of time which they can devote to political activity. In addition to the professionals, the people in business have a greater likelihood of becoming politically active. This is because the businessmen can develop verbal skills (especially those in sales jobs) which can spill over to politics; their frequency of contact with like minded persons and exposure to mass media is also high. Again, their stakes in government decisions and public policy may be vital. This last factor is especially true in India where the government has sought to control business through a labyrinth of licenses, permits, and quotas.[3]

Government employees would also be expected to have higher than average involvement. This is because most public servants are surrounded by politics; some may even be targets of pressure from organized groups. Again, their stakes in government decisions are high and their job security and promotion depend on what the politicians decide. Public servants can be expected to turn out at the polls in greater proportion because through voting they choose in a sense their own employers. Farmers and those involved in agriculture also have higher incentive to become active in politics. This is because farmers' stakes in political decisions are higher than ever before. The establishment of the Panchayati Raj in the villages, of the Community Development programmes, and of the Cooperative Societies in rural India—all have large scale consequences for agriculturists.

Let us now turn to actual analysis of the IIPO data in TABLE 5.1. We will take each occupational group separately and see how it compares with other groups in terms of political participation.

Professionals: People in the professions appear to be the most active of all groups in several political activities. They indicate the highest interest in politics (60 per cent) and their participation in political discussions with relatives, neighbours and fellow-workers is also higher than that of any other group (46 per cent). Further, a large proportion of them also attend public meetings (46 per cent in Delhi, and 30 per cent in a north Indian town). But the activity where professional people leave other occupations clearly behind is in attempting to influence political decisions. Here they are ahead by about 12 percentage points of their nearest follower (34-35 per cent as against 22-23 per cent). At the same time, however, voting turnout among professionals is not particularly high; nor do they

TABLE 5.1

POLITICAL PARTICIPATION AND OCCUPATION

	Professions	Farmers	Businessmen	White-collar Workers	Unskilled Workers	Agricultural Workers	Not in Labour Force
Percentages							
1967 national poll	64	82	75	58	68	79	38
1964 national poll	69	78	71	67	69	69	42
Delhi Area Study	69	85	82	65	67	—	45
1966 urban poll	66	—	—	66	70	—	49
1966 metro poll	63	—	71	62	—	—	49
Percentage Attending Meetings							
Delhi Area Study	46	51	47	31	37	—	17
Law & Order Poll	30	26	16	22	13	—	—
Percentage Interested in Politics							
1961 national Poll	60	44	44	53	21	26	10
Percentage Discussing Politics							
Delhi Area Study	46	41	21	25	16	—	14

Percentage Participating in Activities to Affect Decisions

1967 national poll	35	23	22	21	17	7	17
1964 national poll	34	20	16	22	10	5	15

Percentage Giving Money to Parties

Delhi Area Study	0	3	19	5	4	—	5

Number of Cases

1967 national poll	417	1141	1117	1120	679	204	740
1964 national poll	122	365	422	381	188	128	131
Delhi Area Study	13	59	68	105	94	—	64
1966 urban poll	317	—	—	364	245	—	118
1966 metro poll	82	—	99	160	—	—	95

support partisan campaign activities through financial contributions. About 65 per cent of them exercised their franchise (it varies from 63 per cent to 69 per cent in different polls), but not a single member of this group reported having contributed money to parties.   These findings are not surprising, for they reveal the effect of education on participation; indeed they further support that higher status, whether it is measured through formal schooling or by occupational characteristics, has differential impact on different political activities. People in the upper strata are highly interested in politics and in trying to influence decisions, they do not turn out at the polls in the same proportion as do members of the other strata.

Farmers: In TABLE 5.1, this group includes owner-cultivators and a small proportion of absentee landlords but not agricultural labourers or tenants.   Data in this table clearly suggest that, like professionals, farmers are highly active in politics.   Indeed, as far as voting is concerned, farmers report the highest turnout.   Three different studies confirm this: the 1967 poll, the 1964 poll, and the Delhi Area Study; unfortunately, the 1966 polls do not have data on farmers as both studies had their samples drawn from large urban centres. The respective voting percentages for farmers in the first three studies are: 82, 78, and 85—outranking all other occupational groups in each instance. On other measures of participation, however, farmers do not rank at the top but rather at a second place. This is roughly true for the following activities: attending public meetings (51 per cent in the Delhi area and 26 per cent in the Dehra Dun area); discussing politics (41 per cent); interest in political matters (44 per cent) and participation in political influence activities (23 per cent in 1967 and 20 per cent in 1964).   Their financial contribution to parties at the same time is very low (3 per cent).

This may sound surprising to those who think that farmers stand on the fringes of social systems and consequently are only minimally involved in politics. But in a society such as India where three-fourths or more of the population depends directly or indirectly on agriculture, farmers are close to the centre of the social system. Policies of the Indian government and the Congress party bear testimony to this. Some of the biggest government programmes in India concern villages and agriculturists: programmes like the Community Development scheme for rural construction, the Panchayati Raj system for devolution of power, the National Extension Service, irrigation programmes, distribution of miracle seeds, land reform legislation and various other social and educational projects.

Businessmen: This group in TABLE 5.1 includes big business-men, petty traders and shopkeepers. Most of them show only a few years of schooling although economically they indicate a much better status. A majority of them also live in urban centres. These social characteristics are reflected in their political be-haviour. Their financial contribution to political parties is of the highest order: 19 per cent. Our data do not tell us how much money the businessmen contribute to campaign funds, but it is a common belief that some business houses make sizable contri-butions to the treasury of the ruling party.[4]

On measures other than monetary donations to parties, the business class occupies a position roughly midway between the most and the least activity. This applies equally to activities like attending public meetings, voting, interest in politics, political discussions, and attempting to influence political decisions.

White-collar Workers: Government is the biggest employer in India. This is because private enterprise is not developed to the same extent as it is in the Western industrialized countries. Most of the persons classified as white-collar workers in TABLE 5.1 are therefore employees of the central or state governments. This fact has large scale consequences for their political behaviour. On the one hand, the very nature of the government job makes the public servant keenly aware of political considerations; in some cases he may be subject to pressures from special interests, while in others he may be influenced by politicians who want to affect his beha-viour on behalf of their constituents. On the other hand, public service also carries restrictions on political and electoral involve-ment by state employees. For example, public servants are not supposed to be partisan advocates; nor can they stand for public offices while continuing in government service. The latter is prohi-bited by law.

An important factor to remember about the white-collar workers is their economic status; we will discuss this point in some greater detail under "Income" in a later chapter, but briefly, the mem-bers of the white-collar class, even though many of them have received higher education, have made about the lowest economic gains as compared with other social segments, thus leading to feel-ings of pessimism among them.

These factors are reflected in the data that we are analysing.

We see in TABLE 5.1 that, as compared with other occupational groups, the white-collar workers rank close to the top on interest in political matters, but they do not participate in other political activities in the same proportion. For example, their participation in attending meetings and discussing politics is moderately high, and on voting turnout they rank toward the bottom of the scale, ahead only of the unemployed. Similarly, a very small percentage (5 per cent) reported that they donated money to parties. In addition to their high interest in politics, the only other area where the white-collar workers seem particularly active is in attempting to influence government policies. But this seems entirely reasonable, for many of them may be close to the decision-making centres in the national or state governments.

Unskilled Workers and Agricultural Labourers: The first group includes semi-skilled and unskilled labourers, and the second agricultural labourers and farm tenants. These two groups represent the lower strata in the Indian social hierarchy. Most of them are illiterate and their income levels are also low. The working men do not develop skills on their jobs, nor do they have the social position to carry much political weight. During elections, however, they can be expected to be mobilized to turn out at the polls through their caste, factional, or, more recently, party loyalties. These characteristics are reflected in the data in TABLE 5.1. We note that unskilled workers and agricultural labourers, as compared with other occupational groups, are only minimally engaged in politics. They have little interest in politics (21 per cent and 26 per cent) and their participation in other activities (talking politics, political influence, and donations) is also of a very low order.

In contrast, their turnout rate is quite high. In fact, according to the 1967 poll, the turnout rate among the agricultural labourers is second only to those of the farmers. This differential participation in different political activities fits with the pattern that has so far emerged—that is, the lower classes are little interested in political things, they talk little politics, their participation in political influence activities is very low, but their turnout rates are quite high. (See chapters "Education" and "Conclusions" for some explanatory hypotheses of this phenomenon.)

Not in Labour Force: This group is made up of students, the retired, and the unemployed. These people do not occupy the centre position in the Indian society, or as in the case of students they have not yet entered its mainstream. Respondents in this group indicate the lowest degree of political involvement in all activities including turnout. There is close to unanimity among the Gallup polls in this respect.

Conclusions

As far as job differences and political participation is concerned, we may draw the following conclusions: the professionals, government employees, businessmen, and farmers are more active in politics. People in the professions are about the most active on all measures of participation discussed in this book except on voting. The farmers, on the other hand, turn out at the polls in higher proportion than any other group, although their participation in other activities is not as high as among the professionals. As far as businessmen and the white-collar workers are concerned, they are moderately involved; the former group is particularly active in donating money to parties, and the latter in trying to effect government laws and policies that they disagree with. The less active groups include the unskilled and the semi-skilled workers, the farm tenants and agricultural labourers, and those not in the labour force (students, the retired and the unemployed). The last group—those not in the labour force—is the least active of all.

We also ran correlations between occupation and political activities by holding education constant; in general, the above association did not change even when the effect of education was neutralized (tables not reported in the text).

NOTES

[1] Robert E. Lane, *Political Life* (N. Y.: The Free Press, 1959), p. 331.

[2] Lester Milbrath, *Political Participation* (Chicago : Rand McNally, 1965), p. 125.

[3] In a speech in 1956, W. H. J. Christie, president of the (largely European) Upper Indian Chamber of Commerce, said, "There is scarcely a thing we can do in our business without Government's permission, and the delays attendant on it. . . . We cannot raise capital or distribute shareholders the reserves which are their property without permission. We cannot appoint a new Director, a

Director cannot retire, without Government's consent. Much that we buy and much that we sell is subject to official controls. In some industries, for instance sugar, the price of 75 per cent of all that enters into the cost of production is controlled by the Government. . . . We cannot reduce our labour force without Government's consent and without severe penalty. About the only thing we are free to do without consent is to pay a bonus to our labour, provided of course we pay enough. All this—and taxation too." *The Statesman*, Feb. 27, 1956, as reported in Myron Weiner, *The Politics of Scarcity* (Princeton: Princeton University Press, 1962), pp. 100-101.

⁴In this connection, the following information from Weiner's *The Politics o Scarcity* may be useful. Information on financial contributions by business to parties is not public information. The companies do not publish such information nor are they required by law to do so. The only public leakage concerning the size of any individual businessman's contribution to the Congress party is a statement by Mundhra, a leading Marwari enterpriser in Calcutta, who had been accused of successfully bribing officials of the Life Insurance Corporation of India to buy shares of his companies at higher-than-market prices. Mundhra said that he had given Rs. 1,00,000 to the Congress chest and that other businessmen had donated even more. See p. 75. It is commonly believed that much of business money goes into the election chests either of the Congress party or of the relatively young Swatantra party.

CHAPTER SIX

Income

It is almost universally true in the West that the more prosperous people are more likely to be active in politics and to vote proportionately in greater number than the less prosperous. This relationship is supported by Tingsten,[1] Campbell, *et al.*,[2] and Lane,[3] among many others. Several reasons are given for this. The richer persons are more likely to come in contact with those who are active in politics; this is unlike the lower status persons who tend to avoid social contact in mixed groups and who generally reveal a lack of self confidence. The more prosperous are also likely to possess those characteristics which facilitate comprehension of politics. For example, they are more likely to have gone to schools and colleges and received some higher education. Furthermore, the more affluent are also likely to have received more political stimuli through exposure to mass media. This would be especially true in a poor country like India where only the economically secure persons can subscribe to newspapers or buy radios.[4]

Data from the Indian political system only partly support research findings in the West. Table 6.1 summarizes information on participation levels of various economic groups. Two patterns seem to emerge clearly from the figures in the table. First, interest in politics, political influence, and talking politics are positively correlated with income. The relationship with attempted political influence is particularly striking. Very few people at lower income levels have tried to influence political decisions; in contrast about one-third of those with high incomes report participation in this activity.

On a second point these data offer suggestive evidence that there is an economic threshold of political involvement in the sense that below a certain economic level very little political activity can be expected. In India such an economic threshold appears around

TABLE 6.1

POLITICAL PARTICIPATION AND INCOME
(Rs. per month)

	Very Low About Rs. 50	Low About Rs. 150	Medium About Rs. 300	High About Rs. 600	Very high Above Rs. 600
Percentages					
1967 national poll	—	70	63	62	56
1964 national poll	58	71	77	72	—
Delhi Area Study	55	71	74	68	—
1966 urban poll	—	66	62	63	66
1966 metro poll	—	65	61	66	65
1961 national poll	47	55	56	66	69
Law & Order Poll	—	76	78	71	—
Percentage Attending Meetings					
Delhi Area Study	14	35	44	33	—
Law & Order Poll	15	29	22	22	—
Percentage Interested in Politics					
1961 national poll	25	42	51	56	73
Percentage Discussing Politics					
Delhi Area Study	13	23	23	28	—
Percentage Participating in Activities to Affect Decisions					
1967 national poll	—	12	20	25	30
1964 national poll	3	12	23	36	—
Percentage Giving Money to Parties					
Delhi Area Study	3	5	10	7	—

TABLE 6.1—(Contd.)

NUMBER OF CASES

	Very Low About Rs. 50	Low About Rs. 150	Medium About Rs. 300	High About Rs. 600	Very high Above Rs. 600
1967 national poll	—	4939	2390	1441	707
1964 national poll	122	974	384	316	—
Delhi Area Study	37	143	218	100	—
1966 urban poll	—	283	725	540	271
1966 metro poll	—	185	283	262	172
1961 national poll	1595	1074	530	188	59
Law & Order Poll	—	413	84	81	—

Rs. 50 per month, for as we see from TABLE 6.1, the income-partici-pation relationship is marked by a discontinuity around this income level. In other words, Rs. 50 per month is the income level below which participation is noticeably less likely than it is for persons just above this level. This is supported by all the studies which provide a coding for such a low income. (It should be clear from TABLE 6.1 that not all the IIPO polls provide similar codes for income.) This finding is significant in another sense. It applies with some variation to all forms of participation discussed in this book. That is, whether we are concerned with turnout at the polls and attending public meetings, or interest in politics, discussing politics and doing something to influence decisions, those who live on the fringes of the Indian society and have barely a subsistence level are very much less likely to be politically involved.[5]

Beyond a threshold impact, the data on voting turnout, how-ever, are very irregular. There is no consistent pattern that emer-ges from all the polls. The 1967 and the 1964 national polls and the Delhi Area Study indicate that persons who are in the highest economic status classification vote somewhat less than those who have a slightly lower economic status. But the 1966 metro and the 1966 urban polls reveal no major difference in the voting frequency of various economic groups, and the 1961 national poll shows even a slight positive correlation between voting frequency and rise in income. The only safe conclusion that can be drawn from this evidence is that beyond a threshold impact, rise in income is not significantly related to voter participation.

Data on attending meetings and rallies are also irregular : according to the Delhi Area Study, those in the high economic category are less likely to attend meetings than those in the medium economic category. The Dehra Dun Study shows that there is no difference in the participation rates of these two groups. On donating money to political parties, we find the unexpected pattern that those in the highest economic bracket are less likely to give money than those in the medium bracket. But the number of persons who donated money to parties is so small, only 37 persons out of 492, that a shift in the number of a few persons from one cell to another can make a major difference in the percentages. We cannot therefore regard the information on contributions to parties as very reliable.

CONTROLS FOR EDUCATION

But could it be that the above associations are distorted because of the effect of education on turnout? From our previous chapter, we know that education shows a somewhat negative relationship with voter turnout. That is, persons with the highest degree of education vote less than those who have a little education or none at all. In this chapter we find that contrary to our expectations, the economic status of a person is not positively related to voter turnout. But it is possible that if we controlled the effect of education, a positive relationship would indeed emerge between income and voting. In other words, in each educational group, voting would increase as income levels climbed. There is strong reason for us to hypothesize in this fashion, for education and income usually tend to go together.

Yet, this is not always true in India where education does not bring financial remunerations commensurate with its level. Indeed, the reverse of the above proposition can also be argued. The lower voting rates among the educated of India may in fact be a function of their poor economic conditions. Every student of India knows about the existence of high unemployment rates. What is, however, not readily apparent to an outside observer is that the bulk of the unemployed are educated persons. The disparity between rapidly expanding educational system and the rate of economic growth adds hundreds of thousands of educated people to the unemployed cadres. On the basis of 1961 census data, for instance, only 22 per cent of the unemployed in the country were estimated to be illiterates, but 25 per cent had high school or more education. In many states, the number of unemployed who are educated exceeds that of the illiterate and the barely educated. In terms of the people who are registered with employment exchanges, the total number of unemployed rose from 700,000 in 1955 to 1.8 million in 1961. Within this total figure, the number of registered educated unemployed (those with at least high school education) rose from 216,000 in 1955 to 600,000 in 1961. A 1967 report (*India 1967, A Reference Annual*) shows a similar pattern. Of those registered at employment exchanges, over 724,000 were matriculates or above, while another 153,000 were classified as "professional, technical and related workers" and another 94,000 as "clerical, sales and related workers."[6] These figures do not reveal the full dimension of the problem since only about a quarter of the total unemployed are believed to register with the government agencies. Another important feature of the unemployment situation in India is that a vast majority of those seeking work are young persons. In the 1961 census tables, 82 per cent of all the unemployed population belonged to 15-34 age groups. This situation is quite the reverse of that found in the United States, where unemployment is most common among older persons and those with least education.

The economic condition among the educated sections of the Indian population is thus not very happy. The groups that are worst affected are the white-collar members of the lower middle class in the employment of government and business firms. The Indian Gallup data show that only 25 per cent of the college educated persons in the 1967 sample were making Rs. 600 or over a month, and as many as 41 per cent were earning less than Rs. 300 a month. Among high school graduates in the same sample, 9 per cent had incomes of Rs. 600 or over a month, while 65 per cent were earning less than Rs. 300 a month. Even when we make allowance for lower cost of living in India, these are pitifully low figures

($14 roughly equal to Rs. 100 at the 1974 exchange rate; before devaluation of the rupee in 1966, $21 equalled Rs 100). The educated middle classes therefore have sound reasons for their discontent and even anti-Congress bias. As compared with gains made by certain other groups—labour, agriculture, business—the incomes of the white-collar, educated employees, have tended to lag—a lag that is both relative to other groups, and in some cases, even absolutely in relation to the cost of living.[7]

If economic conditions are responsible for poor turnout rates among the educated, then we should expect to find two participation patterns among the educated: one among those who earn wages which are commensurate with their qualifications, and the other among the unemployed and the under-employed educated who do not make enough money. If this hypothesis is correct, then the affluent educated would tend to vote in heavy numbers, and the non-affluent educated would tend not to vote in the same proportion.

TABLE 6.2 which presents materials on voter turnout among different economic groups with controls for education permits us to examine the participation rates among persons with the same degree of education but differential incomes, and vice versa, among persons with the same income but with differential education.

When we examine TABLE 6.2 in detail we discover that the data are very irregular and that results from various polls do not perfectly match. There is some support for the above thesis that turnout among the educated increases when their income levels rise. This is seen from entries under high education in 1966 Metro and Delhi Area surveys. But this finding is not uniformly supported from other polls. Indeed, in the 1967 data, the affluent educated seem to have lower voting frequency than the non-affluent educated. For those with low education (illiterates or a little education) also, income shows no uniform relationship. Thus in the 1967 poll, the turnout rate among all income groups under low education is about 71 per cent. From these data the only safe inference to be drawn is that the income level of a respondent is not significantly associated with his voting act. Knowing the economic status of a person tells us very little about whether he is a voter or a non-voter.

The finding that most clearly emerges from data in TABLE 6.2

TABLE 6.2

VOTING FREQUENCY AND INCOME, WITH EDUCATION HELD CONSTANT

Income	1967 Poll Low Edu.	1967 Poll High Edu.	1964 Poll Low Edu.	1964 Poll High Edu.	Delhi Area Low Edu.	Delhi Area High Edu.	1966 Urban Low Edu.	1966 Urban High Edu.	1966 Metro Low Edu.	1966 Metro High Edu.
					Percentages					
Low	72	61	71	61	71	—	67	64	70	50
(about Rs. 150)	(4411)	(535)	(459)	(18)	(170)	(9)	(200)	(83)	(141)	(44)
Medium	71	53	75	54	80	60	64	61	67	57
(about Rs. 300)	(1333)	(1053)	(445)	(155)	(157)	(52)	(174)	(551)	(120)	(163)
High	71	58	84	70	78	61	62	63	53	70
(about Rs. 600)	(469)	(969)	(244)	(457)	(87)	(51)	(77)	(463)	(66)	(196)
Very High	70	52	—	—	—	68	60	67	62	66
(above Rs. 600)	(136)	(571)			(3)	(19)	(27)	(244)	(29)	(143)

NOTE: The numbers in parentheses are the bases on which the percentages were computed.
Low Education includes illiterates and those with a little education, whereas High Education includes matriculates and college graduates. The 1966 urban and 1966 metro polls include no illiterates.

is that education is negatively correlated with voter turnout at all income levels. Irrespective of their earnings, the educated vote less often than do the poorly educated. Fifteen out of eighteen comparisons in the table support this inference. We can thus conclude that education is independently associated with voting frequency; this relationship emerges even when the effects of income or place of residence (Chapter Three) have been neutralized.

We had noted previously that economic level shows a positive relation with the following of our dependent variables: interest in politics, discussing politics, and trying to influence decisions. We introduced controls for education to test the above relationships, and it was discovered that the positive correlation between income and these political activities diminishes somewhat in strength but does not altogether disappear (tables not given in the text).

Conclusions

This chapter was concerned with the effect of economic status on political participation. It was found that rising economic level was positively associated with the following activities: discussing politics, taking interest in political matters, and attempting to effect laws and policies. This direct relation was independent of the impact of education.

On a second point, it was seen that very few persons earning below Rs. 50 per month tended to participate in any political activity. Persons who make such low wages were not only uninterested in politics but they also tended to stay away from the other political activities included in our study.

On voter turnout, the data were less uniform. It was seen that income had very little effect on who voted and who did not. Education emerged as an independent variable having negative effect on turnout.

NOTES

[1]Herbert Tingsten, *Political Behaviour* (London: P. S. King, 1937), pp. 144-48.

[2]Angus Campbell, *et al.*, *The American Voter* (N.Y.: John Wiley, 1964), Section IV.

[3]Robert Lane, *Political Life* (N.Y.: The Free Press, 1959), Ch. 16.

[4]In gross figures, newspaper circulation in India is impressive. Some 9 million copies are sold daily. But when divided by total population of 550 million, the circulation rate is 16 copies for each 1,000 people. See *Annual Report of the Registrar of Newspapers in India*, 1970 (New Delhi: Ministry of Information and Broadcasting), p, 44. The above percentage compares as follows for other countries: U.S.—311, Japan—420, and U.K.—490.

[5]For comparative purposes, it may be noted that the economic threshold of political involvement in the United States appears around $2,000 a year (1948, 1952). According to Lane, very few people below this level are likely to vote or engage in other political activities, *op. cit.*, p. 327.

[6]See Rajni Kothari, *Politics in India* (Boston: Little, Brown, 1970), pp. 366-74; and George Rosen, *Democracy and Economic Change in India* (Berkeley: University of California Press, 1967), pp. 155-56. Our data are largely drawn from these two sources.

Myron Weiner cites results of a survey done at the University of Calcutta, which found that approximately 10 per cent of the job seeking population was unemployed. Only 15.5 per cent of the unemployed were illiterates, while 22 per cent were persons with high school and college education. Another 37 per cent had attended secondary schools. *Party Building in a New Nation* (Chicago: University of Chicago Press, 1967), p. 323.

[7]As a class, the lower middle classes in urban areas constitute the greatest source of disaffection in the Indian political system. Kothari writes, "The usual threat of a class war waged by an industrial proletariat is less potent in India where the real threat comes from a disaffected lower middle class, the typical *lumpenproletariat*, and its coalition with an intellectual class that has been disinherited from its earlier status and power." *Ibid.*, p. 366.

CHAPTER SEVEN

Age and Marital Status

MANY STUDIES the world over have found that people vote in greater proportion as they grow older; participation grows steadily till
it reaches the peak around the age of 60, and then gradually drops
with old age. But the decrease in old age is not sharp enough to
return the elderly to the very low participation rates of youth.

Why should older people participate more than the young? Robert Lane, after a careful perusal of the literature, suggests several
reasons:

> In maturity certain things occur in the normal lifetime which
> tend to increase motivation and the pressure to take part in
> the political life of the community. A person acquires property,
> hence one of the most important forces politicizing the local
> citizen comes to bear upon him—the question of the assess-
> ment and tax on his house. Then too, the family includes child-
> ren who need playgrounds and schools and therefore the
> mother finds new stakes in politics. Because of the children . . .
> the parents become conscious of themselves as civic models . . . .
> They are geographically less mobile. . . . Dreams of solving
> status and income problems through rapid personal mobility
> may suffer erosion, and a more solid alignment with class and
> ethnic groups emerge. Vocational interests become more sali-
> ent. The increased economic security associated with middle
> age provides freedom of attention and psychic energy for politi-
> cal matters often not available at an earlier stage in life.[1]

Political activity is also habit-forming—older people have had
more opportunities to acquire the habit. Political activity here is
conceived as being the result of cumulative political experience—
all other things being equal, the longer a person lives, the more

TABLE 7.1

POLITICAL PARTICIPATION AND AGE

	Below 35		36—50		Above 51	
Percentages						
1967 national poll	54	(4803)	77	(3563)	77	(1626)
1964 national poll	58	(1083)	76	(652)	80	(277)
Delhi Area Study	60	(206)	81	(177)	75	(100)
1966 urban poll	50	(846)	68	(981)	66	(166)
1966 metro poll	52	(515)	74	(322)	80	(162)
1961 national poll	44	(1688)	60	(1132)	59	(656)
Law & Order Poll	61	(187)	84	(262)	79	(140)
Percentage Attending Meetings						
Delhi Area Study	35	(206)	38	(177)	39	(100)
Law & Order Poll	18	(187)	25	(262)	24	(133)
Percentage Interested in Politics						
1961 national poll	40	(1686)	37	(1131)	30	(653)
Percentage Discussing Politics						
Delhi Area Study	27	(206)	22	(177)	18	(100)
Percentage Participating in Activities to Affect Decisions						
1967 national poll	15	(4414)	18	(3167)	20	(277)
1964 national poll	16	(1083)	18	(652)	18	(277)
Percentage Giving Money to Parties						
Delhi Area Study	8	(206)	8	(177)	5	(100)

NOTE: The numbers in parentheses are the bases on which the percentages were computed.

TABLE 7.2

AGE AND FREQUENCY OF VOTING
(1964 Poll)

Age Group	Percentage of Voting	Percentage Points increase over the Previous Age Group	N
Below 25	48	—	(280)
26-30	68	+20	(382)
31-35	73	+ 5	(359)
36-40	75	+ 2	(301)
41-45	78	+ 3	(208)
46-50	78	+ 0	(143)
51-60	82	+ 4	(196)
Above 61	75	— 7	(81)

interested and active he is likely to become.

TABLE 7.1, which shows political participation levels of three age groups (21-35, 36-50, 51 & above), gives the expected pattern for voting: those in their twenties vote considerably less frequently than those who are older. But when we turn to other indices of political participation the picture is less clear. Such activities as attending public meetings, giving money to parties, and contacting officials to influence decisions do not seem to be significantly related to variation in age. With respect to interest in politics and engaging in political discussions we even find the unexpected relation that involvement decreases with age. Let us explore these differences more closely and see if they make any sense.

Concerning voting we discover that persons below the age of 35 are markedly less likely to turn out at the polls than those belonging to the two older groups in TABLE 7.1. We have the widest confirmation for this finding: seven IIPO polls conducted at different times, some national and others regional, support this finding. Further, the difference in rates of participation of age groups is substantial; it ranges from 15 to 23 percentage points, the average difference being 20 points. But TABLE 7.1 hardly gives an idea of the full dimension of the relation between age and voting. Instead, TABLE 7.2, which provides a detailed breakdown for age, presents a better picture (unhappily, this detailed breakdown can be presented only for the 1964 national study; other polls either do not provide such a detailed coding for age, or if they do, as does the Delhi Area Study, their sample is not large enough to permit adequate numbers in each cell). We discover that the age group which contributes most to non-voting is the one below 25 years—the group most recently enfranchised. After an initial jump, voting turnout continues to grow as age advances, although this increase takes place at a much smaller rate. The highest turnout is recorded by those in their forties and their fifties (around 78 per cent). Voting frequency again declines for the "above 61" age group, but the decline is not sharp enough to return the elderly to the very low participation of youth; even the elderly vote in greater number than those who have just reached adulthood.

The positive relationship between advancing age and high voting turnout might be explained in several ways. It may be the result of cumulative political experience—the longer a person has lived, the greater the likelihood of his becoming engaged in politics. The greater voting turnout among the older persons may also be the result of "generational effect"—a result produced not by years as such but by the experience peculiar to a given generation. Those who are today in their forties and fifties were in their twenties and thirties at the time of Indian Independence (1947). Since they grew up in a period when the struggle for freedom was most intense, they may constitute a special generation of activists.[2]

Turning to other forms of participation, we see that variation in age is not significantly related to attending public meetings, donating money to parties, or to participating in activities to influence decisions. There are small differences: the older persons are more active on the first and third forms of participation listed above, but the differences are not significant. Regarding two other forms of participation, however—interest in politics and talking politics—we find that the younger persons are somewhat more involved than the older ones. This finding concerning greater participation in political discussion among the youth can perhaps be explained by the fact that younger persons are less sure of their beliefs and hence more likely to invite discussion to examine their positions. Younger people, particularly the students, are also more likely to be exposed to greater political stimuli in schools and colleges.

Briefly, then, our data indicate that advancing age is positively related to turnout, that it has slight effect on attending meetings, political influence, and donations, and that it is negatively related to political interest and to talking politics. We should however sound a note of caution before fully accepting these findings. Could it be that education is reflected in the above associations? We know from our previous discussion that education is positively related to taking interest in politics, discussing politics and political influence, and negatively correlated with voter turnout and attending meetings. It is also true that the younger persons are more likely to have gone to schools and colleges. For example, in the 1964 poll sample, only 6.5 per cent of the elderly (those above 51) as opposed to 20 per cent of the younger group (those under 35) had some college education. Greater educational facilities in the recent years have become available in India and the disparity in the level of formal schooling between the old and the young is likely to be sharp. Therefore, the relationship between age and political activities should be tested by introducing controls for education.

This has been done in TABLE 7.3. We find that variation in age is still related to voter turnout even when the effect of education has been partialled out. For example, at all levels of education, the older people are more likely to vote than the younger.

TABLE 7.3

AGE DIFFERENCES ON POLITICAL PARTICIPATION
BY EDUCATION

	Illiterate	Some Schooling	Matric & College
Percentages			
(Delhi Area Study)			
Below 35	69 (52)	64 (101)	47 (53)
36 and above	75 (87)	87 (109)	68 (78)
Difference	+6	+23	+21

TABLE 7.3 — *(Contd.)*

Percentage Attending Meetings

(Delhi Area Study)

Below 35	29*	37	36
36 and above	33	44	38
Difference	+4	+7	+2

Percentage Discussing Politics

(Delhi Area Study)

Below 35	8*	27	45
36 and above	15	20	24
Difference	+7	—7	—21

Percentage of Political Interest

(1961 poll)

Below 35	10 (518)	46 (614)	62 (524)
36 and above	13 (711)	46 (727)	52 (323)
Difference	+3	+0	—10

Percentage of Political Influence

(1967 poll)

Below 35	5 (111)	16 (1650)	21 (1653)
36 and above	7 (1629)	23 (1908)	26 (1144)
Difference	+2	+7	+5

NOTE: The numbers in the parentheses are the bases on which the percentages were computed.

* The number of cases on which the percentages were computed are the same as those under "Percentage of Vote."

The difference between the two age groups (below 35, and over 36) are wider at higher educational levels than among the illiterates.

Advancing age is also positively related to attending meetings and contacting officials to influence decisions, although the relationship is not very strong. Regarding discussing politics and interest in politics, however, our data are less consistent: in general, when the effect of education is controlled, the relationship between age on the one hand and political interest and discussing politics on the other tends to disappear; this is particularly so for the poorly educated (no education or a little education), although for the highly educated, advancing age appears to be associated with decrease in the level of political interest and talking politics.

Let us now turn to marital status, another variable which, like age, is expected to be positively related to political participation.

MARITAL STATUS

If variation in age is strongly related to frequency of voting, variation in marital status should also be similarly related, for both maturity in age and acquiring a family have similar impact on the person: they tend to enhance his group and factional attachments as well as his stakes in political decisions.

TABLE 7.4

PERCENTAGE TURNOUT AND MARITAL STATUS

	Single	Married	Difference
Percentages			
1964 national poll	45 (309)	74 (1615)	+29
Delhi Area Study	45 (20)	75 (429)	+30
1966 urban poll	50 (554)	67 (1407)	+17
Law & Order Poll	58 (514)	78 (45)	+20

NOTE: The numbers in parentheses are the bases on which the percentages were computed.

TABLE 7.4 reports data on the frequency of voting of married and unmarried respondents in India. Unfortunately, we cannot present data on other indices of participation. The 1967 and the 1961 national polls do not give information on the marital status of a person. The Delhi Area Study does, but the number of unmarried respondents is only 20, too few for a reliable analysis.

Evidence in TABLE 7.4 suggests that marital status is strongly related to frequency of voting. Those who are married turn out at the polls in considerably larger numbers than those who are not married. The difference between the two groups ranges from 17 to 30 percentage points, the average difference being 24 points.

But, is marital status independently related to voting turnout or is it a reflection of something else? One does not need to stretch one's imagination to realize that marital status may reflect variation due to age. This is true in the sense that most unmarried respondents in the sample are likely to be young in years. Accordingly, our discovery of strong relationship between marital status and voting might be expected to disappear when controls for age are introduced.

TABLE 7.5

MARITAL STATUS AND VOTING FREQUENCY WITH CONTROLS FOR AGE

Age Group	1964 Poll		1966 Poll	
	Single	Married	Single	Married
Percentages				
Below 35	42 (274)	70 (797)	48 (484)	61 (348)
Above 36	68 (35)	77 (817)	59 (41)	69 (1059)
Diffrnce	+26	+7	+11	+8

NOTE: The numbers in parentheses are the bases on which the percentages were computed.

Data in TABLE 7.5 indicate that this is *not* the case. Marital status is independently related to frequency of voting; that is, no matter which age group we look at, being married leads to greater turnout at the polls. This is supported by data from two polls; the 1964 national poll and the 1966 urban study. We can therefore conclude that at least as far as voting is concerned, married persons are much more likely to exercise their franchise than are unmarried persons.

We can indeed go further than this and document that the size of one's family is also correlated with frequency of voting: respondents with bigger families are more likely to cast their ballots than those with smaller families. This is clear from data from the 1964 national poll, which contains information on the number of children that married respondents in the sample have (see TABLE 7.6). Unmarried persons vote the least, those who are married but have no children vote more than do the unmarried, and those who have more children vote more than those with fewer or no children. Introduction of controls for age made no difference to this correlation. The evidence is based on one survey, however, and on that account the findings should be regarded at best as tentative.

TABLE 7.6

FAMILY SIZE AND VOTING FREQUENCY

(1964 Poll only)

Family Status	Percentage of Turnout	N
Unmarried	45	(309)
Married but no Children	62	(144)
Married & 1-2 Children	65	(576)
Married & 3-5 Children	73	(802)
Married & 6 or more Children	76	(181)

In the United States several studies have found that couples with young children do not have time for politics, and accordingly their participation is lower than that of other married persons.[3] This reasoning does not have the same significance in India where the joint-family system prevails—the system in which the parents live with their married children and help in rearing the youngsters.[4]

Conclusions

The relationship between political participation on the one hand and age and marital status on the other was explored in this chapter. We found that variation in age is very strongly correlated with turnout at the polls. Those in their middle ages (35 to 60) are much more likely to use the ballot box than those in their twenties and early thirties or those in their sixties and seventies. This finding is valid even when the effect of education is controlled. At the same time, younger persons seem to display greater interest in political matters and in political discussions. But we found that this was partly a consequence of higher educational attainments of the younger generation.

In addition to advancing age, marriage was also found to be positively related to rate of voting: those who were married were more likely to vote than those who were single. This relationship ran independent of the effect of age on voting. Further, acquiring a family and the size of family also seemed to lead to higher turnout rates.

These data suggest that integration into the community may be the main intervening variable that is related to political participation. Unmarried, young persons are likely to have the least identification and those with families are likely to have the most integration with the community. It may be because of this factor that the young unmarried citizens are the most apathetic.

NOTES

[1]Robert Lane, *Political Life* (N.Y.: Free Press, 1959), p. 218.

[2]This seems to be supported from the American experience. According to Lane's analysis, while the number of persons eligible to vote has increased continuously since the American Revolution, the proportion of eligible voters making use of their franchise has gradually decreased. This is true since at least 1856 onward, the period for which Lane reports data. *Ibid*, Ch. 2, pp. 16-26.

[3]Lester Milbrath, *Political Participation* (Chicago: Rand McNally, 1965), pp. 134-35.

[4]The joint-family system is more prevalent among the upper castes, and on that account it is also prestigious. In his study of a North Indian village, Oscar Lewis found that 68 per cent of the Jat and Brahmin (upper caste) families and 33 per cent of the lower caste families lived as extended or joint families. See his *Village Life in North India* (N.Y.: Vintage Books, 1958), pp. 13-19.

CHAPTER EIGHT

Male-Female Differences

VOTING TURNOUT

One of the most widely documented research findings is that women all over the world participate less in politics than men do. In some countries women still do not have voting rights, but even in those countries where they have access to the ballot box they consistently use it less than men.[1] In the United States, although the gap is gradually becoming narrower, the voting rate of women is about ten per cent lower than that of men.[2] The gap is the widest among low status people, and the narrowest among upper status people; that is, at the lower status levels, very few women participate, but among the highest status levels, among the college educated women, for example, political participation rates are little different from those among men.

We might expect sex differences in voting turnout in India to be even greater than among Westerners in general. Although women in ancient India supposedly stood on an equal footing with men in many walks of life (there were said to have been in ancient India women philosophers, women kings and even women warriors), their position for the last several hundred years has been anything but that of equality with men. They have been secluded in typically female roles: keeping the home and rearing the children. Even the buying and procuring of family daily needs like foodstuffs, apparel, and furnishings, which in the West are typically under female jurisdiction, have been the preoccupation of men in most parts of India. All this flows from the fact that women were to be protected from the roughness of the marketplace. If women in India participate so little in activities outside the home, they can hardly be expected to turn out at the polls and exercise their voting rights which the Indian Constitution confers on them.

But there is evidence which may lead us to reach just the oppo-site conclusion. Much is known about the prominent role that women played in India's freedom struggle; women like Sarojini Naidu and Aruna Asaf Ali rank among the giants in the freedom movement. In our own times, women have occupied many envi-able positions. India is one of the very few countries in the world to have elected a woman prime minister in the 1960s. The United Nations General Assembly was one time headed by Mrs. Vijaya Laxmi Pandit, who hailed from India. Before the 1967 general elections, at least one Indian state was led by a female chief minis-ter (Sucheta Kripalani in Uttar Pradesh), and another state had a woman governor (Padmaja Naidu in W. Bengal). Mrs. Sushila Nayyar and Mrs. Tarakeshwari Sinha were cabinet ministers, while Maharani Gayatri Devi and Mrs. Renuka Chakravarthy were vigorous representatives in Parliament. Additional evidence may be cited to make this point. In the second general elections for the Lok Sabha in 1957, 44 women ran for elections and 21 of them succeeded; in the third general elections in 1962, 62 women ran for elections and 31 succeeded.[3] Thus women representatives constituted 6.3 per cent of the total third Lok Sabha membership (31 out of 494 members). This is a much higher percentage than that in the U.S. House of Representatives or the Senate, for exam-ple, where in the 89th Congress there were only 2 female Senators out of 100 and only 9 Representatives out of 435.[4]

Whatever the reason for political involvement among women in India at the leadership level, we see from TABLE 8.1 that at the mass level women are much less active than men. Seven different IIPO polls indicate that women turn out at the polls in considerably smaller numbers than men do. The difference ranges from 4 to 26 percentage points, with the average difference being 12 points. The smallest difference in male-female voting rates is represented by the 1966 urban poll, but the sample of this poll was drawn from ten large cities in India, and the urban character of the sam-ple may constitute a special factor. We will have more to say about the effect of urban-rural differences on female turnout else-where in this chapter.

We should however be somewhat careful about placing too much confidence on sex differences in voting rates as indicated by IIPO polls. This is because women in general are highly under-represent-ed in the IIPO samples. For example, women constituted only 22

TABLE 8.1

PERCENTAGE OF MEN AND WOMEN WHO VOTE

Survey Data	Male	Female	Difference
1970 U.P.-Bihar	92 (1270)	84 (80)	—8
1967 national poll	69 (7802)	56 (2191)	—13
1964 national poll	72 (1720)	55 (292)	—17
Delhi Area Study	72 (452)	64 (40)	—8
1966 urban poll	63 (1816)	59 (182)	—4
1966 metro poll	66 (756)	55 (243)	—11
1961 national poll	57 (2836)	31 (701)	—26
Actual Returns			
1967 Elections	66.7	55.4	—11.3
1962 Elections	62.0	47.0	—15.0
1957 Elections	55.7	38.7	—17.0

NOTE: The numbers in parentheses are the bases on which the percentages were computed: Lok Sabha election returns are derived from published *Reports* of the Election Commission.

per cent of the total sample in the 1967 poll, 14.5 per cent in the 1964 poll, 8 per cent in the Delhi Area Study, 9 per cent in the 1966 urban poll, 24 per cent in the 1966 metropolitan polls, and 20 per cent in the 1961 poll.[5] Happily, however, the limitations of the Gallup samples concerning sex differences on voting are remedied by the availability of data from the Election Commission of the Government of India. The *Reports* published by the Election Commission contain actual turnout figures separately for men and women and are summarized in TABLE 8.1. As compared with female turnout, male turnout for lower house elections was higher by 17 percentage points in 1957, by 15 percentage points in 1962, and by 11.3 points in 1967. We can therefore see that the average difference of 12 percentage points between male and female turnout rate, as computed on the basis of IIPO polls, is indeed very close

TABLE 8.2

VOTING TURNOUT IN THE INDIAN STATES IN 1967, BY LITERACY, INCOME, URBANIZATION, AND MODERNITY LEVEL

	1 Total Percentage	2 Male Percentage	3 Female Percentage	4 Difference Percentage	Rank	5 Literacy Percentage	Rank	6 Per Capita Income Rs.	Rank	7 Urbanization Percentage	Rank	8 Overall Level of Modernity Rank
Kerala	75.6	77.1	74.2	2.9	1	46.8	1	213	11	15.1	9	6
Madras	76.6	79.1	74.1	5.0	2	31.4	2	233	8	26.7	2	3
Panjab*	71.7	74.4	68.7	5.7	3	24.2	7	283	3	20.1	6	5
Maharashtra	64.7	68.7	60.5	8.2	4	29.8	3	292	2	28.2	1	1
Mysore	62.9	67.2	58.2	9.0	5	25.4	6	234	6	22.3	5	7
Andhra P.	68.7	72.1	62.9	9.2	6	21.1	9	218	10	17.4	7	8
U. P.	54.5	59.3	49.0	10.3	7	17.6	12	210	12	12.8	11	11
W. Bengal	66.0	71.0	60.2	10.8	8	29.3	4	319	1	24.4	4	2
Gujarat	63.8	69.2	58.1	11.1	9	20.4	10	275	4	25.8	3	4
Rajasthan	58.3	65.0	51.0	14.0	10	15.2	14	243	5	16.3	8	10
Assam	59.3	66.4	50.9	15.5	11	27.4	5	233	7	7.7	13	9
Bihar	51.5	61.3	40.8	20.5	12	18.4	11	144	14	8.4	12	13
Orissa	43.7	53.5	33.0	20.5	13	21.7	8	157	13	6.3	14	14
Madhya P.	53.5	64.4	42.5	21.9	14	17.1	13	228	9	14.3	10	12
India	61.3	66.7	55.4	11.3		24.0		232		18.0		

*Panjab includes Haryana.

Source: The data on electoral participation is taken from Election Commission *Report* of the Fourth general elections. Data in columns 5 to 8 are derived from M. Weiner (ed.) *State Politics in India* (Princeton, 1968), 11-34, and Paul Brass, "Political Participation, Institutionalization and Stability in India," *Government and Opposition*, 4 (1969), p. 28. The overall Modernity index was constructed by Brass on the basis of income, literacy, urbanization, workers in manufacturing, number of persons per radio, and newspaper circulation. For want of space, data on the last three variables are not included in this table.

to the actual difference reported by the Election Commission. The government data also testify to a gradually narrowing gap between the sexes from 1957 to 1967. Both men and women turned out in greater numbers in 1967 than they did ten years earlier, but female rise is steeper. The Indian Gallup data also lend support to this narrowing gap over the years.

MODERNIZATION

We have seen above that in 1967 women voted less than men by 11.3 percentage points. It is reasonable to expect that this 11.3 per cent gross differential is not equally distributed among all the Indian states. Sex differences may be expected to vary with the level of modernization. States that have a higher proportion of literate, richer, and urban residents may exhibit higher voting rates among women. This thesis is tested in TABLE 8.2. Here we have reproduced data on voting turnout of men and women by states, as well as data on education, per capita income, urbanization and overall modernity level by states. In general, female turnout lags in less modernized states. In 1967, the states which indicate large differential between male and female turnout (Madhya Pradesh, Orissa, Bihar, Assam and Rajasthan) are also among the less modern states in India. The best index of voting turnout by sex is literacy. The voting rates of women in more literate states are more like those of men than in the less literate states. The correlation coefficient between literacy and male-female voting differences by state is —.652. Both Kerala and Madras rank at the top in literacy, and both also indicate very high turnout frequency among women.

Male-female differences are also related to the level of urbanization, and per capita income. The correlation coefficients for these variables are: —.493 for income; and —.639 for urbanization. These negative correlations mean that the higher the level of income or of urbanization in a state, the lower the difference between male-female turnout rates.

Modernization indices (education, place of residence, etc.) are associated with female turnout not only at the aggregate level but also at the individual level, for survey data from India also show that education and urban living are importantly related to female turnout. TABLE 8.3 permits us to examine the distinctiveness of

TABLE 8.3

SEX DIFFERENCES ON VOTING TURNOUT, BY
RESIDENCE, EDUCATION AND RELIGION

	1967 Poll			*1964 Poll*			*1957 Elections*		
	Male	*Female*	*Diff.*	*Male*	*Female*	*Diff.*	*Male*	*Female*	*Diff.*
Percentages									
Residence									
Urban	64	54	—10	70	62	—8	55.4	52.0	— 3.4
	(3854)	(1145)		(880)	(159)				
Rural	73	57	—16	73	50	—23	55.8	38.2	—17.6
	(3947)	1046)		(840)	(133)				
Education									
Illiterate	77	58	—19	70	47	—23			
	(1689)	(1079)		(343)	(123)				
Primary	75	57	—18	79	67	—12			
	(3194)	(761)		(752)	(104)				
Matric	61	47	—14 ⎫						
	(1401)	(146)	⎬	65	60	— 5			
College	53	41	—12 ⎭	(608)	(62)				
	(1518)	(187)							
Religion									
Hindu	69	57	—12	72	56	—12			
	(6201)	(1884)		(1498)	(249)				
Muslim	66	40	—26	72	50	—22			
	(836)	(143)		(131)	(14)				

NOTE: The numbers in parentheses are the bases on which the percentages
were computed. Male-female turnout for both urban and rural areas is available only for the 1957 general elections.

political sex roles across place of residence and education. We
notice that sex differences among rural residents are generally
sharper than among urban residents. The urban-rural differential
may reflect a lag in sex-role change, relatively sheltered as women

are from the impact of modernization and social change in rural areas. Concerning education, the sex differences on voting become narrower as education increases. Obviously the college educated women are somewhat more like men than are their illiterate sisters.

In addition to place of residence and education, this writer explored a number of factors for their possible relationship with male-female voting frequency. It was found that religious affiliation of female respondents had a sizable effect on political participation. This is seen in TABLE 8.3 where turnout difference by sex among Muslims is much larger than among Hindus. Clearly, there is little difference between Hindu and Muslim men: both have roughly the same participation rates. But Muslim women indicate characteristically low participation rates. Cultural differences between the two religious communities may explain these differences. The *purdah* system (seclusion of women to the extent that they are required to wear veils in public) is typically a Muslim custom; Hindu women, except in areas which came under heavy Muslim influence, have been relatively unsecluded and free to move about in the world outside the home.

SEX DIFFERENCES ON OTHER POLITICAL ACTS

If women lag behind men in terms of voting frequency, they would be expected to lag still further behind on other forms of political participation. Voting takes place in a highly charged political atmosphere; it is an activity in which even the least involved do sometimes participate. Male members in the electorate may themselves pressure their womenfolk to vote for the candidate of their (men's) choice, thus increasing turnout among women. No similar positive factors are present in affecting female involvement in other acts. For example, few women could be expected to take part in contacting officials; this is an activity which requires a certain amount of education, self-confidence, outgoingness, and political knowledge—characteristics which indeed very few women are likely to possess.

Our expectations are borne out by data in TABLE 8.4. From three to four times as many men as women take interest in politics, attend meetings, discuss politics, or try to influence decisions. These are obviously large differences. But are these differentials

TABLE 8.4

POLITICAL PARTICIPATION, BY SEX

	Male	Female	Difference
Percentage Attending Meetings			
Delhi Area	39 (452)	10 (40)	—29
Law & Order Poll	43 (2833)	11 (698)	—32
Percentage Taking Interest in Politics			
1969 Madras	52 (727)	33 (273)	—19
1961 national poll	25 (452)	8 (40)	—17
Percentage Discussing Politics			
Delhi Area Study	21 (7026)	5 (2069)	—16
Percentage Participating in Activities to Affect Decisions			
1967 national poll	19 (1726)	5 (292)	—14
1964 national poll	8 (452)	3 (40)	—5

NOTE: The numbers in parenth eses are the bases on which the percentages were computed.

equally distributed over all segments of society? Or, can we expect that women who have received education or those who live in the cities would be more active ? Unfortunately, we cannot answer this question with respect to attending meetings, discussing politics or contributing money to parties, for our data on these variables come from the Delhi Area Study which has a very small female sample (only 40 respondents are females). We can, however, study this question with respect to political influence, on which we have data from both the 1967 and the 1964 national polls.

TABLE 8.5

SEX DIFFERENCES ON POLITICAL INFLUENCE, BY
EDUCATION AND RESIDENCE

	1967 Poll			1964 Poll		
	Male	Female	Diff.	Male	Female	Diff.
Education						
Illiterate	9 (1649)	2 (1091)	—7	5 (343)	1 (123)	—4
Primary	23 (2871)	6 (688)	—17	19 (752)	6 (104)	—13
Matric	22 (1208)	9 (126)	—13	21 (318)	6 (34)	—15
College	29 (1298)	16 (164)	—13	36 (292)	14 (28)	—22
Residence						
Urban	20 (3317)	7 (1073)	—13	23 (380)	6 (159)	—17
Rural	21 (3708)	2 (996)	—19	17 (840)	2 (133)	—15

NOTE: The numbers in parentheses are the bases on which the percentages were computed.

TABLE 8.5 helps us to examine variation due to urban-rural and educational differences among male and female respondents. We find that women living in the cities and those possessing college education are somewhat more likely to have tried to affect unfair laws than their counterparts. But the differences between men and women continue to be large at all levels of education. Only a small percentage of women (no matter what their education) are likely to take part in activities designed to affect laws. Men with only a few years of schooling show greater activity than women with a college education (23 per cent against 16 per cent in 1967). From this it would follow that attempting to exercise political influence is a special kind of political involvement, one which female citizens, no matter where they live or what their level of education, find it very hard to engage in.

SUMMARY

In this chapter, we examined evidence pertaining to political participation rates of men and women. On the basis of Indian survey data and the Election Commission aggregate data, it was found that turnout rate among women is about 12 per cent lower than that among men; the gap is gradually narrowing. Sex differences on turnout were sharper among the illiterate, among those who lived in the villages, and among Muslims. At the level of states, those regions which are less modernized are also backward on female participation in electoral politics.

With respect to other forms of participation treated in this book, differences between male and female involvement rates were even larger. From three to four times as many men as women were likely to be interested in politics, to attend meetings, to discuss politics, or to try to influence decisions. Finally, few women at any educational level felt confident about affecting governmental policies.

NOTES

[1] See Herbert Tingsten, *Political Behaviour* (London: P. S. King. 1937), p. 29. Also see, Lester W. Milbrath, *Political Participation* (Chicago: Rand McNally, 1965), pp. 135-36; and Robert Lane, *Political Life* (New York: Free Press, 1959), pp. 209-16.

[2] See Angus Campbell, *et al.*, *The American Voter* (N.Y.: John Wiley, 1960), p. 256; and Donald R. Matthews and James W. Prothro, *Negroes and the New Southern Politics* (N.Y.: Harcourt, Brace & World, 1966), pp. 65-70.

[3] These figures have been computed from the data reported by the Government of India Election Commission, *Report on the Third General Election in India*, 1963, New Delhi.

[4]These figures were computed from the data reported in the *1966 World Almanac*, pp. 101-3.

[5]Concerning the extent to which this under-representation of women in the IIPO samples may affect our findings in this study, see Ch. 1 above.

CHAPTER NINE

Religion and Caste

INDIA IS a land of many religions; all of the world's major religions are represented amongst its people. According to 1971 census data, there are first some 453 million Hindus, who constitute 83 per cent of the total population; then there are 61 million Muslims, constituting 11 per cent of the population; Christianity ranks third with about 14 million adherents; there are also 4 million Buddhists and 35,000 Jews in India.[1] In addition to these major world religions, India has a few other religious groups which are found only in India. First there are 10 million Sikhs; these are the people who follow the religion of the ten Gurus—the first and the last being Guru Nanak and Guru Gobind Singh. Almost all of the Sikhs inhabit the present state of Punjab and its vicinity, with only sprinklings in other parts of India. They wear their hair long which necessitates their also wearing turbans. A second religious group which is also limited to India are the Parsis; these are the people who fled from Persia when Islam made inroads into that part of the world. They came over to India around the 6th century A.D. and have maintained their Zoroastrian identity since then. In addition to the Sikhs and the Parsis, there are Jains or the adherents of Jainism. This religion was founded by Lord Mahavira in the 6th century B.C. Like Buddhism, Jainism arose as a reform movement in Hinduism, but over the years it became a separate religion.

More than religion, India is a land of many castes. Properly speaking, only the Hindus believe in the caste hierarchy, but other religions in India have not been able to shed its influence, if only for the simple reason that many of the converts to these religions (Islam, Christianity and Sikhism) came from Hinduism and brought with them the Hindu ideas of social organization.[2] There are four major castes or *varnas* : Brahmins, Kshatriyas, Vaishyas, and Shudras. Each of these major castes has a number of endo-gamous sub-castes or *Jatis*. Whereas *Varnas* or major caste division have been popular in textbook accounts, the more relevant social groupings are *jatis* which are particular to each region. One can identify caste hierarchy in a particular village only after empirical investigation. A typical village might have from a half-dozen to twenty castes within it. Each caste is hierarchically ranked accord-ing to the ritual purity of its traditional occupation, whether or not the occupation is still being followed. In general, one caste or a configuration of closely knit castes will be dominant in a commu-nity. A "dominant" caste usually holds higher caste status in relation to others in the community and is often wealthy as far as material things (land for example) are concerned. If minority reli-gious groups, such as Muslims and Christians, are present in such a village, they too are placed somewhere within the status hierarchy and are expected to behave in accordance with the social tradi-tions of the village.

Religion and caste have played an important role in Indian politics. The Indian subcontinent was divided in 1947 on the basis of religion. However the religious and communal problems did not disappear with partition. There are in India today communal parties which appeal to the electorate primarily on the basis of religion. For instance, there is the Muslim League which seeks to represent only the Muslim community; the Jana Sangh on the other hand appeals primarily to the orthodox Hindus; the Sikhs also have their own political party called the Akali Dal. All this would indicate that religious differences are very much a part of political conflict in India.

Like religion, caste also plays an important role in Indian poli-tics. Many students of the Indian political scene now agree that caste is among the most important factors which guide the electo-ral choice of the majority of the people.[3] According to Myron Weiner "debate over issues of public policy plays a negligible role in the election campaign and presumably in affecting the way in which individuals vote."[4] According to the Rudolphs, "Within the new context of political democracy, caste remains a central element of Indian society even while adapting itself to the values and methods of democratic politics. Indeed it has become one of the chief means by which the Indian electorate has been attached to the process of democratic politics."[5] Thus, far from disintegrating under the impact of modernization, caste feelings have been politicized. Karl Deutsch observed some time back, "Men discover sooner or later that they can advance their interests in the competitive game of politics and economics by forming coalitions — coalitions which will depend to a significant degree on social communication and on the culture patterns and personality structure of the participants."[6] It can be said that in post-Independence India, politicians have discovered caste and communal factors as particularly expedient vehicles of mobilizing electoral support. Thus, in the selection of candidates, building of party coalitions, mobilization of voters, and factionalism within political parties, the factor of caste has frequently been prominent. Jayaprakash Narayan is reported to have remarked in 1960 that under the present system of elections, "caste has become the strongest party in India."[7]

But whereas large scale research is now available on how different castes have been politicized, and on how different castes try to further their economic and political power by aligning with one political party against another, little work has been done on the participation rates of different castes. We do not know which caste or communal groups are more active than others; or under what circumstances caste groups begin to exercise their franchise in large proportion. It is this narrower question that we will try to explore in this chapter with the aid of data collected by the Indian Institute of Public Opinion.

Before analyzing the IIPO data, this writer hypothesized that minority groups would be more active in politics than the majority community. This is especially true of those minority groups which may fear discrimination and domination from the majority community. Such minority groups would want to forestall any use of governmental machinery for oppression. Groups without these fears would have less motive for political participation. If this reasoning is correct, then members of the Muslim community in India would be more involved in political matters. Let us see if this expectation comes true.

TABLE 9.1 permits us to examine the participation rates of several religious groups in India. However, data are available only on two measures of political participation: voting and participation in political influence activities. This is for the reason that not all IIPO polls contain information on religious affiliation of respondents. The Delhi Area Study—a poll from which three of our six

TABLE 9.1

POLITICAL PARTICIPATION BY RELIGIOUS
AFFILIATION

	Hindus	Muslims	Christians	Sikhs
Percentages				
1970 U.P.-Bihar	91	97	—	—
	(1172)	(164)	(8)	(6)
1967 national poll	66	63	52	71
	(8084)	(981)	(301)	(183)
1964 national poll	69	70	66	76
	(1747)	(145)	(93)	(21)
1966 urban poll	62	57	59	68
	(1738)	(51)	(83)	(90)
1966 metro poll	63	85	—	66
	(865)	(48)		(32)
1961 national poll	52	52	59	50
	(3009)	(295)	(114)	(57)
Law & Order Poll	76	71	—	—
	(542)	(55)		
Percentage Participating in Activities to Affect Decisions				
1967 national poll	17	15	16	20
	(7596)	(935)	(300)	(182)
1964 national poll	17	15	26	5
	(1747)	(145)	(93)	(21)

NOTE: The numbers in parentheses are the bases on which the percentages were computed.

dependent variables come—does contain information on religion, but the number of persons in the sample belonging to minority communities is so small as to prohibit any reliable analysis. Out of 492 respondents in this study, 440 or 90 per cent are Hindus, 28 Muslims, 19 Sikhs, 2 Christians, and the remaining 3 belong to other religions. We therefore cannot use data from this poll to explore the relationship between religion on the one hand and attending meetings, discussing politics, and giving money to parties on the other.

Statistics in TABLE 9.1 do not sustain our expectation about minority religious groups being more active. Although the 1966 metropolitan and the 1970 U.P.-Bihar polls indicate that members of the Muslim community vote in greater proportion than those of other communities, this is not supported by other polls. In a few polls the Sikhs seem to have turned out at the polls in greater proportion than other religious groups, but even this is not confirmed in all the polls. There is thus little agreement among the several studies on voting rates of various religious communities. But all polls do indicate that percentage differences are rather small and are not statistically significant. Therefore, the only inference that we can draw is that, in our data, religious affiliation of respondents has very little effect on their voting frequency; accordingly, we will accept the *null* hypothesis that religious affiliation and voting frequency are not significantly related.

Looking now at participation in influential activities, again the results from the two national surveys do not match in all respects. The two polls agree concerning the political activity level of the Hindus and the Muslims, but they do not agree concerning the political activity level of Christians and Sikhs. Thus, in both surveys, 17 per cent of the Hindus and 15 per cent of the Muslims reported that they had done something to try to influence local or national decisions. The difference in these two communities is small—2 percentage points which is not significant. Concerning the two other religious groups, the 1964 poll indicates that Christians are most influential with 26 per cent of them saying that they participate in influence activities, and the Sikhs the least active with only 5 per cent of them indicating this type of involvement. The respective percentages for these two groups according to the 1967 poll are 16 and 20. But since the 1967 poll has a much bigger sample, and since in this poll each cell has an adequate number of cases, the results of this poll should be given greater weight than those from the 1964 poll. If we assume this, then the political participation does not vary significantly by religious affiliation. In short, we will accept the null hypothesis that religion has little impact on attempting to influence local and national decisions.

CASTE

Turning now to the relationship between caste and voting frequency, we notice from TABLE 9.2 that there is no marked difference among various caste groups regarding their rate of voting. Shudras and the Untouchables vote roughly in the same proportion as do the upper castes (Brahmins, Kshatriyas, and Vaishyas) or as do the non-Hindu. On political influence, however, the Shudras and the Untouchables are less active than the upper castes. Notice in TABLE 9.2 that twice as many members belonging to the upper castes, or those who are not Hindu, as those belonging to the Shudra or the Untouchable category, say that they have done something in an effort to influence political decisions. This is entirely understandable for we know that Untouchables have less education than the upper castes and we also know from our previous discussion that education is strongly related to degree of participation in political influence activities. Even so, we should be very cautious in interpreting the data from a single IIPO poll and attaching importance to it. We should await the confirmation of this finding from future studies before fully accepting it.

TABLE 9.2

CASTE AFFILIATION AND POLITICAL PARTICIPATION

(1964 National Poll)

	Percentages	Percentage Taking part in Activities to Affect Laws	N
Cas			
Brahmins	71	21	(509)
Kshatriyas	73	16	(390)
Vaishyas	68	18	(282)
Shudras	68	11	(414)
Untouchables	72	9	(74)
Not Hindu	71	21	(203)

CONCLUSIONS

On the basis of IIPO data we can conclude that religious and caste affiliations at the all-India level are not significantly related to rate of political participation. Hindus are little different from Muslims, Christians or Sikhs as far as their turnout at the polls and their political influence are concerned. Similarly, there is no significant difference between Brahmins, Kshatriyas, Vaishyas, Shudras and Untouchables regarding their voting turnout. At the same time, the Untouchables and Shudras were found to be somewhat less prone to do something to affect decisions than members of other castes.[8]

We should not however dismiss the relevancy of caste and religious factors for political participation. The IIPO studies have used the popular four-fold caste classification with Brahmins at the top and the Untouchables at the bottom. But it has become abundantly clear that this kind of classification is over-simplified. As a veteran Indian anthropologist remarks, "The caste system of even a small region is extraordinarily complex and it does not fit into the varna-frame except at one or two points. For instance, the local caste-group claiming to be Kshatriya may be a tribal or near-tribal group or a low caste which acquired political power as recently as a hundred years ago."[9] Because caste hierarchy varies from place to place, studies of caste ought to be conducted at the regional level. Such studies may indeed find that caste and religion are meaningful factors for understanding political participation. The data from political sample surveys, though limited, do indicate that there are no national or all-India patterns among religious and caste communities in India.

NOTES

[1] See *India : A Reference Annual* (New Delhi : Government of India Publications Division).

[2] According to a recent account of caste in modern India, "Caste system is not confined only to the Hindus. The social organization of the majority community will naturally influence the life patterns of other communities. Moreover, most of the Muslims, Christians and Sikhs in India originally belonged to the Hindu stocks.... Therefore, social organizations of almost all

the communities in India have been shaped and patterned with certain variations on the basis of Hindu social system." A. P. Barnabas and Subhash C. Mehta, *Caste in Changing India* (New Delhi : Indian Institute of Public Administration, 1965), p. 23.

[3] A large body of research has been accumulated on the role of caste in the Indian politics. Most studies, however, have been conducted at the village or constituency level, and only a few at the state or the national level. Social anthropologists have authored a large proportion of the village studies. Among the more prominent ones, see the following: M.N. Srinivas, *Caste in Modern India and Other Essays* (Bombay: Asia, 1962); F.G. Bailey, *Politics and Social Change,* (Berkeley: University of California, 1963); Andre Beteille, *Caste, Class and Power* (Bombay: Oxford University Press, 1966); McKim Marriot, ed., *Village India,* (Chicago: University of Chicago Press, 1955); Henry Orenstein, *Gaon: Conflict and Cohesion in an Indian Village* (Princeton: Princeton University Press, 1965); Lloyd and Susanne Rudolph, *The Modernity of Tradition* (Chicago: University of Chicago Press, 1967); Rajni Kothari, ed., *Caste in Indian Politics* (New Delhi: Orient Longman 1970); Bashiruddin Ahmed, "Caste and Electoral Politics," *Asian Survey,* 10:11 (Nov. 1970), pp. 979-92; and H. W. Blair, "Caste, Politics and Democracy in Bihar State, India: The Elections of 1967," (Ph. D. Thesis, Duke University, 1969). For an extended bibliography of general works on caste in rural and urban India, see George Rosen, *Democracy and Economic Change in India* (Berkeley: University of California Press, 1967), Appendix B.

[4]Myron Weiner and Rajni Kothari, eds., *The Indian Voting Behaviour* (Calcutta: F.K.L. Mukhopadhyaya, 1965), p. 7.

[5]Lloyd Rudolph and Susanne Rudolph, "The Political Role of India's Caste Associations," *Pacific Affairs,* 33:1 (1960), p. 5.

[6]Karl W. Deutsch, "Growth of Nations," *World Politics,* 5:2 (Jan. 1953), p. 183.

[7]Quoted by Donald E. Smith, "Emerging Patterns of Religion and Politics," in his, ed., *South Asian Politics and Religion* (Princeton: Princeton University Press, 1966), p. 37.

[8]Verba, Ahmed and Bhatt in their comparative study of Harijans and Caste Hindus found that the two groups had roughly the same voting rates but the Harijans were less active when it came to influencing the government via citizen-initiated contacts. See their *Race, Caste and Politics* (Calif.: Sage, 1971).

[9]M. N. Srinivas, *op. cit.,* p. 7.

CHAPTER TEN

Exposure to Mass Media of Communication

RECENT CONCEPTUALIZATION in the social sciences has built a rather sophisticated communications theory.[1] Communications has been conceived as forming the "web of human society". It is contended that all social life can be studied in terms of communications structure; this is because the very relations between man and man depend on his capacity to communicate. Thus, it is argued that (1) the kinds of materials that flow through the communications channels determine the value system of a society; (2) the size of communications structure—the mass media and their audiences, reflects the economic development of a society; (3) the patterns of communications networks which determine where information flows and who shares it with whom reflect the homogeneity of a people; and (4) the ownership of the communications facilities, i.e. the purposeful use and control of communications, reflects the political philosophy in a system.[2]

Perceived in this fashion, the term communications means the whole business of human intercourse, i.e. man's capacity to send and receive in countless ways both intended and unintended messages. The term communications, however, is also applied to a particular institution or industry, that of the mass media—the press, radio, TV, and films. In this book the prime use is in terms of the narrower concept of communications as an institution. We shall be concerned with the question of how exposure to mass communications affects the level of political participation among the Indian electorate.

Many claims have been made in the name of communications. It is contended that the so-called Revolution of Rising Expectations is in reality a Revolution of Mass Communications. The mushrooming of desires and needs which this Revolution implies have been precipitated by the spread of mass media—radio and films in particular, for these do not require reading and writing skills. Daniel Lerner, who is the author of this viewpoint, regards the development of the mass media as the key step in a society's march from a state of traditionalism to that of modernity. A major thesis of Lerner's study is that "high empathic capacity" is the predominant personal style only of the modern man. Empathy is the capacity to imagine oneself in another person's position; an empathic person is psychologically mobile: he can identify personal opinions with public issues. One of the characteristics of this modern, empathic man is that he is a participant individual—he has opinions, he is a cash customer, and he votes.[3]

According to Lerner, geographical mobility played the key role in generating empathy in the Western countries. "Many generations ago, in the West, ordinary men found themselves unbound from their native soil and relatively free to move. Once they actually moved in large numbers, from farms to flats and from fields to factories, they became intimate with the idea of change by direct experience." The role that physical mobility played in the West is being played by mass communications in the new nations. "The earlier increase of physical experience through transportation has been multiplied by the spread of *mediated* experience through mass communications."[4] Thus, few may leave the village to come to Bombay, Cairo or to New York, but today, as it were, Bombay, Cairo and New York come to the village, too. With this spread of mass communications, people are now brought into the participant style of life—a style of life which in the West came about only with near-universal literacy, with urbanization and with industrialization.

A recent study of the American rural South, an area much like the developing nations, further certifies to the political effects of mass communications. Matthews and Prothro in their book, *Negroes and the New Southern Politics*, found that communications were contributing to the modernizing of the South, especially the South of low class Negroes. Associated with this modernizing ethos are new beliefs : there are alternatives to the traditional way of life; personal efforts and initiative are meaningful; one can improve one's lot through political activity; and it is one's duty to participate in civic activity.[5]

COMMUNICATIONS REVOLUTION

Consistent with this view of mass communications, some developing countries have made bold use of newspapers, radio and films as agents of modernization. Egypt is a prime example among these countries. President Nasser sought to lead his nation through social, economic and political revolutions simultaneously by means of a unifying communications revolution. Radio was his chosen weapon. He is noted to have remarked:

> It is true that most of our people are still illiterate. But politically that counts far less than it did twenty years ago .... Radio has changed everything .... Today people in the most remote villages hear of what is happening everywhere and form their opinion.[6]

According to the UNESCO figures, the number of radio receiving sets in Egypt has increased tremendously since the early 1950's from 238,000 in 1950 to 1,705,000 in 1961 (this represents an increase of 600 per cent), Lerner's figures agree that radio was available to most people, no matter what their class. On the basis of his sample, which no doubt over-represented media consumers, it was found that 89 per cent of the professionals, 82 per cent of the white-collar workers, 78 per cent of the blue-collar workers and 42 per cent of the farmers were more or less regular radio listeners.[7]

India has not made the same advances in the permeation of mass media as Egypt and some other developing countries have. In 1964, compared with 66 radio sets per 1,000 persons in Egypt, 14 in Iraq, 40 in Jordan, 63 in Greece, India had only 12 sets per 1,000.[8] Broadcasting in India is controlled by the government; All-India Radio operated 106 medium wave and 32 short wave transmitters in 1971. In the same year, there were some 12.7 million receiving sets licensed by the government.[9]

As for the press in India, there were 12,218 newspapers and periodicals registered with the Registrar of Newspapers for the year 1971. Of these 12,218, 889 were daily newspapers, 3,608 weeklies, and the remaining were publications brought out less frequently (monthlies, annuals, etc.). Not all the publications reported circulation figures to the Registrar of Newspapers, but some 60 per cent did and their total circulation was 29.6 million copies.

Of this, the dailies had a total circulation of 8.9 million. This makes an average of only 16 copies to every 1,000 persons in India.[10] Because of high illiteracy rate, this low circulation is not surprising.

Regarding movies and TV, there were 433 full-length feature films produced in 1971, placing India at the top of film-producing countries in the world. This was in addition to 2,340 short films (documentaries, etc.) produced in the same year. During 1971, there were 7,291 cinema houses in India, including touring talkies numbering about 2,500. Television has been slow in coming to India. The experimental television service in the Capital has been in operation only as recently as 1959. During 1971, there were in all less than 38,000 licensed TV sets around Delhi, most of these acquired within the previous two or three years. [11]

These figures tell their own story: mass media are not wide-spread in India. Furthermore, these inadequate communication facilities are confined mainly to the upper status people in the urban areas. TABLE 10.1 bears this out. Persons who are male, young and with upper income, who are at least high school matriculates and who live in cities, expose themselves to more than one medium regularly, i.e. they tend to read newspapers and listen to the radio daily and go to movies at least once a month. Low status persons, on the other hand, have little or no exposure, and if they make use of media at all, these are likely to be radio and films, which do not require skills of literacy.

Our information on media exposure patterns in this chapter comes from two survey studies: the 1964 national poll and the Delhi Area Study. The former survey contained the following items "Have you ever listened to a radio?" If yes, "how often do you listen to a radio?" "Do you read a newspaper? (or have a newspaper read to you?)" If yes, "how often do you read a newspaper?" And, "Have you ever seen a movie?" If yes, "how often do you go to a movie?" The Delhi Area Study did not use the same questions but it did enquire what newspapers and magazines the respondent read and what other sources of information, if any, he relied on most.

These questions were used to devise a mass media exposure index. The index allowed us to group respondents in one of the four categories: persons in the 'no' exposure category had never listened to a radio, read a newspaper or seen a movie; those in the 'high'

TABLE 10.1

EXPOSURE TO MASS COMMUNICATIONS BY DEMOGRAPHIC VARIABLES

(1964 National Poll)

	Exposure to Mass Media				
	None	*Low*	*Medium*	*High*	*N*
			Percentage of Vote		
Residence					
Rural	27	26	26	21	(975)
Urban	6	18	34	42	(1035)
Sex					
Female	35	23	27	15	(292)
Male	13	21	31	35	(1723)
Age					
21-25	9	22	24	45	(343)
26-35	12	19	29	40	(740)
36-50	19	21	34	26	(654)
Above 51	30	31	32	7	(277)
Income					
0-99 Rs.	37	34	22	7	(485)
100-199	11	24	30	34	(611)
200-349	5	12	37	46	(365)
Above 350	1	9	37	53	(317)
Education					
Illiterate	48	39	10	3	(466)
Some schooling	10	26	38	25	(857)
Matric	1	6	35	58	(350)
College	0	2	33	64	(321)

classification, on the other hand, had *often* been exposed to these three media. Persons in the 'low' group had been exposed to only one communication and those in the 'medium' group to two communications.[12]

The main question that we are concerned with in this chapter is: how is the consumption of mass media related to different political activities? Does greater exposure lead to greater participation, or to lesser participation? Is media exposure related to all the activities similarly or does it have a differential effect on different activities? These questions are examined in TABLE 10.2.

TABLE 10.2

POLITICAL PARTICIPATION AND MEDIA EXPOSURE

	Mass Media Exposure			
	None	*Low*	*Medium*	*High*
Percentages				
1964 national poll	63 (327)	74 (438)	75 (607)	64 (642)
Delhi Area Study	69 (181)	72 (141)	73 (112)	70 (58)
Percentage Attending Meetings				
Delhi Area Study	27 (181)	35 (141)	47 (112)	52 (58)
Percentage Discussing Politics				
Delhi Area Study	11 (118)	18 (141)	35 (112)	50 (58)
Percentage Participating in Activities to Affect Decisions				
1964 national poll	5 (327)	11 (438)	22 (607)	24 (642)

NOTE: The numbers in parentheses are the bases on which the percentages were computed.

Two different patterns seem to emerge: one for voting turnout and the second for other political activities. Mass media exposure is positively related to attending public meetings, discussing politics, and trying to influence decisions, but it shows a curvilinear association with voter turnout. On attending meetings, for instance, we find that 27 per cent of those who have never listened to a radio, read a newspaper or seen a movie, as contrasted with 52 per cent of those who have made use of the three media, attend meetings and rallies. Similarly, from three to five times as many persons in the medium and high exposure groups, as those in the no exposure group, engage in political discussions; and four to five times as many persons in the medium and high consumption group, as those in the no consumption group, do something in an effort to affect decisions.

TABLE 10.3

PARTICIPATION IN POLITICAL INFLUENCE ACTIVITIES,
BY EDUCATION AND MEDIA EXPOSURE

(1964 National Poll)

	Mass Media Exposure			
	None	*Low*	*Medium*	*High*
Percentage of Vote				
Illiterates	2 (226)	3 (181)	11 (45)	14 (14)
Some Schooling	11 (90)	15 (222)	21 (329)	17 (216)
Matriculate	— (2)	19 (21)	19 (123)	20 (204)
College	— (0)	— (8)	32 (106)	34 (207)

NOTE: The numbers in parentheses are the bases on which the percentages were computed.

The positive relationship is not merely a reflection of the effect of other variables like education, income and place of residence, for when controls for these variables are introduced, the linear relationship between media exposure and political activities named above does not disappear. TABLE 10.3 presents data on communications exposure and political influence with controls for education. Tables for other political activities are not given here but they show roughly a similar pattern. Data presented here clearly indicate that both education and mass media exposure are independently associated with political influence—for example, the highest percentage (34 per cent) of participation in political influence activities is indicated by those persons who have both college education and high media consumption. At the same time, we also note that media exposure has greater significance for the illiterates than for the highly educated individuals: at higher levels of education, participation does not vary a great deal with increase in the level of media consumption, but among the illiterates, it does.

Though our data are limited, it is clear that persons who expose themselves to mass media are more likely also to engage in political activities. This is indeed as we would expect, for one of the best documented research findings in political science is that the more stimuli about politics a person receives, the greater the likelihood that he will participate in politics. Our research will not, however, tell us whether reception of political stimuli *causes* political participation. All we can say is that the two phenomena are associated; persons who receive more stimuli are more likely to participate in such activities as discussing politics, attending meetings, and joining groups or contacting officials in order to influence decisions, and persons who do these things are more likely to expose themselves to political stimuli.

VOTING TURNOUT

The positive relationship between media exposure and political participation does not apply, however, to one political activity: voting turnout. In examining data in TABLE 10.2 above, we find that exposure to mass communications has curvilinear relationship with voting frequency: those who have medium exposure vote more by about 10 per cent points than persons at either end of the media consumption scale.

This finding is so puzzling and contrary to expected results that

TABLE 10.4

VOTING TURNOUT AND MEDIA EXPOSURE WITH CONTROLS FOR EDUCATION AND AGE

(1964 National Poll)

| | *Mass Media Exposure* | | | | |
	None	*Low*	*Medium*	*High*	*Total*
		Percentages			
Education					
Illiterate	60 (226)	67 (181)	73 (45)	64 (14)	64 (466)
Some Schooling	70 (90)	82 (222)	82 (329)	68 (216)	77 (857)
Matric	— (2)	62 (21)	66 (123)	61 (203)	63 (349)
College	— (0)	— (8)	66 (106)	64 (207)	64 (321)
Age					
21-25	33 (30)	59 (74)	48 (83)	3 (156)	45 (343)
26-35	64 (92)	73 (138)	76 (26)	69 (294)	71 (740)
36-50	61 (122)	76 (140)	82 (220)	77 (172)	76 (654)
Above 51	75 (83)	86 (86)	81 (88)	80 (20)	80 (277)
Total	63	74	75	64	

NOTE: The numbers in parentheses are the bases on which the percentages were computed.

we should be careful that it is not a spurious finding. Could the relationship between media exposure and voting turnout in reality be a reflection of the effect of education on turnout? There is cause for this speculation because the degree of media consumption is related to the degree of formal education. Thus the initial rise and the later decline in voting associated with the consumption of mass communications might be seen as the result of educational differences rather than of anything learned from the media. TABLE 10.4 shows that this is not true: for each level of education, turnout at the polls rises as media consumption rises upto a point, and then declines with further increase in media exposure.

A more severe test is provided when we introduce controls for age. We would remember from our discussion in a previous chapter that age was even more strongly related to political participation than was education. Young persons have woefully low voting rates (see the 5th column in TABLE 10.4 under "Total"). At the same time, young persons as compared with older people have higher exposure to mass communications (see TABLE 10.1 above). The lower voting rate among those with regular exposure to mass communications might therefore be viewed as the result of strong age-voting relationship. But again TABLE 10.4 shows that this is not the case. Among persons of the same age, the curvilinear media-voting relationship as reported above holds true. It is therefore clear that media exposure is related to voting, independently of variations due to age or education. It is well to remind ourselves however, that our results are derived from one national and one regional poll, and for that reason, we cannot place as high a confidence in the validity of findings reported in this chapter as in those reported at other places.

Though our data are limited, they do nevertheless conform to what we have so far discovered: that voting is a special kind of political act in India in the sense that persons who are most competent to participate in politics do not exercise their franchise. It may be speculated that mass communications, like education, geographical mobility and urban residence, foment what has been called the Revolution of Rising Expectations. Mass communications create images of a different and a better world, and thus help expand the range of desires. But the creation of these images is one thing and their satisfaction quite another. Since India, like most other Asian and African countries, is at a stage of development when demands cannot be satisfied as quickly as they arise, a certain amount of alienation and frustration is generic in the process of modernization. This alienation and frustration is widest not among the most destitute and the illiterate, but among the comparatively better off and the educated, for it is these people who are most aware of the gaps between what they seek and what they can get. We provided evidential support for this view in previous chapters: on several different measures, it was seen that governmental criticism and political alienation were prevalent exactly in those groups which were urbanized or exposed to modernizing influences. If these findings are correct then lower voting frequency among those exposed to media may be a consequence of their unhappiness (see chapters on Education and Urban-Rural Differences for the development of this theme).

SUMMARY

In this chapter we have presented data on the reading and listening habits of the people and their effects on political participation. Unhappily, only two of the 11PO polls analysed in this study had information on mass communications. But on the basis of these two polls, there is some evidence that every rise in media consumption is not accompanied by a corresponding increase in voting turnout. Beyond a certain point, further exposure to the media is curiously associated with a declining voting rate. This is yet another indication that voting is a special kind of political activity in India.

Participation in political discussions, attending meetings, and trying to influence decisions show the expected and normal relationship with media exposure. Participation in these activities rises as the consumption of mass media rises.

NOTES

[1]Karl W. Deutsch has been a pioneer in this field. See his *Nationalism and Social Communications* (The M.I.T. Press, 1953); see also his *The Nerves of Government* (N.Y.: The Free Press of Glencoe, 1963). Lucian Pye's (edited) *Communications and Political Development* (Princeton, Princeton University Press, 1963) is an anthology of recent theorizing in this field.

[2]Wilbur Schramm is the author of this viewpoint. See his "Communications Development and the Developmental Process," in Lucian Pye, *ibid.*, p. 34.

[3]Deniel Lerner, *The Passing of Traditional Society* (N.Y.: The Free Press of Glencoe, 1958), Ch. 2.

[4]*Ibid.*, pp. 47-52.

[5]Donald R. Matthews and James W. Prothro, *Negroes and the New Southern Politics* (N.Y.: Harcourt, Brace & World, 1966), p. 263.

[6]Quoted in Lerner, *op. cit.*, p. 214.

[7]*Ibid.*, pp. 232-33.

[8]These figures are calculated from the data in UNESCO'S *World Communications* (Paris: 1950, 1961, 1964),

[9]*India: A Reference Annual*, 1973 (New Delhi, Ministry of Information and Broadcasting, 1973), pp. 124-51. Some social scientists contend that the problems of turmoil and disorder prevalent in most developing societies are caused by too rapid a growth of mass communications. Modernization is a multi-dimensional phenomenon: there must be a balanced growth in several sectors of modernization—economic, social, political, and communications. Too much growth in one sector can retard the overall developmental process. For instance, schools and the mass media create desires and images of a better world. If the economic and industrial sectors do not keep pace with the expansion in the educational and media sectors, frustration and unhappiness are likely to follow, which in turn create political instability. In this view, India's stability, in contrast to instability in many other Afro-Asian countries, can be explained as partly a consequence of the better balance achieved between development of the media and development in the other sectors. See Lerner, *op. cit.*, and Samuel P. Huntington, *Political Order in Changing Societies* (New Haven: Yale University Press, 1969).

[10]*Press in India, 1972* (New Delhi: Registrar of Newspapers, 1972).

[11]*India: A Reference Annual 1973*, and *The Times of India Directory and Yearbook, 1971.* A 1967 issue of the *Seminar* magazine published from Delhi (No. 98 entitled "Mass Communication") raises important questions regarding difficulties faced by the various media in India, and also contains useful bibliography on the subject.

[12]See the Appendix at the end of the book for further details on the mass media exposure index.

CHAPTER ELEVEN

Geographical Mobility

THE 1964 NATIONAL POLL contains several questions which form the basis of inquiry into geographical mobility of respondents. They were asked: "How about travelling? Have you ever been on a train or a bus?" Those who answered in the affirmative to this question were further queried: "When was the last time you travelled on a train or a bus?" Two additional questions complete the exploration of the travelling habits of respondents; these were: "Have you ever been to another state?" and "Have you ever been to another country?"

A 4-step mobility index was constructed using these four items. Some 230 persons (out of 2014) had never been on a train or a bus and had never been to another state; they were classified as having 'no' mobility. Some 746 persons in the sample had travelled as recently as the past week and had in addition been to another state and some of them (94 persons) even to another country; these were classified as having 'high' geographical mobility. The two other classifications, 'low' and 'medium,' fall in between these two extremes—the first includes those persons who had travelled within the past one year, and the second includes those who had travelled within the past one month and had also visited another state.[1]

As might be expected, geographical mobility is strongly associated with place of residence, sex, social position, age and education of the respondents. The urban residents, males, the more affluent, the middle aged persons and the more educated also travel more often. The best indicator of physical mobility remains the educational attainments of the respondents (see TABLE 11.1): whereas only 9 per cent of the illiterate and 32 per cent of those having a few years of schooling reported that they had been on a train or a bus within the past week and had also been to another state, as many as 58 per cent of the high school educated and 68 per cent of the college

TABLE 11.1

URBAN-RURAL, SEX, INCOME, AGE AND EDUCATION CORRELATES OF GEOGRAPHICAL MOBILITY

(1964 National Poll)

	Geographical Mobility				
	None	*Low*	*Med.*	*High*	*N*
Place of Residence		Percentages			
Rural	17	25	29	28	(975)
Urban	6	23	25	45	(1035)
Sex					
Female	19	36	28	17	(292)
Male	10	22	27	40	(1722)
Income (Rs. a month)					
-99	18	32	37	12	(485)
-199	8	24	28	40	(611)
-349	0	18	28	43	(385)
350 & above	2	19	15	64	(316)
Age					
21-25	11	22	34	34	(342)
26-35	9	21	29	40	(740)
36-50	14	25	22	40	(654)
51 & above	12	35	27	27	(277)
Education					
Illiterate	29	36	25	9	(465)
Some Schooling	9	24	35	32	(857)
Matriculate	2	18	22	58	(350)
College	0	16	16	68	(321)

graduates reported the same. Also all those 94 persons who said that they had visited another country were at least matriculates. It is evident that physical mobility fits well with the SES syndrome as well as the modernization syndrome.

If we did not know the pattern of Indian findings we would expect to see a positive relationship between travel and voter turn-out. But now that we have knowledge of some of the peculiarities of participation patterns of the Indian population, we should expect to find a curvilinear relationship between physical mobility and voter turnout.

Our latter expectation is borne out by the data in Table 11.2: those with low or medium mobility report a higher turnout rate than those who had never travelled anywhere or those who had travelled extensively. For example (see under Total), 52 per cent of those with no mobility, 72 per cent with low mobility, 75 per cent with medium mobility, but only 69 per cent with high mobility report having used the ballot box. TABLE 11.2 also demonstrates that the above relationship is not lost when controls for education or for age are introduced. That is, no matter what educational or age group is examined, individuals at either pole of our physical mobility index vote less than those in the middle. This would indicate that travelling has an independent effect on voter participation.

The effect of geographical mobility on voting turnout is thus similar to that of education and media exposure. All these variables have a curvilinear relationship with voting frequency. But then all these factors may have a similar impact on attitudinal and psychological make-up of an individual. Physical mobility broadens an individual's outlook through *actual* experiences of far away people and places; mass communications and education have the same effect through *vicarious* experiences of these things. In his book on the Mideast, Daniel Lerner argues that factors like education, mass media exposure, travel, urbanization (each one of them separately, or all of them together) lead to personality changes. The hallmark of this new personality, according to Lerner, is "empathy" or the capacity to see oneself in somebody else's position.[2]

In one sense, then, our data support Lerner's thesis—education, income, media exposure and travel are related to one another, and a person who possesses these attributes is a person with opinions on a variety of issues; those who have no education or no mass media exposure or no travel are much more likely to just say "don't know". In another sense, our data do not support Lerner's thesis. Education, media exposure and travel may lead to "empathy," but empathy does not necessarily lead to greater participation, when participation is defined as turnout at the polls. This should be abundantly clear from evidence presented in this and previous chapters.

TABLE 11.2

VOTING FREQUENCY AND GEOGRAPHICAL MOBILITY
WITH CONTROLS FOR EDUCATION AND AGE

(*1964 National Poll*)

	Illiterate	Some Schooling	Matric	College	Total
			Percentages		
Mobility					
None	51 (136)	58 (79)	— (8)	— (1)	52 (230)
Low	66 (109)	82 (204)	65 (62)	58 (50)	72 (491)
Medium	76 (117)	80 (299)	66 (76)	66 (50)	75 (546)
High	70 (43)	77 (275)	62 (204)	65 (220)	69 (746)
	21-25	26-35	36-50	Above 51	
Mobility					
None	46 (37)	51 (68)	51 (92)	64 (33)	
Low	57 (75)	67 (159)	78 (161)	83 (96)	
Medium	47 (115)	79 (297)	89 (260)	84 (77)	
High	34 (115)	74 (297)	75 (260)	78 (77)	

NOTE: The numbers in parentheses are the bases on which the percentages were computed.

TABLE 11.3

ATTEMPTED POLITICAL INFLUENCE AND GEOGRAPHICAL
MOBILITY, WITH CONTROLS FOR EDUCATION AND AGE

(1964 National Poll)

	Percentage Trying to Influence Decisions				
	Illiterate	Some Schooling	Matric	College	Total
Mobility					
None	1 (136)	13 (79)	— (8)	— (1)	5 (230)
Low	1 (109)	12 (204)	20 (62)	24 (50)	10 (491)
Medium	3 (117)	17 (299)	21 (76)	34 (50)	17 (560)
High	17 (43)	22 (275)	25 (204)	35 (220)	25 (746)
Mobility	21-25	26-35	36-50	Above 51	
None	0 (37)	3 (68)	5 (92)	15 (33)	
Low	9 (75)	9 (159)	12 (161)	10 (96)	
Medium	13 (115)	17 (297)	18 (141)	23 (74)	
High	15 (115)	28 (216)	27 (260)	25 (77)	

NOTE: The numbers in parentheses are the bases on which the percentages were computed.

POLITICAL INFLUENCE

Turning now to participation in political influence activities, TABLE 11.3 shows that physical travel is positively associated with attempted political influence, i.e. an increase in one is accompanied by an increase in the other. Thus (see under Total), only 5 per cent of those with no mobility, 10 per cent of those with low mobility, 17 per cent of those with medium mobility, but as many as 25 per cent with high mobility reported that they had joined groups or contacted officials in an affort to affect local or national decisions.

But since education is so strongly associated with travel, the positive relationship between travel and attempted political influence might disappear when the effect of education is "partialled out." An examination of TABLE 11.3 reveals that education is indeed strongly related to political influence, as we already know. But this does not mean that mobility itself has no independent effect on attempted political influence. When we make our comparisons between people with the same degree of education, the strength of association between travel and attempted political influence decreases, but by no means disappears. At every level of education, those who have travelled more are more likely to have tried to affect political decisions. TABLE 11.3 also shows that geographical mobility has a greater meaning for the illiterates than for the highly educated; that is, physical travel is much more strongly associated with attempted political influence among the illiterates than among the high school or college graduates. On the basis of these data, it can therefore be inferred that travel can partly compensate for a lack of education as far as attempts to influence political decisions are concerned.

Since age is also associated with mobility (those under 50 have travelled more than those over 51), it was thought necessary to test the correlation between travel and attempted political influence by holding age constant. This has been done in TABLE 11.3, and reading down each column, we find that the positive relationship between travel and participation in political influence activities persists even when variation due to age is controlled. Another finding is that, at higher levels of mobility (indicating greater modernization), advancing age as such does not lead to greater participation; at lower mobility levels, however, advancing age is associated with increased participation in political activities. The latter may represent the traditional situation where age is supposedly seen as a basis for political influence without reference to competence.

Conclusions

In summary, then, it is evident that physical mobility forms a part of the modernization syndrome. Persons who are on the upper ladders of the modernization scale—those who have received education, been exposed to more media, lived in cities, etc. are much more likely to have also had travelling experiences. It was found that, like other modernization factors, physical travel was curvilinearly related to voter turnout. This relationship persisted even after variation due to age and education was controlled. At the same time, travel was positively related to participation in political influence activities. Unfortunately, the data in this section were derived from a single poll, and the generalizations must remain qualified on this account.

NOTES

[1]See the Appendix for further details on this index.

[2]Daniel Lerner, *The Passing of Traditional Society* (N.Y.: The Free Press, 1958), Ch. 2. See Chapters Three and Ten in this book for a discussion of Lerner's "empathy" concept.

PART III

INDIVIDUAL ATTITUDES, BELIEFS
AND
POLITICAL PARTICIPATION

So far we have been concerned with socio-economic cha-
racteristics and their impact on political participation.
Now we turn to another class of variables: individual
attitudes and beliefs. In this section, we shall examine
the impact on political participation of the following
five variables: political information, attitudes toward
political recruitment, party preference, party evaluation
and feeling of subjective effectiveness. These five vari-
ables form a group in another sense: they are a measure
of political attributes and cognitions. For this reason,
the five factors can also be labelled as "political"
variables, as contrasted with socio-economic variables.

CHAPTER TWELVE

Political Information

THE 1967 AND THE 1964 NATIONAL POLLS provide us with an opportunity to test the relationship between the amount of political information a person possesses and the level of his political participation. Two identical questions asked in these polls were: "Now, will you please name three important or well-known leading men in the Congress party today?" After the person had responded to this question he was asked: "And, who are two important national leaders outside the Congress party?" The answers to these questions were coded 0, 1, 2, 3, etc.—each digit corresponding to the number of leaders the respondent could identify. On the basis of these answers an index of political information was constructed by this writer as follows: all those persons who could identify neither any Congress nor any opposition leaders were classified as having 'no' political information; on the other hand, those who identified three to four of the Congress leaders and two of the opposition were classified as having 'high' information; persons in between these two polar categories were classified as 'low' or 'medium'.[1]

It should be noted that the above questions only tangentially tap the political information level of a person. It would have been better if several questions exploring political information had been available and a Guttman scale built using these questions. Since such was not the case, it is well to keep in mind that the political information index used in this chapter is at best only an approximation of the level of political knowledge of a respondent.

With this qualification in mind, an examination of TABLE 12.1 shows that the degree of political information is directly related to participation in activities designed to affect political outcomes. The more information a person commands, the more likely he is to have tried to influence national and local decisions. Thus, according to the 1967 national survey, only 6 per cent of those having no information, 13 per cent with low information, 20 per cent with medium information, but 29 per cent with high information have done something to affect the decision making process (the corresponding percentages for the 1964 poll are : 5, 10, 19, and 30). But as we might expect, voting and information do not show a similar positive relationship : the two are curvilinearly related. Both the 1967 and the 1964 surveys support this correlation (see TABLE 12.1).

These findings should surprise no one. We know from our previous discussions that factors like education, media exposure, and social status show a *linear* relationship with political influence but a *curvilinear* relationship with voting turnout. We also know that the level of political information follows closely the degree of media exposure and the level of educational attainment. TABLE 12.2 demonstrates this : twice as many urbanites as ruralites, about

TABLE 12.1

POLITICAL PARTICIPATION AND POLITICAL INFORMATION

	No Information	*Low Information*	*Medium Information*	*High Information*
Percentages				
1967 national poll	62 (2588)	71 (1852)	66 (1996)	65 (2712)
1964 national poll	60 (500)	76 (417)	73 (467)	70 (630)
Percentage Participating in Activities to Affect Decisions				
1967 national poll	6 (2588)	13 (1852)	20 (1996)	29 (2712)
1964 national poll	5 (500)	10 (417)	19 (467)	30 (630)

NOTE : The numbers in parentheses are the bases on which the percentages were computed.

TABLE 12.2

POLITICAL INFORMATION, BY PLACE OF RESIDENCE, SEX, EDUCATION AND LEVEL OF MEDIA EXPOSURE

	No Information	Low Information	Medium information	High information	N
	1967 National Poll				
Residence	*Percentage nf Vote*				
Rural	37	21	20	22	(4740)
Urban	19	19	23	38	(4405)
Sex					
Female	53	21	14	12	(2071)
Male	22	20	24	35	(7074)
Education					
Illiterate	61	24	10	5	(2746)
Some Schooling	20	24	27	29	(3595)
Matriculate	7	12	29	51	(1344)
College	7	11	25	57	(1463)
	1964 National Poll				
Media Exposure					
No Exposure	68	27	5	1	(327)
Low ,,	37	33	20	9	(438)
Med. ,,	14	18	30	38	(607)
High ,,	5	12	28	55	(642)

three times as many males as females, about eleven times as many college educated persons as illiterates belong to the 'high' information category. The media exposure index from the 1964 poll is even more strongly related to political information scale. Whereas only 1 per cent of those not regularly exposed to newspapers, radio and cinema

TABLE 12.3

VOTING FREQUENCY AND POLITICAL INFORMATION, WITH CONTROLS FOR EDUCATION AND MEDIA EXPOSURE

Information	Education				Mass Media Exposure			
	Illiterate	Some schooling	Matric	College	None	Low	Medium	High
Percentages								
No Information	64 (1679)	64 (710)	53 (101)	34 (98)	58 (221)	66 (164)	59 (86)	41 (29)
Low "	77 (667)	71 (860)	62 (164)	53 (161)	76 (88)	80 (145)	77 (108)	76 (76)
Medium "	82 (262)	72 (982)	54 (388)	50 (364)	— (16)	83 (88)	77 (181)	65 (182)
High "	83 (138)	73 (1043)	58 (691)	53 (840)	— (2)	68 (41)	77 (232)	65 (355)

NOTE: The numbers in parentheses are the bases on which the percentages were computed.

TABLE 12.4

POLITICAL INFLUENCE, BY POLITICAL INFORMATION AND EDUCATION

(*1967 National Poll*)

Information	Percentage Trying to Influence Decisions			
	Illiterate	Some Schooling	Matric	College
No Information	3 (1674)	9 (709)	9 (100)	22 (98)
Low ,,	8 (667)	13 (856)	21 (164)	26 (161)
Med. ,,	19 (260)	20 (972)	17 (387)	24 (363)
High ,,	19 (138)	32 (1021)	24 (638)	30 (840)

NOTE: The numbers in parentheses are the bases on which the percentages were computed.

were able to name three Congress and two opposition party leaders, as many as 55 per cent of those regularly exposed to these media could identify these leaders. This is indeed as it should be, for even in an underdeveloped country, a great deal of political information is gained through mass media as compared with face-to-face communications.

The real meaning of political information for political participation can be discerned only when controls for education and mass media exposure are provided. These controls are given in TABLE 12.3. When education is controlled, an increase in political information does seem to be associated with an increase in voting frequency. This relationship is especially true for the less educated persons (illiterates and those with a little education). Thus, taking the first row, 83 per cent of those with 'high' information, as compared to 64 per cent of those with 'no' information, reported that they turned out at the polls. The pattern is less consistent in the case of the highly educated (high school and above); each rise in the level of political information is not accompanied by a corresponding rise in voting frequency. On the basis of these data, it is therefore fair to conclude that generally for the highly educated, the level of political information plays little role in determining whether or not they vote; but in the case of less educated persons, a rising level of information is accompanied by a rise in voting frequency. Indeed, the highest voting rate (83 per cent) is recorded by those illiterates who are highly knowledgeable, and, in contrast, the lowest voting rate (34 per cent) is among those who have college education (a factor associated with declining frequency), and who are oblivious of the political world around them.

The relationship between voting turnout and political information, with controls for media exposure, is also clearly highlighted in TABLE 12.3. Reading across each row provides a picture of the influence of media exposure with political information held constant. At each level of information, voting frequency rises when we move to medium and high exposures. Taking the second row for instance, turnout increases from 76 per cent to 80 per cent and then declines to 77 per cent and 67 per cent. Reading down each column, we see the effect of different levels of political information on people with the same amount of media consumption. In all columns (except column six), turnout increases sharply when we move from no information to low information and *does not* significantly decline with further rise in the level of information. Taking the seventh column for instance, a column that has an edequate number in each cell, turnout rises from 59 per cent to 77 per cent and stays at that level. This is an indication that, unlike the modernization factors like education and media exposure, political information is an important correlate of voting turnout.

POLITICAL INFLUENCE

We now turn to the relationship between political information and political influence with controls for education. TABLE 12.4 provides these data from the 1967 All-India poll, and we see that political information is positively related to political influence for all levels of education, i.e. no matter which educational group we consider, a rise in the level of political information is associated with a rise in political influence. But we also notice that a rise in the level of political information has quite a different meaning

for the illiterates than for the college educated. Among the illiterates and those with a little education, political influence rises
sharply as political information increases, but no such sharp rise is
registered by the college educated (among the illiterates it rises
from 3 per cent to 19 per cent, among those with a little education
from 9 per cent to 32 per cent, and among the college educated from
22 per cent to 30 per cent). It appears that once a person has
received a college education, he acts like a politically efficacious
person whether he is politically knowledgeable or not; in the case of
the illiterates, on the other hand, only those who can command political information have the confidence to try to influence decisions.
In fact it would seem that political knowledge can go a long way
to compensate for the lack of education. Nearly as high a proportion of the *highly informed* illiterates (19 per cent) as that of the *ill-
informed* college educated (22 per cent) reports participation in political influence activities.

The relationship between political influence and political information with controls for media exposure was also tested. It was
found (table not given here) that for every level of media exposure,
a rise in political information was positively correlated with attempts
to influence decisions. All this indicates that political information
is an important factor which facilitates political participation in
India.

SUMMARY

Here, we have presented evidence from the 1967 and the 1964 national studies on the level of political information among people, and the
effect of this level on political participation. We found that people
who live in cities, who are males, who have high education and
who are regularly exposed to mass media are much more likely to
be able to identify Congress and Opposition national leaders than
people with the opposite characteristics.

It was discovered that political information was linearly related
to attempted political influence but curvilinearly related to voting
turnout. An interesting finding was that when we make comparisons between people of similar education, political information had
significant effect on participation rates especially of the poorly
educated. That is, the well-informed illiterates were more likely

to vote and to attempt to influence decisions than the ignorant illiterates. The differences between well-informed and the ignorant college educated persons, at the same time, were not as distinct.

NOTES

[1] Further details on this and other indexes are available in the Appendix at the end of the book.

CHAPTER THIRTEEN

Politicizatian

THERE IS a common impression among social scientists that politics plays an unduly important role in the new nations, and that political considerations pervade even day to day social relations. For example, Lucian Pye in his study of the Burmese society writes: "There are few cultures that attach greater importance to power as a value than the Burmese. Considerations of power and status so permeate even social relationships in Burma that life tends to become highly politicized. . . . The appreciation of power is in many ways similar to the American feeling about love: namely, it is a thing of the highest value, to be pursued, but once grasped it is far too precious to be used for any material gain, at least not openly or explicitly. . . ."[1]

Kwame Nkrumah, the former President of Ghana, epitomized this power theme by having inscribed under his statue: "Seek ye first the political kingdom and all other things shall be added unto it."

This writer cannot speak for the whole underdeveloped world, but at least as far as India is concerned, the above impression about the primacy of politics is largely correct. Politics is a highly sought after vocation in India and it attracts persons from all walks of life. This can be seen from the large number of candidates who contest a limited number of electoral seats, and from the increase in the number of contesting candidates. For instance, in the 1957 lower house elections, 2,281 persons were nominated for 494 Lok Sabha seats (4.6 persons to a seat), and after withdrawals and rejections, 1,522 candidates actually fought for these 494 seats (3.1 persons per seat). In 1967, 2,369 candidates contested 520 constituencies, increasing by 19 per cent over 1962 and by 55 per cent over 1957. These data are reported in TABLE 13.1, and two patterns are evident: more candidates contested each seat in 1967 than in the previous elections; state legislative assembly elections attract more candidates for each position than do national parliamentary elections. This second phenomenon is perhaps indicative of the fact that some local parties contest elections only at the state level, and that independent candidates are more confident about winning a state office than a national office which requires greater organizational resources. Another index of the attractiveness of political offices in India is provided in TABLE 13.2, which reports data on the proportion of constituencies that were contested by a varying number of candidates. Sixty-five per cent of the 1967 and 57 per cent of 1962 parliamentary constituencies fielded four or more candidates. Firozabad constituency in U.P. had the unique distinction of fielding 17 candidates in 1962.[2]

TABLE 13.1

NUMBER OF CANDIDATES WHO WERE NOMINATED AND
WHO CONTESTED LOK SABHA AND VIDHAN SABHA SEATS

	No. of Seats	No. of Candidates Nominated	No. of Average Candidates Nominated for each Seat	No. of Candidates that contested after withdrawals & rejections	Average per Seat
1957 Election					
Lok Sabha	494	2,281	4.6	1,522	3.1
Vidhan Sabha	2,906	16,475	5.6	10,176	3.5
1962 Election					
Lok Sabha	494	2,763	5.6	1,985	4.0
Vidhan Sabha	2,855	18,582	6.5	12,646	4.5
1967 Election					
Lok Sabha	520	3,244	6.2	2,369	4.5
Vidhan Sabha	3,487	23,838	6.8	16,503	4.7

TABLE 13.2

NUMBER AND PERCENTAGE OF CONSTITUENCIES THAT
WERE CONTESTED BY TWO OR MORE CANDIDATES

	2 Candidates	3 Candidates	4 Candidates	5 Candidates	6 Candidates	7 or more Candidates
1962 Election						
Lok Sabha	69 (14%)	141 (28%)	126 (25%)	78 (16%)	45 (9%)	32 (7%)
Vidhan Sabha	359 (13%)	654 (23%)	662 (23%)	489 (17%)	315 (11%)	363 (13%)
1967 Election						
Lok Sabha	61 (12%)	115 (22%)	125 (24%)	80 (15%)	54 (11%)	80 (15%)
Vidhan Sabha	396 (11%)	789 (23%)	729 (21%)	516 (15%)	376 (11%)	647 (19%)

Why is the political world so attractive in India? Why do so
many persons want to get into public offices even when running in
elections is expensive in terms of time and money? One can argue
that there is a high rate of unemployment in India and those who
do not find suitable jobs elsewhere turn to politics. But this argument fails when it is realized that running in elections costs money,
and a person who is not already established in a profession or a
business, or who does not have inherited sources of wealth, can
hardly afford to run for public office. The prime reason why so
many persons pursue public office would therefore appear to be the
status that accompanies an office of authority in India. The status
that is attached to government position is partly a remnant of
the British days when government and bureaucracy were the heart
of the colonial rule and when many of the elite in society were
government officers. But also, the traditional sources of authority
and status, like caste, are gradually being obliterated under the
impact of modernization. This further intensifies the struggle for
public offices—the one certain venue for prestige and status.[3]

The evidence that public office is highly desired in India is also available from survey research. One of the IIPO studies conducted in Delhi in 1964 contained the following item: "If you had a son who was thinking of going into politics, would you encourage him, discourage him, or say nothing?" The same question was also asked in a metropolitan survey in the United States (Detroit Area Study).[4] The frequency of answers to this question was :

	Delhi Per cent	Detroit Per cent
Encourage him	27	13
Discourage him	11	28
Say nothing to him	47	55
Don't know	15	

Although there might be some question regarding cross-national comparisons of this kind, particularly since neither of the samples was national, it is clear that twice the percentage of persons in Delhi as in Detroit would encourage their sons to enter politics. The prestige levels of government service in India are also very high. In another study conducted in the Delhi state, the same general question which had been asked in a few other countries was posed: "If the pay were the same would you prefer to work for the government or for a private firm?" In urban Delhi 76 per cent of the respondents and in rural Delhi 89 per cent of the respondents said that they would prefer public employment. This compares with a 56 per cent prestige level in the U.S. in 1954, a 44 per cent level in an Australian study in 1948, and a 36 per cent level in Canada in 1948.[5]

SOCIAL CORRELATES

What kind of Delhi residents would "encourage" their sons to seek political careers? Are they rich or poor? More educated or less educated? More exposed to mass media or less exposed? These questions are examined in TABLE 13.3.

TABLE 13.3

EDUCATION, INCOME AND MEDIA EXPOSURE CORRELATES OF POLITICIZATION

(*Delhi Area Study*)

"If you had a son who was thinking of going into politics, would you encourage him, discourage him, or say nothing?"

	Would Encourage	Would Discourage	Say Nothing	Don't Know	N
Education		*Percentages*			
Illiterate	18	10	49	23	(141)
Some Schooling	31	10	46	14	(216)
Matric	35	11	43	12	(95)
College	16	22	51	11	(37)
Income per month					
0-100 Rs.	20	13	45	23	(164)
101-250	32	8	47	12	(211)
Above 251	25	15	47	13	(100)
Mass Media Exposure					
None	17	10	47	25	(181)
Low	25	9	54	11	(141)
Medium	36	12	43	9	(112)
High	47	12	33	9	(58)

The more educated persons are not necessarily more politicized. Our data indicate that the most politicized of the Delhi residents are those who have middle or high school education. Data indicate that the college educated persons are least likely to answer that

they would encourage their sons to go into politics. Another interesting finding is that the range of opinion becomes considerably
wider as the level of education increases. The more educated are
simply more likely to have opinions, although these opinions may
not be in the same direction. Thus, in answer to the question on
recruitment, 23 per cent of the illiterates had no opinion; this
compares with 14 per cent of those who had a few years of schooling, 12 per cent of high school matriculates and 11 per cent of
college graduates.

Income shows a similar relationship. The most favourably disposed toward political careerism are members of the middle earning groups (those who make between Rs. 101 and 250 a month).
We again note that the proportion of "don't knows" declines as
we move from the poor to the relatively rich. In contrast to education and income, the mass media exposure is positively related
to the level of politicization: namely, those who are exposed to
more than one mass medium are more likely to say that they would
encourage their sons to enter politics. There is also some evidence
indicating that rural residents may be more willing to see their
sons pursue political careers than urban residents. In answer to
"would you like to see your son enter politics?" 25 per cent of
rural respondents as against 14 per cent of urban respondents in a
1965 poll answered "yes".

The basic and primary query for us, however, is whether the
feelings toward recruitment are significantly correlated with political participation levels. Do we find that the more politicized are
more active in politics than those who are not? The data for this
query are unhappily available only in the Delhi Area Study. It
may also be noted that although the question on political recruitment has been taken as a measure of politicization, it is far from
being a good or an adequate operationalization of what is nor-
mally meant by this concept.

The above questions are examined in TABLE 13.4, and we find
that those who would "encourage" their sons to enter politics report higher participation than those who would "discourage," or
"say nothing," or who say "don't know." This relationship holds
true for all forms of political participation on which data are available from the Delhi Area Study. Furthermore, the difference in
the participation rates of those who would "encourage" and those
who gave other answers is sizable: it varies from 14 percentage

points on voting turnout to 27 percentage points on discussing political matters. This is an indication that the independent variable under discussion is quite powerful in explaining political behaviour in India.

TABLE 13.4

POLITICAL PARTICIPATION AND POLITICIZATION

	Percentage of Vote	Percentage Attending Meetings	Percentage Discussing Politics	Percentage Giving Money	N
Would encourage Son to enter Politics	81	56	43	18	(133)
Other Answers	67	30	16	4	(359)
Difference	—14	—26	—27	—14	

But before fully accepting this conclusion, we must examine whether the relationship between politicization and political participation holds when variance due to such factors as education and mass media is neutralized. It is necessary to do so because education and mass media exposure are strong determinants of political attitudes of people.

Considering first controls for *education*, we see (TABLE 13.5) that no matter what the level of education, the more politicized are more active. For instance, turnout among the illiterates (first column), declines from 96 per cent to 66 per cent when we move from those who would encourage their sons to enter politics to those who gave other answers. On the other end of the educational ladder (third column), voting turnout declines from 67 per cent to 58 per cent.

As in the case of voting turnout, the positive relationship between politicization and other forms of participation (attending public meetings and discussing politics) continues to hold even after education has been controlled.

It is thus clear that the positive relationship between attitudes

TABLE 13.5

POLITICAL PARTICIPATION AND POLITICIZATION WITH CONTROLS FOR EDUCATION AND MEDIA EXPOSURE

	Education			Media Exposure		
	Illiterate	*Some Schooling*	*Matric & Coll.*	*None*	*Low*	*Medium & High*
Percentages						
Would Encourage	96 (26)	85 (66)	67 (37)	90 (30)	81 (36)	78 (67)
Other Answers	66 (115)	75 (150)	58 (93)	64 (151)	70 (105)	70 (103)
Difference	—30	—10	—9	—26	—11	—8
Percentage Attending Meetings						
Would Encourage	58	56	54	40	61	60
Other Answers	26	33	30	24	26	42
Difference	—32	—23	—24	—16	—35	—18
Percentage Discussing Politics						
Would Encourage	35	41	54	30	36	51
Other Answers	8	17	25	7	12	33
Difference	—27	—24	—29	—23	—24	—18

NOTE: The numbers in parentheses are the bases on which the percentages were computed. The bottom rows have the same bases as the top rows.

toward recruitment and political participation is not merely a reflection of education. The most striking entry in TABLE 13.5 is the one which shows that participation among the politicized illiterates is extremely high. Almost all of them (96 per cent) turned

out at the polls and as many as 58 per cent reported having attended public meetings. Both these percentages are the highest among
all educational groups. It would seem that the world of politics
has quite a different attraction for the lower strata of society in
Delhi than for the upper strata; politics may be the vehicle which
the uneducated and the under-privileged use to break away from
their traditional and depressed status.

What about the relationship between politicization and political
participation when the effect of mass media is controlled? Data in
TABLE 13.5 indicate that when the effect of mass media is neutralized, the relationship between politicization and political participation remains strong. Briefly, then, attitude toward political
recruitment has emerged as a significant explanatory variable of
political participation in India. The authors of *The American Voter*
have argued that psychological orientations are a better predictor
of human behaviour than are socio-economic variables.[6] The large
differences between the politicized and the non-politicized indicated
in our data are a confirmation of this thesis in India.

Another interesting point that emerges from these data is that
turnout levels decrease with higher education, whether or not respondents are favourably oriented to political recruitment of their
sons. This is a further documentation of one of the key findings in
this study, that voting rates among the highly educated are lower
than among the less educated and that they vary only slightly with
differences in other attributes.

CONCLUSIONS

The relationship between attitudes toward political recruitment
and political participation was examined in this chapter. It was
seen that a large number of Delhi residents were favourably disposed toward political careerism. Data from the Election Commission
also supported our contention that political offices are highly sought
after positions in India.

The middle educated and the middle income groups in Delhi
were more politicized than others. At the same time, exposure to
mass media was positively related to attitudes toward political recruitment.

It was further found that politicization and political participation were positively related. Those who "would encourage" their sons to enter politics were more likely to vote, to attend meetings, to engage in political discussions, and to give money to parties. This positive relationship persisted even when controls for education, mass media exposure and other relevant variables were introduced.

The measure of politicization was derived from answers to the question: "If you had a son who was thinking of going into politics, would you encourage him, discourage him, or say nothing?" Those who answered "encourage him" were taken to be favourably disposed toward political recruitment, or to be more politicized than others.

NOTES

[1]Lucian Pye, *Politics, Personality and Nation Building: Burma's Search for Identity* (New Haven: Yale University Press, 1962), p. 146.

[2]These data were derived from the *Reports* of the Election Commission, Government of India, 1957, 1962, 1967.

[3]In this context Myron Weiner writes: "The rush for office is bound to be great in a hierarchical social system. Furthermore, where authority is esteemed, as it almost universally is in traditional societies, individuals in a hierarchical system look with covetous eyes on all positions of power accessible to them. . . . Struggles for power become particularly intense and emotional when other criteria for status become fuzzy. Caste in changing rural India is no longer as clear a mark of status as it once was. . . .Many villagers now report that in the 'old days' it was not necessary for men to contest panchayat elections since everyone recognized who the village leaders were. That this is becoming less and less so suggests that criteria for status are no longer clear; todaymen must often stand for public office to assert their claims to status." See his "India's Two Political Cultures," in *Political Change in South Asia* (Calcutta: F.K.L. Mukhopadhyay, 1963), p. 124. Also see Pye, *op. cit.*, Ch. 11.

[4]Samuel J. Eldersveld, *Political Parties: A Behavioral Analysis* (Chicago: Rand McNally, 1964), p. 440.

[5]Data are derived from Samuel J. Eldersveld, *et al., The Citizen and the Administrator in a Developing Democracy* (Glenview, Ill.: Scott, Foresman, 1968), p. 27.

[6]Angus Campbell, *et al., The American Voter* (N.Y.: John Wiley, 1960).

CHAPTER FOURTEEN

Party Preference and Party Evaluation

THE REGIONAL, linguistic, caste, racial, economic, social and cultural diversity of the Indian society—in short, the "fragmented" nature of its political culture—has given rise to a multiplicity of political parties. The number of political parties in India changes continuously as old groups from new coalitions, or as once unified parties split along factional lines. Because of this it is difficult to arrive at any exact count of all the political parties in India at any one time. Here the findings of the Indian Election Commission are revealing. In 1952 it listed 14 parties on an all-India basis and 59 other parties as state parties. In 1957, the number was significantly reduced: the Commission recognized only 4 parties as national parties and 19 others as state parties; there were, however, 36 other additional political groups and parties which contested elections in 1957. In 1962, the number increased again and the Election Commission recognized 9 national parties and 22 state parties. The number of parties that emerged after the 1967 elections increased again; some 17 different political parties were represented in the Indian lower house, the Lok Sabha.[1]

Though there are a number of parties, it would be difficult to categorize the Indian party system as simply a multi-party one in the classical European sense. The Congress party has dominated Indian politics to such an extent that some political scientists find it useful to classify the Indian party system as a "one-party dominance" system, the Congress being the dominant party. Under this system, opposition parties have not constituted alternatives to the ruling party. Their role has been to constantly criticize and influence the governing party.[2]

The "Congress system" appeared to break down after the 1967

leections, and it looked as if the tide might be changing. For the first time, the opposition parties together scored widespread successes. The Congress was replaced as the governing party in about half the Indian states, and at the centre, the Congress retained power only with the smallest majority (54 per cent of seats). This proportion was further reduced when in 1969 some 60 MP's left the ruling Congress to sit on the opposition benches. Indian political life took on a new look that brought predictions that it was entering a new stage.[3] However, a number of the coalitions collapsed before the next elections. When Mrs. Gandhi's Congress party made a stunning comeback in the 1971 and 1972 elections, the 1967 results began to look more like a deviation than a re-alignment.

Barring unforeseen developments, the hegemony of the ruling Congress is likely to continue, at least at the centre. The trouble with the opposition is that it is split among innumerable parties; in the Lok Sabha alone, there are over a dozen parties. In the distant future these parties may form one single group, thus bestowing some sort of a two-party system in India, but at the time of this writing there are too many differences among them and a reconciliation does not seem possible in the near future. The 1969 left-right split in the Congress did not lead to a duality of political conflict either. Thus, despite the fact that India has adopted the simple majority, single-ballot electoral system, the two-party system is nowhere in sight.[4]

Since there are a number of opposition parties in India, many of them quite small and some of them limited to only a single state, or even a single region within a state, our data will not allow us to examine the strength of all of them. Instead we shall be concerned primarily with only the major, all-India parties and these include: the Socialists (the Praja Socialist Party or the P.S.P. and the Samyukta Socialist Party or the S.S.P.), the Communists (both the Right and the Left wings), the Jan Sangh, and the Swatantra. At times, we shall treat all these opposition parties as a bloc, and to highlight the differences between Congress on the one hand and these opposition parties on the other, we shall use a summary term "the opposition" to refer to these parties. At the same time, we will preserve individual party cells, so that the reader could make his own independent judgment with respect to the several opposition parties individually.[5] "The Congress" includes both the "Old" and the "New" wings of the party, unless otherwise identified.

What are the bases of social support for major Indian parties? To what extent, if any, are political affiliations related to social backgrounds? What kind of people prefer one political party rather than another? Secondly, how is party affiliation related to political participation? Are adherents of one party more likely to be active in politics than those of another party? These are some of the questions that will be explored in this chapter. The literature on political parties, though vast, has been predominantly concerned with the history and organization of parties, highlighting workings of the top political leadership. More recently, survey data have been employed linking party fortunes to voter attitudes and orientations.[6] The present study focuses on data in exploring social bases of party support, and on comparing participation levels among the supporters of various parties. A word of caution is in order. Most of the data analysed here were gathered in 1967 and earlier. Knowing the fluid political conditions in India, we cannot be perfectly certain that patterns discovered in 1967 necessarily hold true today, or will prevail in the future. Secondly, the social bases of party support discussed here apply to the parties at the national level. The regional nature of Indian politics is only too well known. Therefore, the statewise breakdown of the data might well alter the results significantly.

Social Support

It is commonly believed that a large part of the Congress support in India comes from the rural, the less educated, and the minority communities in the country. It is further believed that Congress is proportionately more popular among the older generation than among the youth. This is because the older generation was socialized during India's freedom struggle under the leadership of such national heroes as Mahatma Gandhi, Jawaharlal Nehru and Sardar Patel. The opposition parties, on the other hand, are believed to be proportionately more popular among the youth, in urban areas, and among the better educated persons. Myron Weiner writing in 1957 observed: "Recruitment of party members, especially by opposition parties, appears to occur largely in the cities and is conducted, for the most part, among office employees, shopkeepers, members of professions, and others in the middle

classes. The Hindu communal parties, the Communists, the Socialists, and the Marxist parties all seem to recruit from similar social
groups."[7]

In general, these views are confirmed by the IIPO studies.
Although Congress draws support from all sections of the Indian
society, it is proportionately more popular among the older generation, among the less educated, in the rural areas, and among the
religious and ethnic minorities.   TABLE 14.1 reports the bases of
social support for various major Indian parties. These data are in
response to the question: "Generally speaking, do you prefer one
of India's political parties?" If yes, "which of the parties comes
nearest to your views?"[8]

Regarding age differences on party support, TABLE 14.1-A indicates that the Congress draws relatively more support from among

TABLE 14.1

DISTRIBUTION OF PARTISAN CHOICES IN INDIA, BY AGE,
EDUCATION, RESIDENCE AND RELIGION

A. *AGE*		
	1967 Poll	
	21-35	*36 & Above*
	Percentages	
Party Choice		
Congress	46	54
All Opposition*	54	46
PSP-SSP	47	53
Communist	56	44
Swatantra	52	48
Jan Sangh	61	39
Hindu Mah.	49	51
No Preference	48	52
Total Sample	49	51

TABLE 14.1—(Contd.)

B. EDUCATION

Party Choice	1967 Poll		1964 Poll	
	Illit. or Some Sch.	High Sch. & Coll.	Illit. or Some Sch.	High Sch. & Coll.
Congress	69	31	66	34
All Opposition	62	38	52	48
PSP-SSP	56	44	62	38
Communist	57	43	54	46
Swatantra	62	38	37	63
Jan Sangh	65	35	45	55
Hindu Mah.	92	08	—	—
No Preference	73	27	74	26
Total Sample	69	31	66	34

C. URBAN-RURAL

Party Choice	1967 Poll		1964 Poll	
	Urban	Rural	Urban	Rural
Congress	45	55	47	53
All Opposition	57	43	62	38
PSP-SSP	60	40	60	40
Communist	61	39	63	37
Swatantra	54	46	49	51
Jan Sangh	63	37	70	30
Hindu Mah.	35	65	—	—
No Preference	46	54	47	53
Total Sample	50	50	50	50

TABLE 14.1—(*Contd.*)

D. *RELIGION*

Party Choice	*Hindu*	1967 Poll *Muslim*	*Other Minorities*
Congress	82	12	6
All Opposition	86	8	6
PSP-SSP	80	10	10
Communist	79	17	5
Swatantra	83	9	9
Jan Sangh	95	2	3
Hindu Mah.	100	0	0
No Preference	84	10	6
Total Sample	84	10	6

*"All opposition" also includes those persons who offered a non-Congress party other than the five listed here.

NOTE: For number of cases, see Table 14.3.

the older people than do the opposition parties. Whereas 54 **per** cent of the support for the opposition parties comes from those between the ages of 21 and 35, only 46 per cent of the Congress support comes from this age group. This may suggest a shrinking constituency for the Congress. The age differences on party support may be related to the socializing experience of the individual. In a 1967 election study (Centre for the Study of Developing Societies) voters were queried what first made them aware of politics. The group under 35 cited "independence movement" only in 10 per cent of the cases; in contrast, the group over 35 mentioned the independence movement in 39 per cent of the cases.[9] Clearly, persons who were drawn to politics during the national struggle **are** more inclined to support the Congress. When the opposition parties are examined individually (TABLE 14.1-A), the Jan Sangh and

the Communists are found to be the most active among the youth—
61 per cent and 56 per cent of their suppport respectively comes
from the under 35 age group. This is understandable, for the Jan
Sangh recruits much of its membership from the RSS, which in
turn attracted students and other young people largely from urban
areas of northern and central India.[10] The Communists are also
known to be most active among students and other young intellectuals. Another important point suggested in the data is that older
persons are as likely as young ones to have no partisan affiliation.

Regarding educational differences, we have evidence that the
Congress draws somewhat more support from among the illiterates
and the less educated than do the opposition parties. Thus TABLE
14.1-B shows that 69 per cent of the Congress following, as contrasted with 62 per cent of the opposition following, comes from the
less educated groups. In this connection, the 1964 poll shows even
greater difference: 66 per cent of the Congress following, as contrasted with only 52 per cent of the opposition following, is made up
of illiterates, and those persons who had no partisan preference are
more likely to be illiterates than the highly educated.

The data above lend evidence to the view held by some political
scientists that there is a tradition of oppositionalism among the
educated elite in India.[11] Before Independence, Congress was the
main opposition to the British rule, and the educated flocked to
the ranks of the Congress. Now that the Congress party is the ruling authority, the members of the intelligentsia are more inclined
to join one of the opposition parties. The reason for this may be
the intellectual's view of politics, which he assails as an essentially
dirty game, or as something from which he should stay away.
Several years ago, Edward Shils found that when intellectuals were
asked to name which leading politicians they admired most, only
three from the Congress party fared well at all—Prime Minister
Nehru, C.D. Deshmukh and Pandit Pant. The first two were
noted intellectuals, and both were educated at Cambridge in
England. Shils' data also indicate that the opposition members,
Socialists, Communists, and the Jan Sangh leaders were given a
higher rating than the members of the Congress—except for the
three leaders named above—even by those who had no sympathy
with the opposition parties.[12]

The educational differences on party support spill over to urban-
rural differences. Congress is more of a rural party than any of

the opposition parties except perhaps the Hindu Mahasabha. Part of the reason for this is that the urban residents are more educated than rural residents. But many of the urban residents are also likely to be without strong community roots, as well as less homogeneous, in contrast to rural residents, and they may be more open to the influence of extremist parties.[13] Thus we see in TABLE 14.1-C that 55 per cent of the Congress following is made up of rural citizens as contrasted with only 43 per cent of the opposition support from the villages—a difference of 12 percentage points. The data from the 1964 poll closely support those from the 1967 poll.

Differences between the Congress and the opposition parties on the basis of religion are slight. Both receive more than 80 per cent of their support from the Hindus. But this is not surprising because Hindus constitute about 85 per cent of the Indian population and about 84 per cent of the IIPO samples. However, the Congress and the opposition parties draw somewhat differential support from the Muslim community, the biggest minority community in India. Whereas 12 per cent of the Congress following is made up of Muslims, only 8 per cent of the opposition parties following comes from this community. This is understandable, for the Congress is committed to a secular and non-sectarian ideology under the leadership of such champions of minority rights as Mahatma Gandhi and Jawaharlal Nehru. When we look at the opposition parties individually, the results are even more interesting. Notice that the Communist party draws more of its support from Muslims than does any other party, including even the Congress. At the same time, the Jan Sangh and the Hindu Mahasabha are almost entirely Hindu based (95 per cent and 100 per cent respectively). These results confirm what we know of the character of Indian political parties. The Communist party is inspired by a secular ideology, but both the Jan Sangh and the Hindu Mahasabha are Hindu communal parties, although the former (Jan Sangh) is officially a secular party and in order to project a nonsectarian image has admitted Muslims as its members.[14]

In summary, it can be stated that the Congress is proportionately more popular among the rural residents, the less educated, the older, and the non-Hindu sections of the Indian society. The opposition parties taken together, on the other hand, are propor-

tionately more popular in the cities and towns, among the educated, the youth, and among the Hindus.[15] Our data also indicate
that the illiterate, the rural, and in general the low-status persons,
are more likely just to have *no* party preference at all. It may be
noted that there are significant differences among the opposition
parties, when examined individually. Another important point
(not reflected in our data) about the opposition parties is significant regional differences among them; their support has not been
evenly distributed across states. Thus the Communists recruit
mostly in West Bengal, Kerala and Andhra Pradesh, the Jan
Sangh in Uttar Pradesh, Madhya Pradesh and Haryana, the Swatantra in Gujarat, Rajasthan and Orissa, and the Socialists in
Bihar and Assam. Only the Congress party has strength in all parts
of the country, receiving about 40 per cent of the vote.

CONGRESS SPLIT

What can we say about the Left-Right split in the Congress party?
Do the two rival groups draw their strength from different or similar social strata? Unfortunately, most of the data analysed for this
book were gathered before the Congress party broke up in 1969.
The U.P.-Bihar 1970 poll is the only survey bearing on the questions posed here, but the regional nature of the survey seriously
qualifies any inferences that are made.

Notice in TABLE 14.2 the somewhat greater popularity of the
New Congress among the urban residents, the below 35 years age
group, the less educated, and members of the minority religions,
although the differences are not all that striking. Significantly, however, larger proportions of Muslim and urban voters felt that the
New Congress represented the interests of the poor, whereas the
Old Congress was the party of the rich. The need for validation of
these findings through additional research is self-evident.

In answer to another question in U.P., only 7 per cent gave cre-
dence to the Old Congress claim that it represented the Congress
rank and file ; the corresponding figure for the New Congress was
48 per cent. In urban areas as many as 74 per cent held this view.
In rural areas, significantly, most of the village leaders (Panchas
and Sarpanchas) also upheld the claim of the New Congress as the
true representative of rank and file.

TABLE 14.2

DISTRIBUTION OF PARTISAN CHOICES IN U.P. AND BIHAR
BY RESIDENCE, AGE, EDUCATION, AND RELIGION

"Which party would you vote for, if there was an election tomorrow".

| | Total | Residence | | Age | | Education | | Religion | | N |
		U	R	−35	36+	Low	High	Hindu	Muslim	
					Percentages					
New Congress	30	27	73	40	60	78	22	80	19	(406)
Old Congress	8	24	76	34	66	72	28	91	8	(106)
Jan Sangh	18	45	55	43	57	72	28	99	1	(242)
Socialists	17	35	65	40	60	75	25	93	6	(231)
BKD	12	13	87	36	64	91	9	85	13	(157)
Communists	6	54	46	55	45	68	32	83	14	(78)
Others	10	9	91	46	54	93	7	76	22	(129)
Total Sample	100	30	70	40	60	78	22	87	12	(1350)

Is party preference related to the level of political participation?
Are people who belong to one party more active in politics than
those who belong to a different party? It is to these questions that
we now turn.

POLITICAL PARTICIPATION

The effect of party affiliation on political participation is reported
in TABLE 14.3. Notice first that persons who profess no party affiliation are the least active; that is, their participation is lower than
those who either identify with the Congress or with one of the
opposition parties. If we take the 1967 poll figures on turnout, we
see that non-partisan persons turn out at the polls 24 percentage
points less than Congress supporters, and 9 percentage points less
than opposition supporters. Other polls indicate roughly the same

trend. The difference between the partisan and the non-partisan on other measures of participation (attending meetings, discussing politics, trying to affect decisions, giving money to parties, taking interest in political matters) is similarly quite large. The image of an independent, non-partisan citizen who is at the same time involved in politics therefore does not hold, just as it does not hold in other countries. It is now well established that the less partisan are also less interested as well as less involved in politics.[16] The Indian data conform to this pattern.

More importantly, note that those who identify with the Congress party have a higher turnout than those who identify with the opposition. No matter which opposition party is compared with the Congress, the opposition followers are more likely to stay at home on the election day than the Congress followers. When the opposition parties are taken as a group, the difference in the turnout rate of Congress and the opposition supporters is substantial— around 14 percentage points. As many as four different opinion polls—3 national and one regional—support this finding.

TABLE 14.3

POLITICAL PARTICIPATION, BY PARTISAN AFFILIATION

	Percentages				Percentage Attending Meetings
	1967 Poll	1964 Poll	Delhi Study	1961 Poll	Delhi Study
Party Choice					
Congress	78	86	77	78	40
All Opposition	63	72	64	65	52
PSP-SSP	70	77	—*	69	—
Communist	64	66	—	66	—
Swatantra	53	70	—	46	—
Jan Sangh	70	75	—	46	—
Hindu Mahasabha	57	—	—	—	—
No Preference	54	47	61	38	24

TABLE 14.3—(*Contd.*)

	Percentage of Political Interest	Percentage Discussing Politics	Percentage Trying to Affect Decisions	
	1961 Poll	Delhi Study	1967 Poll	1964 Poll
Party Choice				
Congress	69	27	19	16
All Opposition	86	33	21	32
PSP-SSP	76	—	28	49
Communist	89	—	23	35
Swatantra	93	—	17	26
Jan Sangh	—	—	21	20
Hindu Mahasabha	—	—	13	—
No Preference	17	11	12	11

	Number of Cases			
	1967 Poll	1964 Poll	Delhi Study	1961 Poll
Congress	3686	941	310	1068
All Opposition	2079	356	49	372
PSP-SSP	337	65	—	62
Communist	471	68	—	151
Swatantra	493	76	—	33
Jan Sangh	579	73	—	20
Hindu Mahasabha	49	9	—	2
No Preference	3392	717	133	2100

*The Delhi Study has a small sample and does not allow individual examination of opposition parties. The blanks mean that there were too few cases to deserve separate entry.

Note : Keeping with our usual practice, the percentages in this table do not add to 100, because only those persons have been reported who indicated participation in a particular activity. To calculate the proportion of persons who are inactive or who said "don't know," subtract the reported figure from 100.

Another interesting pattern that emerges from TABLE 14.3 is that when the measure of participation is activities other than voting, the picture is reversed. In this case, supporters of the opposition parties are more active than Congress adherents. Thus we note from TABLE 14.3 that 52 per cent of the opposition supporters, as opposed to 40 per cent of the Congress supporters, attend public meetings; 86 per cent of the opposition supporters, as opposed to 69 per cent of the Congress supporters, take an interest in political matters; 33 per cent of the former, as opposed to 27 per cent of the latter, engage in political discussions; and 21 per cent of the former, as opposed to 19 per cent of the latter, according to the 1967 poll, try to influence political decisions (according to the 1964 poll, the difference on political influence between these two groups is even larger: 32 per cent as against 16 per cent).

In short, our data clearly indicate that the opposition party followers are more involved in such political activities as attending meetings, discussing politics, taking interest in political matters and trying to affect laws, but do not at the same time turn out at the polls in the same proportion as do the Congress followers. This finding is interesting and fits well with the pattern discovered so far, in that voting is a special kind of political act in India. The question that we want to pose is: Why do those who prefer one of the opposition parties not implement their choice on the election day in the same proportion as do those who have preference for the Congress party?

One reason for the depressed voting rates among the non-Congress supporters may be their level of education and social status. We would recall that those who possess high education and occupy the upper levels of the social status are less likely to turn out at the polls than are illiterates or those who possess only a little education. It is possible then that the lower voting rate among the opposition supporters may be a reflection of their education. That is, if we controlled the effect of education, the relationship between party identification and turnout rate may disappear. There is reason for this line of argument, because the more educated are also more inclined to support one of the opposition parties.

TABLE 14.4, which presents data on voting frequency of various party supporters with controls for education, indicates that the relationship between party preference and voting frequency does not disappear when the effect of education is "partialled out."

Among the highly educated (high school and above), as well as among the illiterates and the less educated, those who prefer the Congress party are more likely to exercise their franchise than the opposition supporters. Thus, taking the 1967 poll data, among those with a little or no education, 82 per cent of Congress supporters, as opposed to 68 per cent of opposition supporters, and among the highly educated, 69 per cent of the former, as opposed to 55 per cent of the latter, went to the polls.

TABLE 14.4

VOTING FREQUENCY, BY PARTY PREFERENCE AND EDUCATION

Party Preference	1967 Poll		1964 Poll	
	Illiterate or Some Schooling	High School & Coll.	Illiterate or Some Schooling	High School & Coll.
	Percentages			
Congress	82 (2549)	69 (1138)	89 (617)	79 (315)
Opposition	68 (1280)	55 (766)	81 (185)	61 (171)

NOTE : The numbers in parentheses are the bases on which the percentages were computed.

Indeed, both education and party preference are related to voting frequency. If we were to build an ascending scale of voting turnout, the top of this scale would belong to those persons who have less education and who belong to the Congress party, and the bottom of the scale would be occupied by persons with just the opposite characteristics, i.e. high education and identification with one of the opposition parties. The middle of the scale would be occupied by those who have only one of these traits, i.e. those who have less education but choose one of the opposition parties, or those who have high education but remain in the Congress fold. It may be that those who are educated are somewhat alienated from the political system, and as a consequence of this, they do not vote as frequently as they would otherwise (see the chapter on "Education" for evidential support of this thesis). At the same time, their alienation leads them into the fold of an opposition party, and this further depresses their voting rates.

From TABLE 14.4 it is evident that the depressed turnout rate among the opposition party identifiers is not solely a function of their high education. The Indian party system is a relevant and significant factor in explaining political participation in India. The relationship between party identification and voter turnout was further tested with controls for such factors as urban-rural dichotomy, age, and religion. When the effect of these variables was neutralized, party identification was still found to be significantly related to voting frequency (tables not shown here). That is, no matter whether we consider rural residents or urban residents, young or old, Hindus or Muslims, those who identify with the Congress are more likely to vote than those who choose one of the other parties. Party identification feelings are therefore an important variable in the study of political participation in India. Those who belong to the Congress party must feel that they get a great deal more out of the act of voting. The opposition rank and file on the other hand do not find the same satisfaction in exercising their franchise. The uncompetitiveness of the Indian party system might have something to do with these feelings.

From our previous discussion in this chapter, it should be clear that although a multiplicity of political parties contest elections in India, it is difficult to classify the Indian party system as a multi-party one. The Congress has been the dominant party and all other parties have remained in its shade. The Election Commission statistics testify to this. In the first three general elections, the Congress managed to secure about 75 per cent of the Lok Sabha seats even when the share of its popular vote never reached 50 per cent. Of course the simple-majority, single-ballot electoral system is responsible for this. Even though the combined popular strength of the opposition parties exceeded 50 per cent in these elections, they received no more than 25 per cent of the legislative seats. To take just one example, the Socialist parties (the P.S.P. and the S.S.P) polled 9.5 per cent of the total vote in 1962, but received only 3.6 per cent of the Lok Sabha seats.

The large number of opposition parties, as well as the presence of many differences among them leads to a diminution of their strength in the national legislature. Even in the 1967 election, when a larger majority of the Indian electorate was disenchanted with the Congress rule, and when the opposition parties made the greatest gains, the governing party won 54.6 per cent of the Lok Sabha seats even though it received only 40 per cent of the popular vote.

We do not quite know why opposition party supporters have lower turnout rates, but it may be argued, as Duverger argues, that the simple-majority, single district electoral system works against smaller parties, not only mechanically but also psychologically.[17] Supporters of smaller parties have less incentive to vote for they realize that, under the existing system, their votes are wasted. Why should one take the trouble of standing in long voting queues when one's ballot does not have an equal impact? There would be some sense in going to the polls if one's candidate had a fair chance of winning. In short, minority party followers do not turn out simply because, under the simple-majority electoral system where the opposition parties are split, their candidates have such a small chance of getting elected. Thus the uncompetitiveness of the Indian party system and the mechanics of the simple-majority electoral system may be responsible for the lower voting rates among the opposition party supporters. This theory further presumes that when, and if, the Indian party system becomes genuinely competitive, many persons who are now reluctant to cast their ballots will return to the ballot box.

Our presumption can be supported from results of the 1967 elections. In the State of Madras, where competition was primarily between the D. M. K. and the Congress, voters registered the highest turnout rate of any state in India (76.57 per cent). Similarly, in Kerala and the Punjab, the element of competitiveness being acute, the voting levels were 75.67 per cent and 71.18 per cent respectively. In contrast, the turnout rates in Maharashtra and Mysore, where Congress was the dominant party, were 64.8 per cent and 63.1 per cent respectively.[18]

So far we have examined the impact of party preference on turnout, and the reasons for it. Now we will turn to an examination of a related question: that of the relationship between the attitudes that people have toward different parties (Party Evaluation) and their voting turnout.

PARTY EVALUATION

In a newly independent country like India, where most political parties date back only to a recent past (except for the Congress party which was founded in 1885), strong psychological attachments to parties do not develop. Accordingly, it is less useful to categorize the Indian public in terms of its psychological identification with one of the parties. That is, we cannot usefully talk of the Indian people as Congressmen, Jan Sanghis, Communists, or Swatantrites. Indeed, it is more meaningful to study the kind of attitudes that people have toward various parties. Accordingly, in this section we shall discuss how Indians evaluate different parties and what effect these evaluations have on turnout.[19]

The Indian Institute of Public Opinion polls contain a wealth of data on peoples' evaluation of the past and present performance of various political parties and groups. The 1967 and the 1964 national polls, for instance, pose the question: "Now just suppose that (name of the party) were to win the national elections. Do you think that this party government might harm the country, that it would have little effect, or that it might help the country?" The question was repeated four times, once each for the Praja Socialist party, the Communist party, the Jan Sangh, and the Swatantra party. In addition to the above question, the 1967 poll asked: "Do you approve or disapprove the move of the opposition parties to form election alliances to defeat the Congress party?" This question, asked when many opposition parties were trying to form some kind of broad coalition to defeat the Congress party, was indeed timely. The 1961 national poll and later the 1966 urban poll sought popular reactions to: "Which party can provide cheaper food? more jobs? better income?" The 1966 metropolitan poll, conducted in the four big Indian cities of Bombay, Calcutta, Delhi and Madras, directly asked how the respondent evaluated the performance of various political parties: "Please tell me about the performance of various political parties in your state. First of all tell me about the Congress party. . . . And how about the Praja Socialist Party? . . . the D.M.K.?"

Answers to these questions provide us with glimpses into the evaluative map that Indians have of their political parties. Party evaluation is not the same thing as party preference or party identification. Although the two concepts are obviously related, two persons may prefer the same party and yet evaluate it differently. For instance, not all those persons who say that they prefer the Communist party necessarily believe that the Communists would "help" the country. In a single dominant party system, especially opposition parties are likely to attract *protest* votes; persons who are disenchanted with the Congress system may express their anger by supporting one of the opposition parties. It is for this reason that some persons who presently prefer the Communist party might withdraw their support if the Communists became a serious contender for majority power. To take another example, all those who support the Congress party might not possess identical views regarding an opposition party. Some Congress followers vehemently reject any opposition party rule; other Congress supporters sincerely believe that an opposition party government might "help the country" by facilitating the development of a two-party system in India. Thus, party preference and party evaluation, though closely related, are not identical concepts.

TABLE 14.5

ATTITUDE TOWARD POSSIBLE GOVERNMENT OF AN
OPPOSITION PARTY, BY PARTISAN AFFILIATION

"Now suppose that [name of party] were to win the national elections. Do you think that this party might help the country, that it would have little effect or that it might harm the country?"—(1967 Poll)

	Jan Sangh Govt.				Communist Govt.			
	Might harm	Might help	No effect	D.K. etc.	Might harm	Might help	No. effect	D.K. etc.
	Percentages							
Party Preference								
Congress	24	8	24	43	33	6	19	42
PSP-SSP	19	22	30	29	39	19	17	25
Communist	29	11	32	28	5	72	10	13
Swatantra	18	12	23	47	33	6	20	41
Jan Sangh	4	66	11	19	34	13	20	32
Hindu Mah.	10	20	10	59	24	16	0	60
No Preference	7	9	18	66	12	11	15	62
TOTAL SAMPLE	16	14	21	50	23	12	17	48

TABLE 14.5—(Contd.)

	Swatantra Govt.				Socialist Govt.			
	Might harm	Might help	No effect	D.K. etc.	Might harm	Might help	No effect	D.K. etc.
				Percentages				
Party Preference								
Congress	23	8	24	45	20	9	27	44
PSP-SSP	16	23	28	33	5	57	17	19
Communist	25	11	31	34	19	15	34	31
Swatantra	5	50	9	36	16	14	23	46
Jan Sangh	22	16	25	37	19	17	24	39
Hindu Mah.	4	6	12	77	6	12	18	63
No Preference	7	10	17	66	6	9	18	65
TOTAL SAMPLE	15	12	20	53	14	12	23	51

NOTE: For number of cases, see Table 14.3.

This is demonstrated in TABLE 14.5. Taking data from the 1967 national poll, we find that of those who say that they prefer the Jan Sangh party, only 66 per cent believe that it 'might help' the country, 4 per cent even believe that it 'might harm' the country, and the remaining 30 per cent hold other opinions. Similarly, of those who prefer the Communist party, only 72 per cent believe that it 'might help' the country, 5 per cent believe that it 'might harm' the country, and 23 per cent gave other answers. The pattern is not at all different when the question is repeated concerning a possible Swatantra or a P.S.P. government. Parenthetically, readers may observe that Communist supporters are more likely to say that their party would 'help' the country (72 per cent) than are supporters of any other party, suggesting a greater commitment among the Communist rank and file.

Party evaluation is not only a different concept, it may be as powerful as, or even more powerful than, party identification in explaining political participation in India. Evaluation requires more information and greater political sophistication. People who do not have knowledge about what a particular party stands for can hardly pass judgment on whether that party could 'help' or 'harm' the nation.

TABLE 14.6

VOTING FREQUENCY BY PARTY EVALUATION

"Now suppose that [name of party] were to win the national elections. Do you think that this party might help the country, that it might have little effect, or that it might harm the country?"—(1967 Poll)

	Percentages			
	PSP	*Jan Sangh*	*Communist*	*Swatantra*
1967 Poll				
Might harm	74 (1280)	72 (1471)	73 (2155)	73 (1415)
Might help	64 (1097)	70 (1237)	59 (1122)	63 (1121)
Other answers	68 (2142)	68 (1936)	69 (1568)	69 (1924)
1964 Poll				
Might harm	76 (201)	73 (419)	75 (614)	73 (551)
Might help	76 (324)	78 (227)	73 (200)	66 (302)
Other answers	74 (388)	75 (344)	77 (277)	78 (275)

"Do you approve or disapprove the move of the opposition parties to form election alliances to defeat the Congress party."—(1967 Poll).

	Percentages	
Disapprove	73	(2340)
Approve	64	(3010)
Don't Know, no opinion	63	(3800)

NOTE: The numbers in parentheses are the bases on which the percentages were computed.

The relationship between party evaluation and political participation is presented in TABLE 14.6 and 14.7. Clearly, those who
favourably evaluate the Congress party have higher turnout frequency than those who favourably evaluate one of the opposition
parties. We have the widest of confirmation for this relationship :
five different polls, using different measures of party evaluation,
support this. Taking first the 1967 national poll, we note that those
who say that the opposition party rule would harm the country
(most of these are pro-Congress people) have a higher turnout rate
than those who say that it would help the country or that it would
have no effect. The difference between the 'might harm' and
'might help' groups ranges from 2 percentage points on Jan Sangh
to 14 points on Communist rule—the average difference being 9
percentage points (1967 poll figures). Figures from the 1964 however do not validate this trend as strongly, although even here
there is a 7-point difference on Swatantra.

Another question asked in the 1967 poll ("Do you approve or
disapprove the move of the opposition parties to form election
alliances to defeat the Congress party?") leads us to the same general conclusion : those who disapprove of the move of the opposition
parties to form alliances to defeat the Congress (these are pro-
Congress people) have a higher voting frequency than those who
approve of such a move. A similar trend is shown by data in the
1961 poll—a poll conducted just before the third general election in
1962. The question posed was: "Would you like to see a liberal but
non-Socialist party such as the Swatantra party in opposition to the
Congress?" Those who replied in the negative were further queried:
"Would you like a party of the Left such as P.S.P. or the Communist
party as the main opposition to the Congress?" When the results of
these two questions are combined, we get the following pattern :

	Turnout	N
Percentages		
Disapprove of both	86	(282)
Approve of Liberal opposition	61	(478)
Approve of Leftist opposition	64	(468)
Don't know, no opinion, etc.	46	(2754)

TABLE 14.7

VOTING FREQUENCY AND PARTY EVALUATION

"Which party can provide cheaper food? more jobs?"

	Percentages		
	1966 Urban Poll		1961 NationalPoll
	More Jobs	Cheaper Food	Cheaper Food
Congress	73 (800)	73 (824)	74 (1293)
Opposition	65 (512)	66 (466)	60 (336)
Don't Know, no opinion	31 (685)	31 (707)	35 (1909)

"Please tell me about the performance of various political parties in your State. First of all tell me about the Congress party? And how about the PSP?... the Swatantra?... the Jan Sangh?... the Communist Party?... and the D.M.K.?"—(1966 Metropolitan Poll).

	Percentages					
	Congress	PSP	Communist	Swatantra	Jan Sangh	D.M.K.
Bad	66 (177)	72 (251)	67 (367)	73 (263)	76 (243)	67 (174)
Fair	53 (312)	62 (248)	63 (239)	59 (244)	62 (236)	57 (143)
Good	71 (398)	63 (44)	62 (85)	62 (69)	63 (83)	56 (73)
Don't Know, etc.	18 (112)	48 (457)	44 (308)	48 (423)	46 (437)	56 (609)

NOTE: The numbers in parentheses are the bases on which the percentages were computed.

It is clear that those who disapprove of opposition parties turn out at least 20 percentage points more than those who approve of the opposition parties, and by 40 percentage points more than those who had no opinion.

Two additional polls, both conducted in 1966, sustain this trend. The 1966 urban poll enquired: "Which party can provide cheaper food? more jobs?" When the answers to this question are correlated with voting frequency we find that persons who say that the Congress party can provide cheaper food and more jobs have a higher turnout rate than those who say that the opposition can provide these things. The 1966 metropolitan poll, similarly, documents that persons who are favourably disposed toward the Congress are more active in voting than those who are favourably disposed toward one of the opposition parties. See TABLE 14.7 for these results.

In addition to the reasons suggested previously for the lower voting frequency among those who favour one of the opposition parties, another significant factor might be the attitude of various parties toward democracy and popular elections. National leadership of the Congress party has been a strong supporter of democracy and constitutionalism in India. The same cannot be said of other parties. The Communists and other revolutionary parties are openly hostile to the democratic process, although their present strategy emphasizes participation in popular elections. On the other end of the spectrum, the rightist parties like the Jan Sangh, the Hindu Mahasabha and the Ram Rajya Parishad pose a threat to the democratic system by reviving Hindu traditionalism. Only the Swatantra party and the Socialists are not openly against the democratic system, although even these parties have resorted to strikes and mass action to change the government.[20]

In light of the above facts, it may be hypothesized that persons who favour the Congress party and the present democratic system are more likely to use their franchise. This is not far fetched, for the act of voting is a powerful instrument of socializing people into democratic values, and vice versa, those who believe in democracy and constitutional methods are more likely to use the ballot box.

But we must strike a note of caution. In interpreting these data we should not lose sight of the fact that a person's attitude towards a political party is more or less congruent with his political preference: those who prefer the Communist party, for example, are also likely to favourably evaluate the Communist party and to believe that the Communist government would help the nation. Yet, under the special circumstances of the one party dominance system of India, this congruency is by no means perfect (see TABLE 14.5 above). And, as TABLE 14.8 shows, the relationship between party evaluation and turnout is not just the result of the close correlation between party evaluation and party identification. When we make our comparisons between people with the same party preference but with different party evaluation, we discover that persons who are unfavourably inclined toward the opposition turn out in greater numbers than those who are favourably inclined. Read the first row in TABLE 14.8 for instance, where 79 per cent of those who say the Communist rule might 'harm' the country were voters; this contrasts with 68 per cent of those who say the Communist rule might 'help' the country.

This clearly indicates that attitudes toward parties and evaluations of party performance are at least as predictive of political participation in India as party preference and party identification.

TABLE 14.8

VOTING FREQUENCY, BY PARTY PREFERENCE
AND PARTY EVALUATION

1967 National Poll

	Percentages		
	Communist Party Rule might		
	'Harm'	No effect., D. K., etc.	'Help'
Party Choice			
Congress	79 (1221)	78 (2263)	68 (218)
Opposition	71 (536)	61 (968)	60 (540)
No Preference	58 (397)	54 (2632)	51 (364)

NOTE: The numbers in parentheses are the bases on which the percentages were computed.

CONCLUSIONS

The Indian Gallup data reveal that political parties in India receive differential support from different social groups. Although Congress is strong among all groups, it is proportionately more popular among the elderly (those socialized during the freedom struggle), among the less educated, in the rural areas, and among the ethnic and religious minorities. The opposition parties, in contrast, are proportionately stronger among the youth, among the more educated, in the cities, and among the Hindus. In terms of age, the Jan Sangh had the distinction of drawing the largest share of its support from the under-35 age group. When the Left and Right wings of the Congress party are compared, the 1970 U.P.-Bihar poll show a clear victory for the Left Congress in these two states. Supporters of the New Congress tend to be younger, urban, less educated and non-Hindu, in comparison with supporters of the Old Congress, although these differences are by no means clearly established.

Regarding the effect of party choice on political participation, it was seen that people who prefer the Congress party are more likely to vote than people who prefer one of the opposition parties. At the same time, however, opposition supporters were found to be more active on these measures of participation—taking interest in politics, attending public meetings, discussing politics, and trying to influence decisions.

One reason for the lower voting turnout among the opposition supporters is their level of education and high social status. From our previous discussion we know that higher education is accompanied with feelings of pessimism, alienation and rejection of the present political system, leading to lower turnout rates. But we saw that these parameters do not fully account for the lower voting frequency among the opposition supporters. That is, identification with an opposition party is independently related to lower voting turnout. It was hypothesized that the erstwhile dominant position of the Congress, and the mechanics of the simple-majority electoral system, may account for this phenomenon.

In the second part of the chapter we examined the significance of attitudes toward parties and evaluation of their performance: The concept of party evaluation is different from that of party preference, although the two are obviously related. It was seen that persons who had positive feelings toward opposition parties were *less* likely to vote than those who had positive feelings toward the Congress. This finding was supported by data from several polls, which used different questions to measure attitudes toward various parties.

NOTES

[1]These statistics are available in The Election Commission *Reports*. Counting big and small parties, including small state parties (and factions within parties, working as independent parties at one time or another) the total number of parties, according to one survey, is 110. See Craig Baxter, *District Voting Trends in India: A Research Tool* (N.Y.: Columbia University Press, 1969), pp. XIX-XXII.

Here a word on the Election Commission criteria for recognition of parties may be useful. The yardstick used by the Commission is that the party to be recognized must have polled at least 4 per cent (3 per cent before 1957) of the total valid votes cast in the previous elections.

Parties are recognized by the Commission for the purpose of reserving election symbols for them. A symbol which has been reserved for one party may not be used by another party. Only the "recognized" parties have uniform symbols throughout the country or the state.

Pictorial election symbols play an important role in the elections. Voters cast their ballots by checking against the symbol (not the name) of their favourite candidate or party. This is necessary because a vast majority of the Indian electorate is illiterate and cannot read the names of the contestants. Political parties lay great stress on choosing proper pictorial symbols.

[2]Rajni Kothari, "The Congress System in India," in Centre for the Study of Developing Societies, *Party System and Election Studies* (Bombay: Allied Publishers, 1967). pp. 2-3. An important criticism of the Kothari model is that the Congress system was never a single, all-India system. Rather, it consisted of an all-India system plus sixteen or seventeen state systems.

[3]For such a viewpoint, see Paul Brass, "Coalition Politics in North India," *American Political Science Review*, 62:4 (Dec. 1968), pp. 1174-91. For the contrary view that the dominant party system is "only modified by fresh forms of competition, not replaced," see W.H. Morris-Jones, "From Monopoly to Competition in India's Politics," *Asian Review* (Nov. 1967), pp. 1-12.

[4]Maurice Duverger is an advocate of the view that there is a direct correlation between a country's electoral system and its party system. According to him the simple-majority, single-ballot system favours a two-party system and proportional representation favours a multi-party system. See his, *Political Parties* (N.Y: John Wiley & Sons, 1966), pp. 216-28.

[5]In addition to the all-India parties listed above, the following are among the major *state* parties: the DMK in Madras, the Akali Dal in the Panjab, the Peasants and Workers party in Maharashtra, the Republican party in Maha-

rashtra, U.P. and the Panjab, the Muslim League in Kerala, the Hill Leaders' Conference in Assam, the Revolutionary Socialist party in Kerala, the Forward Bloc in West Bengal and the Jana Kranti Dal in Bihar.

⁶The 1967 Election Study conducted under the auspices of the Centre for the Study of Developing Societies (New Delhi) is the basis of several articles in this area. For results of a preliminary analysis of this survey, see the special issue of the *Asian Survey*, "Elections and Party Politics in India: A Symposium." 10:11 (Nov. 1970): articles by Kothari, Marvick, Ahmed, Modsen, and Eldersveld. Also see the articles by Kothari and D.L. Sheth in the 1970 Annual Number of *The Economic and Political Weekly*.

Among the earlier important party studies are the following: Craig Baxter, *The Jana Sangh: A Biography of an Indian Political Party* (Philadelphia: University of Pennsylvania Press, 1969); Paul R. Brass, *Factional Politics in an Indian State: The Congress Party in Uttar Pradesh* (Berkeley: University of California Press, 1966); Angela S. Burger, *Opposition in a Dominant Party System* (Berkeley: University of California Press, 1969); Howard Erdman, *The Swatantra Party and Indian Conservatism* (Cambridge: Cambridge University Press, 1967); Robert L. Hardgrave, *The Dravidian Movement* (Bombay: Popular Prakashan, 1965); Stanley Kochanek, *The Congress Party of India* (Princeton: Princeton University Press, 1968); Rajni Kothari, ed., *Party Systems and Election Studies* (Bombay: Allied Publishers, 1967); Baldev Raj Nayar, *Minority Politics in the Panjab* (Princeton: Princeton University Press, 1966): Mohan Ram, *Indian Communism* (Delhi: Vikas, 1969); Robert W. Stern, *The Process of Opposition in India* (Chicago: University of Chicago Press (1970); Myron Weiner, *Party Building in a New Nation* (Chicago: University of Chicago Press, 1967); and Weiner, *Party Politics in India* (Princeton: Princeton University Press, 1957).

⁷Weiner, *ibid.*, pp. 230-31.

⁸It can be readily seen that this question is different from that used in the United States. In the United States, most studies following the example of Survey Research Centre, employ the question, "Generally speaking, do you think of yourself as a Republican, a Democrat, an Independent, or what?" The same question cannot be used in India for two reasons. One, the number of political parties is so large that they cannot be easily enumerated in a question. If the American format were used, the question would read like this, "Generally speaking, do you think of yourself as a Congressi (or Congressman), a Jan Sanghi, a Communist, a Socialist, a Swatantrite, a Hindu Mahasabhai, a DMK man . . . etc., . . . or What?" The awkwardness is readily recognized.

Second, even if such a question were used, the terms like Congressi, Jan Sanghi, a Communist, imply in India a strong commitment to the party. For example, a person who is called a Congressi, would usually wear a Khadi shirt and a white cap (preferred Congress dress) and he would likely be an active party member. Therefore, belonging to a party in India does not have the same casualness as it does in the United States.

Samuel J. Eldersveld and his colleagues employed a slightly different format in their 1964 study: "Generally speaking, what political party do you support at election time?" See *The Citizen and the Administrator in a Developing Democracy* (Glenview, Illinois: Scott, Foresman, 1968), p. 165. The item which the Centre for the Study of Developing Societies used for party identification in 1966 reads:

"Which party do you support?" If the respondent replies "None", he was further queried, "If you had to choose, is there any party that you might prefer?" (Project on Social and Political Change.)

⁹Douglas Madsen, "Solid Congress Support in 1967: A Statistical Inquiry," *Asian Survey*, 10:11 (Nov. 1970), pp. 1004-14, at 1007.

¹⁰The RSS (Rashtriya Swayamsevak Sangh) was founded in 1925 by Keshav Hedgewar as a cultural organization for the purpose of revitalizing the Hindu community. He was succeeded on his death in 1940 by M.S. Golwalkar. It grew into a popular body with a well-disciplined membership of 400,000 to 500,000 in 1947 and the support of another 4 to 5 million Hindus. The organization lost much of its appeal and was banned by the government in 1948 after it became known that Nathuram Godse, Mahatma Gandhi's assassin, was a fanatic Hindu and a former RSS member. See Weiner, *op. cit.*, Ch. 9; and Donald E. Smith, *India As a Secular State* (Princeton: Princeton University Press, 1963), pp. 465-68. For a detailed account of the RSS and its activities, see J.A. Curran, *Militant Hinduism in Indian Politics: A Study of the RSS* (N.Y.: Institute of Pacific Relations, 1951).

¹¹See, for instance, M. Weiner, *op. cit.*, pp. 229-37.

¹²Edward Shils, "Influence and Withdrawal: The Intellectuals in Indian Political Development," in Dwaine Marvick, ed., *Political Decision Makers* (N.Y.: The Free Press, 1961), pp. 41-42.

¹³Even in the city of Bombay, which is regarded as cosmopolitan, extremism appeared in the form of Shiv Sena, a militant anti-South organization. The core of Shiv Sena programme is the replacement of non-Maharashtrians by Maharashtrians in all business and government jobs. Lately, however, in order to widen its appeal, the Shiv Sena has tried to softpedal its hostility to outsiders. See Ram Joshi, "The Shiv Sena: A Movement in Search of Legitimacy," *Asian Survey*, 10:11 (Nov., 1970), pp, 967-78.

¹⁴In an interview with K.K. Sharma, reporter of *The Statesman*, New Delhi (December 7, 1966), the President of the Jan Sangh, Mr. Balraj Madhok, fiercely rejected the charge that the Jan Sangh was a communal organization. He said "We are a nationalistic and democratic party," pointing out further that of more than 2,000 candidates who were contesting elections on the Jan Sangh ticket, many were non-Hindus. But the reporter editorialized: "Respectability and admission to the democratic club on terms of equality is what the Jan Sangh craves. The quest has proved to be unfruitful so far; the stigma of communalism sticks besides desperate efforts to shake it off and, after the Delhi riot of November 7, the party's name has been besmirched further by the allegation that it will take recourse to violence." Also see Donald E. Smith, *India As a Secular State*, *op. cit.*, pp. 469-79; and Craig Baxter, *The Jana Sangh, op. cit.*

¹⁵These generalizations find confirmation in the 1967 election study conducted by the Centre for the Study of Developing Societies (New Delhi). In a preliminary analysis of these data, Douglas Madsen, *op. cit.*, found a 14 point differential between urban and rural support for Congress; among the highly educated, the Congress received substantially less support; and on measures of traditional status the support for Congress is highest among the lower and scheduled castes and lowest among the Brahmins. The variable most strongly associated with party support was age: younger voters were much less inclined

to vote for the Congress party. This supporting evidence indicates that the Indian Gallup data are not as unrepresentative as one might surmise. Madsen also found that compared to attitudinal variables, the social and economic groupings explain very little of the variance in the dependent variable (Solid Congress Support). "Solid Congress Support" is measured by voting record of the respondent. If he voted for the Congress candidate at both the national and the state levels, he was defined as a "Solid Supporter".

[16]See Angus Campbell, *et al.*, *The American Voter* (N.Y.: John Wiley, 1964), p. 83, and Lester W. Milbrath, *Political Participation* (Chicago: Rand McNally, 1965), pp. 50-64.

[17]The mechanical factor consists in the under-representation of the third, i.e. the weakest party, its percentage of seats being inferior to its percentage of the poll. The psychological factor operates on similar lines. "In cases where there are three parties operating under the simple-majority single ballot system the electors soon realize that their votes are wasted if they continue to give them to the third party: Whence their natural tendency to transfer their vote to the less evil of its two adversaries in order to prevent the success of the greater evil." See *op. cit.*, pp. 224-26. Unlike Duverger argument, our position is that opposition party supporters are more likely to simply stay at home.

[18]For the effect of party competition on voter participation, see O.P. Goyal, *et al.*, "The Nature of Party Competition in Five Indian States," *Asian Survey*, 6:10 (Oct., 1966), pp. 580-88, and Peter McDonough, "The Anatomy of Party Competition and Electoral Participation in India, 1952-1967," a paper presented at the Midwest Political Science Conference in Chicago, May, 1968. Data reported in these articles indicate that turnout is higher in districts with keener party competition. Also see Iqbal Narain and Mohan Lal, "Election Politics in India: Notes Toward an Empirical Theory," *Asian Survey*, 9:3 (March, 1969), pp. 202-20.

[19]The concept of "party evaluation" is similar to the Matthews and Prothro concept of "party images," in *Negroes and the New Southern Politics* (N.Y.: Harcourt, Brace and World, 1966), pp. 377-78.

[20]For a discussion of the role and strategy of the Communist and revolutionary parties in West Bengal, see Marcus Franda, *op. cit.* and his "India's Third Communist Party," *Asian Survey*, 10:12 (Dec. 1970).

CHAPTER FIFTEEN

The Feelings of Civic Competence

In many ways, then, the belief in one's competence is a key political attitude. The self-confident citizen appears to be the democratic citizen. Not only does he think he can participate, he thinks that others ought to participate as well. Furthermore, he does not merely think he can take a part in politics; he is likely to *be* more active. And, perhaps most significant of all, the self-confident citizen is also likely to be the more satisfied and loyal citizen.[1]

THE ABOVE QUOTE is from Almond and Verba's *The Civic Culture*. The authors of this study argue that attitudes about one's ability to affect politics and government are crucial to the functioning of a democratic political system. As compared with persons who are low on self-confidence, the persons high on self-confidence are more satisfied and loyal citizens. Furthermore, they are more likely to be active as well, for "if an individual believes he has influence, he is more likely to attempt to use it." Subjective competence should not, however, be confused with actual *political influence*. The latter is defined as "the degree to which government officials act to benefit [a] group or [an] individual because the officials believe that they will risk some deprivation (they will risk their jobs, be criticized, or lose votes) if they do not so act." Defined this way, a sense of competence is not the same as political influence, because thinking that one can influence the government or even attempting to influence it is different from actually influencing it.

Nonetheless, Almond and Verba argue that a sense of civic competence cannot be altogether divorced from objective reality. Persons who exhibit higher subjective competence in fact are more influential than those who have no competence. They found that subjectively incompetent persons tended to shy away from political involvement and because of this they were more likely to be ignored by government leaders as well. Clearly, subjective competence or the belief that one can influence governmental affairs is a key political attitude. The concept of civic competence (or political efficacy) has been a popular one in the social sciences.[2] The major theme of this chapter is the extension of the study of civic competence, through survey data, to India. We will attempt to answer a few simple questions. What sections of Indian society exhibit greater feelings of political efficacy? Do people feel more effective with respect to the local government or with respect to the national government? What "strategies" of influence are likely to be emphasized by people in India? And finally, does civic competence have any effect on the level of political involvement and political participation of the Indian electorate?

Our concept of civic competence differs from the traditional definitions which emphasized cynicism, and the loss of values or like feelings. The frame of reference for this research is the one developed by Almond and Verba in their five-nation study. Political efficacy is the *feeling* that one is capable of influencing the decision-making process. When a person *believes* that he can exert some influence on government officials, he is subjectively efficacious or competent.[3] The following questions in the 1964 and 1967 national polls provide the data for a measure of this attitude.

(1) "Suppose that some action or policy or law were being considered by the Local government unit (specify local unit: village, city government or council) which you disagreed with, because it was unjust or harmful or something like that. What are the possible things you think you could do about it?'

(2) "If you made such an effort, how likely is it that anything good would come of it?''

(3) "If such a case arose, how likely is it that you would actually do something about it?''

A similar set of three questions was asked about an unjust law or regulation being considered by the National government. The results of questions on local and national subjective competence are reported in TABLE 15.1. We have also reproduced the results from the five countries studied by Almond and Verba. The Indian data indicate that the proportion of those saying that they can do something to affect an unfair regulation is reasonably high. A little more than half of our respondents feel that there is something that they can do about a local issue; similarly, about 50 per cent feel that they can do something to affect the decision-making process at the national level. On the other hand, it is also true that roughly 50 per cent of the sample felt that they could do nothing at all to influence political decisions. Nevertheless, the percentages indicated by the Indian data are not too dissimilar from those in Germany, Italy and Mexico, countries which have had relatively a short history of functioning democratic institutions.

TABLE 15.1

PERCENTAGE OF VOTERS WHO SAY THEY CAN DO
SOMETHING ABOUT AN UNJUST LOCAL OR NATIONAL
REGULATION, BY NATION*

"Suppose that some action or policy or law were being considered by a Local/National Government Unit, which you disagreed with, because it was unjust or harmful or something like that. What are possible things you think you could do about it?"

	Can do something about Local Regulations	Can do something about National Regulations
	Percentages	
INDIA		
1967 poll	60	50
1964 poll	52	47
UNITED STATES	77	75
GREAT BRITAIN	78	62
GERMANY	62	38
ITALY	51	28
MEXICO	52	38

*Almond and Verba data are from page 142 of *The Civic Culture*.

Another interesting thing that we find is that self-confidence is prevalent more at the level of the local government than the national government. Evidence from the five-nation study reproduced here indicates that these differences between local and national levels of competence exist in other countries also, more so in Germany and Italy than in Mexico, Great Britain, and the United States. This is not surprising, for people often feel closer to a local governmental unit than to a national governmental unit. The former is physically nearer to them and is also at a level of personal acquaintance. However, there are some parts of the world, for example certain sections in southern United States, where some people view the local government as oppressive and look to the national government for amelioration of their conditions. The success of the Panchayati system of local government perhaps has something to do with the higher level of local competence found in India. *Panchayati Raj* (meaning government by local assemblies) is part of the Indian government's overall plan of decentralization of power to the level of the village. Under this system village leaders with roots in the traditional social order have increasingly come to occupy positions of authority. Thus, as the process of decision making is brought closer to the people through Panchayati Raj, it becomes more susceptible to local influence, and in turn this generates feelings of political efficacy.

STRATEGY OF INFLUENCE

Another significant aspect of subjective political competence is the "strategy" that an individual might use in trying to influence politics. It makes a difference whether an individual would associate with other people to bring pressure on the government or whether he would act alone. Further, it also makes a difference whether an individual would contact an elected politician or an appointed bureaucrat to seek redress for his grievances. These differences are reported in TABLE 15.2. In this table we have also reproduced statistics from *The Civic Culture* for comparative purposes. Because of differences in data this kind of cross-cultural comparison is, however, somewhat risky, and caution is recommended in interpreting the data.

What is most striking in Table 15.2 is the variation from country to country in the numbers who feel they can work with informal, face-to-face, groups to bring pressure on the government.

The Indian pattern of answers is closer to that in the U.S., England and Mexico than that in Italy or Germany. From one-third (1967 poll) to one-fourth (1964 poll) of the Indian respondents indicated that they would try to organize an informal group to counteract an unfair regulation. The difference between the 1967 and 1964 poll data may be a reflection of their timing. The 1967 poll was taken shortly before the fourth general elections—a period when citizens are likely to be more active in politics as well as sought after by politicians than at other times.

TABLE 15.2

WHAT CITIZENS WOULD DO TO TRY TO INFLUENCE THEIR LOCAL GOVERNMENT, BY NATION

	Percentages						
	India		US	UK	Germany	Italy	Mexico
	1967 Poll	1964 Poll					
Work with local groups of friends, neighbours; get them to write letters; go to meetings; sign a petition	33	24	56	34	13	7	26
Work through a Party	7	8	1	1	3	1	—
Work through any formal organization	6	5	4	3	15	1	2
Work by oneself in talking, writing letters, speaking to political leaders (elected)	10	4	20	45	15	12	15
Work by oneself, writing to or telling the govt. department officials (non-elected)	13	13	1	3	31	12	18
Take the matter to court, use a lawyer	4	3	2	1	3	2	2

TABLE 15.2—(*Contd.*)

Vote against offending officials at next election	4	3	14	4	1	1	—
Do something very strong: demonstrate, etc.	6	3	1	1	1	1	1
Other modes of reation	1	1	1	2	—	15	5
Total percentage who would do something, with others or alone*	60	52	77	78	62	51	53
Total percentage who would not do anything, or DK, etc.	40	48	23	22	38	49	47
Number of cases†	(9157)	(2014)	(970)	(963)	(955)	(995)	(1007)

*Total percentages are less than the total of individual cells, since some respondents gave more than one answer.

†Numbers in the parentheses in this and the following tables are the bases on which the percentages were computed.

This capacity to work with others is a significant attribute; a democratic political culture presumes that people have the ability and willingness to work together and associate amongst themselves. Almond and Verba list this attribute as a major characteristic of "the civic culture" in democratic political systems.[4]

Another striking difference indicated in TABLE 15.2 deals with *citizen* competence feelings as opposed to subject competence feelings—that is, whether individuals are more inclined to work through elected officials or through bureaucrats. In the United States and in England, only an insignificant proportion of the respondents (1 to 3 per cent) would want to affect government by working through non-elected officials, i.e. through bureaucrats. In sharp contrast to this, as many as 31 per cent of the German respondents mentioned working through bureaucratic channels as a proper strategy. The picture in India approximates the situation in Italy and Mexico; both in 1967 and in 1964, 13 per cent of the Indian respondents indicated that they would prefer to work through the "output" rather than the "input" structures of the political system. The 13 per cent figure is not large, but it perhaps reflects the fact that subject feelings are still an important residue from the days of the British *raj* when the state was primarily an administrative agency.

It is also worthy of notice that in a country where non-violent methods of social protest were perfected, a number of people mention demonstrations as appropriate method of putting pressure on the government. The Indian percentages are the highest of any country in this category. Significantly, the proportion of these people doubled from 1964 to 1967 (from 3 per cent to 6 per cent). We also note that only a small percentage of the Indian sample (3 per cent to 4 per cent) believes that voting against the offending official is an appropriate strategy to bring pressure on him. In the United States, as many as 14 per cent mentioned voting as one of the effective strategies to influence the government. Readers are reminded that *The Civic Culture* data were collected in 1960, and therefore current attitudes toward violence and elections may not be reflected in these statistics.[5]

Obviously, then, people in India are somewhat different from those in other countries regarding their level of competence feelings and regarding the strategies that they would employ to influence their government. Our next question is: how are efficacy feelings spread among various social groups in India? Is a particular social group more likely to display feelings of competence than another group? We have chosen education to answer this question, for education is about the best single index of a person's overall social position, his degree of modernization, and other similar attributes that are strongly associated with a man's attitudes.

TABLE 15.3 reports data on subjective competence among several educational groups, separately for rural and urban residents. These data pertain to the local level; data with respect to the national level are not reported here, but they indicate a similar relationship to that seen in TABLE 15.3. It is clear that education is positively related to subjective competence. This is true both in rural and in urban India. That is, no matter where a person lives, the more education he has, the more likely he is to consider himself capable of influencing the political world. An overall comparison of urban and rural groups in TABLE 15.3, under "Total" also indicates that, in general, rural residents feel less efficacious than urban residents, but when comparisons are made between

TABLE 15.3

PERCENTAGE WHO BELIEVE THEY CAN DO SOMETHING TO COUNTERACT AN UNJUST LOCAL REGULATION, BY EDUCATION AND RESIDENCE

1967 National Poll

What Citizens would do	URBAN					RURAL				
	Illit.	Some Sch.	High Sch.	Coll.	Total	Illit.	Some Sch.	High Sch.	Coll.	Total
	Percentages									
Work with local groups	14	35	37	48	36	17	42	38	37	31
Work through a party	1	6	7	9	6	3	9	9	10	7
Work through an organization	2	4	9	8	6	3	7	10	11	6
Work by oneself : talk to politicians	4	10	19	14	12	3	9	11	12	7
Work by oneself : talk to bureaucrats	5	14	18	21	15	4	14	15	14	10
Appeal through courts	1	4	7	9	5	1	4	7	10	3
Vote	3	3	4	5	4	2	3	2	5	3
Demonstrate	3	6	9	5	6	3	5	8	13	5
Other modes of reaction	—	1	1	3	1	1	1	1	2	1
Do nothing, DK†	72	37	25	15	34	70	28	31	13	44
Number of Cases	(741)	(1602)	(863)	(1201)	(4407)	(2007)	(1988)	(488)	(267)	(4750)

†The number of percentages do not add to 100 because of multiple answers.

people of similar education, rural residents are as efficacious (if not more) as urban residents. The strong, positive relationship between education and civic competence is indeed not surprising; education is obviously an important factor affecting a man's abilities as well as his perceptions of himself. Thus our finding is consistent with that of Almond and Verba who note that, "No matter what the frequency of local competence within a nation, the incidence of this competence is greater among those with higher education."[6] Our data provide further support on uniform patterns across national lines concerning the effect of education on a person's political attitudes.

POLITICAL PARTICIPATION

That an individual is subjectively competent does not mean that he will in fact try to change what he regards as an unjust law. Thinking that one can do something to influence political leaders is not the same as actually doing it. Our main question, then, in this part of the chapter is: do those who think themselves to be capable of participating in the affairs of the government in fact participate in them? We want to know whether political participation goes along with feelings of civic competence. We shall explore this question with reference to two variables: (1) past attempts to influence politics, and (2) voter turnout—two dimensions of political participation on which data are available from the 1964 and the 1967 polls.

To facilitate our exploration into the relationship between civic competence and political participation, a subjective competence index was constructed. The index was devised from responses to questions dealing with local and national government. Respondents were asked whether they thought they could do anything to counteract a law or a policy that they disagreed with, and if such a case arose, how likely it was that they would in fact do something about it, and further, if they did something, how likely did they think that anything good would come of it. The answers to these questions were divided into positive and negative responses. If a person said that he could do something to affect decisions, he was considered to have answered positively, no matter what he said he could do. The same division was used about the likelihood of action—if an individual said that it was "very likely" or "moderately likely" that something good would come of his efforts or that he would actually do something, he was given a positive score; on the other hand, if he said "slightly likely" or "not at all likely" or "don't know, etc." he was given a negative score. Using this division method, the scale allowed us to group respondents into one of the four categories, ranging from "no competence" for those with no self-confidence at all to "high competence" for those with the most self-confidence.

How does the self-confident citizen differ from the person who considers himself relatively powerless? Is the subjectively competent person more active in politics compared with a subjectively incompetent person? TABLE 15.4 examines these questions with respect to attempted political influence and TABLE 15.5 with respect to voter turnout. The first thing deserving notice in TABLE 15.4 is that although some 60 per cent of our respondents had indicated that they could do something to oppose local legislation

TABLE 15.4

PERCENTAGE WHO TRY TO INFLUENCE DECISIONS, BY
SUBJECTIVE COMPETENCE AND EDUCATION

(*1967 Poll Data*)

Competence	Illiterate	Some Schooling	High School	College	Total
			Percentages		
None	1	3	4	4	2
	(2000)	(1275)	(370)	(250)	(3894)
Low	14	21	24	26	21
	(303)	(760)	(314)	(365)	(1742)
Medium	27	31	22	36	30
	(197)	(617)	(263)	(395)	(1472)
High	23	35	34	35	33
	(248)	(906)	(387)	(452)	(1985)
Total	7	20	21	28	17

that they disagreed with (see TABLE 15.1 above), only a very small proportion of the sample had *in fact* tried to engage in this form of political participation; thus only 17 per cent of the whole sample indicated that they tried to change unsuitable laws, and even for those with a 'high' level of competence, only 1 out of 3 respondents engaged in this political activity (see the last column in TABLE 15.4). In short, a wide gap between a person's claimed potential for political participation and his past record is indicated by these data. There is thus a world's difference between a non-specific, generalized attitude that one can affect government and really trying to do so.

Secondly, it is clear that, as far as the past record in attempting to influence politics and government is concerned, the subjectively efficacious persons have been considerably more active than the inefficacious persons. The percentage of persons who in the past tried to influence decisions rises sharply as we move from 'no' subjective competence to higher levels of competence. The real break occurs between 'no' efficacy and 'low' efficacy; that is, between those who cannot think of anything they can do to oppose unfair legislation and those who can. Here also our data support the generalizations made in the five-nation study. The authors of *The Civic Culture* note, " In all nations those who say they could influence the local government, in comparison with those who say they could not, are at least three times as likely to have attempted such influence."[7] The Indian data provide one more illustration in support of the validity of this statement. Presumably, the relationship between subjective efficacy feelings and past experience in political activity must really exist across several different cultures.

The above relationship between civic competence and attempted political influence is not destroyed when education is held constant. It is necessary to introduce controls for education, because a person's schooling is strongly associated with his self perception. We find that at all levels of education, the more subjectively competent are more likely to have tried to influence government affairs than the less competent. But our data also indicate that higher education is a poor compensation for the lack of civic competence. No matter what the level of schooling, persons who do not possess efficacious feelings rarely have the courage to petition political leaders. The top row in the table, which indicates persons with 'no' competence, shows that only an insignificant proportion of the respondents did anything to try to affect decisions; this is true for illiterates as well as for the college educated (between 1 per cent and 4 per cent). Persons with 'high' competence, on the other hand, have often tried to affect politics; this is true for the less educated (illiterates or some school) as for the highly educated (high school or college).

It is clear from the above that feelings of efficacy are very strongly related (more so than education) to participation in political influence activities. Our data, of course, will not tell us whether it is political participation that leads to change in a person's perception of his ability, or whether it is his competence that leads to greater political participation.

Turnout : What, we may ask next, is the relationship between subjective competence and political participation when political participation is defined as turnout at the poll? A great deal of research in the West indicates that those who are highly efficacious are also regular voters and that they rarely fail to turn out to vote

TABLE 15.5

PERCENTAGE OF VOTER TURNOUT BY SUBJECTIVE
COMPETENCE AND EDUCATION

1967 National Poll

Competence	Illiterate	Some Schooling	High School	College	Total
			Percentages		
None	68	72	63	44	67
	(2002)	(1279)	(371)	(251)	(3903)
Low	83	72	57	51	67
	(305)	(769)	(314)	(365)	(1753)
Medium	75	75	58	49	65
	(199)	(626)	(266)	(395)	(1486)
High	64	67	58	57	63
	(240)	(922)	(393)	(452)	(2007)
Total	70	71	60	52	65

on election day. But our previous information indicatee that voting is a special activity in India and that it differs from other forms of political participation.

Notice in TABLE 15.5 that when the measure of participation is turnout at the polls, subjective competence does not show the same positive relationship with voting as it does with political influence. For instance, Column 5 shows that those with higher effectiveness are not particularly more likely to turn out at the polls than those with lower effectiveness. If anything, the data indicate that the former have a slightly lower turnout rate, although the difference is not large.

When we test the above relationship with controls for education, the picture does not change radically. At all levels of education, except for the college educated, those with 'high' competence turn out at the polls a few points less than those with 'no' competence. Notice that education shows even a stronger negative (or curvilinear) correlation with voting turnout. This somewhat curvilinear relationship is present at all levels of civic competence. Indeed, the lowest turnout rate, 44 per cent, is among the college graduates who report no efficacy feelings. The highest turnout rate (83 per cent) on the other hand, is recorded by illiterates with 'low' competence.

Knowing what we know of the political participation patterns in India, the slightly negative correlation between civic competence and turnout should not surprise the reader. All along we have seen that, as contrasted with those lower on the ladder of education, social status, and media exposure, those higher on this ladder are much more likely to participate in such political activities as taking interest in politics, discussing politics, exposing oneself to political content, and attempting to influence decisions, but they are somewhat less likely to vote. Now, subjective competence should be added to this list of variables which produce differential results for different political activities—slightly negative with turnout but positive with other political acts.

One reason for lower voting rates among the educated and the efficacious persons may be the low regard that these persons seem to have for the act of voting. They do not seem to think that voting is a typically correct strategy to gain their ends. For instance, we would recall that only 3-4 per cent of the Indian respondents (TABLE 15.2, row 7) mentioned voting against the offending official as the appropriate method of influencing policy. Further, education had little bearing on the proportion of respondents who mentioned this strategy. In the United States, as many as 14 per cent mention voting as an appropriate method. It is also true in the Western nations that many citizens regard voting as among the important civic duties. We had presented some data in the chapter on Education which suggested a low incidence of civic duty feelings in India. For instance, in answer to "People speak of duties which they owe to their country. In your opinion, what should every person do for his country?" only 12 per cent mentioned voting as a duty, but more significantly, the college educated people gave less value to voting (11 per cent) than those with a little education (16 per cent). People who mentioned "Love one's country, be loyal, respectful" were divided as follows—illiterate: 20 per cent ; a little education : 41 per cent; high school : 52 per cent ; college education : 43 per cent. These percentages suggest that patriotism, loyalty and citizen obligatory feelings do not rise with college education. Other recently conducted research also supports this inference. For instance, Alex Inkeles discovered that in India the highly educated, informed and "rational" citizens were also less patriotic and more hostile toward government.[8]

It is at this place that our findings diverge rather significantly from those of Almond and Verba. The authors of *The Civic Culture* found a strong relationship between civic competence and system allegiance. They argue that, as compared with persons who are low on self-confidence, the persons high on self-confidence are more "satisfied" and "loyal" citizens. If non-voting can be taken as one index of lower system allegiance, then our data unmistakably indicate that higher education and higher effectiveness, while very strongly interrelated, are not necessary correlates of political loyalty and political happiness in India. The relationship between civic competence and satisfaction is not as universally true as one might be led to believe from the Almond and Verba statement. Our conclusion is that the association between education, efficacy and political satisfaction is culture-bound.

SUMMARY

In this chapter we have presented data on beliefs among the Indian people about their ability to affect an unfair governmental act—or

what Gabriel Almond and Sidney Verba have called "the subjective civic competence feelings." We found that about 50 per cent of
the Indian respondents feel fairly confident that they could do something to change an injurious or harmful decision. This feeling of confidence was found to be more prevalent in hypothetical encounters
with the local government than with the national government.

Regarding "strategy" of influence, we found that from one-
fourth to one-third of the Indian respondents would choose to work
with other people—in informal groups of friends, neighbours and
colleagues—in order to put pressure on the political decision-makers.
Another 13 per cent indicated that they would use "output" rather than "input" structures of the system to affect politics. From
3 per cent to 6 per cent of the Indian respondents also mentioned
demonstrations and violent activity as suitable methods of putting pressure on the government.

In accordance with our expectations, political efficacy and
education showed strong positive correlation. An overwhelming
majority of the highly educated believed that they could do something to influence policy-making in the direction of their liking.

Finally, regarding the relationship between subjective competence
and political participation, it was seen that when political participation is defined as past efforts to affect politics through direct methods
(organizing groups, writing letters, working through a party, etc.),
subjective competence showed a positive relationship with participation. But when voting turnout is taken as the measure of participation, competence showed a slightly negative correlation.

From this it would appear that the highly efficacious persons may
be somewhat cynical about the act of voting, i.e. they may not perceive voting as a particularly effective method of influencing government output. Higher non-voting rates among educated and the efficacious persons may also reflect the lack of citizenship duty feelings
(i.e. a feeling that voting is a citizen's duty), or may even reflect the
existence of political alienation and disgruntlement among them.

NOTES

[1]Gabriel Almond and Sidney Verba, *The Civic Culture* (Boston: Little, Brown,
1965), pp. 206-07.

[2]The literature on political efficacy and its correlates is vast and still growing. For an extensive listing of this literature, see footnote 4 in David Easton and Jack Dennis, "The Child's Acquisition of Regime Norms: Political Efficacy," *American Political Science Review*, 61:1 (March 1967), pp. 25-38. Also see Ada W. Finifter, "Dimensions of Political Alienation," *American Political Science Review*, 64:2 (June 1970), pp. 389-410.

[3]Ada Finifter distinguishes four different meanings of political alienation: powerlessness, normlessness, meaninglessness, and isolation; see *op.cit.* Our concept of political efficacy is the reverse of "political powerlessness". In terms of Easton and Dennis conceptualization, our concept includes second part of their definition. Easton and Dennis write, "As a concept, political efficacy appears in three separate although by no means independent guises: as a norm, as a psychological disposition or feeling, and as a form of behaviour." See *op. cit.*, p. 25.

[4]"In a democratic political system, the belief that cooperation with one's fellow citizens is both possible and an effective political action represents, we suggest, a highly significant orientation. The diffusion of influence over political decisions, by which we define democracy, implies some cooperative ability among the citizenry. This cooperation seems to be necessary, in terms of both the amount of influence the ordinary man can expect to have and the results of his influence on governmental decision," *op. cit.*, p. 152. Edward C. Banfield in *The Moral Basis of a Backward Society* (N.Y : The Free Press, 1967), and Lucian W. Pye in *Politics, Personality and Nation Building* (New Haven: Yale University Press, 1962), also emphasize the importance of "organizational sentiments" for the development of democracy.

[5]In this regard, see Jack Dennis, "Support for the Institution of Elections by the Mass Public," *American Political Science Review*, 64:3 (Sept. 1970), pp. 819-35. In the United States, the general conclusion is that the institution of elections enjoys a broad, and stable, level of public support, and that a vast majority of the people regard voting as their civic obligation. At the same time, however, the belief in the efficacy of elections (i.e., elections have political consequences, they control government) has declined in the 1960's.

[6]*Op. cit.*, p. 164.   [7]*Ibid.*, p. 144.

[8]Alex Inkeles, "Participant Citizenship in Six Developing Countries," *American Political Science Review*, 63:4 (1969), pp. 1120-41. See Chap. Four for a further discussion of these findings.

PART IV

CONCLUSION AND SUMMARY

CHAPTER SIXTEEN

Modernization and Political Participation

THE THEME of this study has been political participation patterns in India. We have sought to know who are the participants and who are the non-participants. The empirical base of this study has been the opinion polls conducted by the Indian Institute of Public Opinion, New Delhi. Some of these polls were national studies, based on urban and rural samples spread all over India, while others were regional studies, restricted to one geographical locality or even to a single city. The sample size for the national studies varied from 2,000 to 10,000. These Gallup surveys contained a variety of information on demographic characteristics, party preferences, political attitudes, and participation patterns of the Indian public. The Gallup surveys therefore provide a rich store of data which are deserving of scholarly analysis. The Indian Gallup samples are not as random as one would like them to be, yet for the limited purpose of establishing relationships between variables, they are quite useful. The present study is one indication of how such data can be utilized for political behaviour research.

For purposes of explaining political participation rates in India, we have employed two groups of variables : (1) individual socio-economic attributes, and (2) individual psychological and attitudinal variables. The first group included place of residence, education, occupation, income, age, marital status, sex, religion, caste, mass media exposure, and geographical mobility. The second group included political information, feelings toward political recruitment (politicization), party identification, party evaluations, and feelings of civic competence.[1]

MAJOR FINDING

Many of our findings support generalizations derived from research in the West while many others suggest a revision in these generalizations. In general, unlike the case in Western democracies, voter turnout in India shows a persistent curvilinear relationship with modernism variables. For instance, it was seen that education was positively correlated with such political activities as discussing politics, taking interest in politics and trying to influence governmental decisions, but that it showed a curvilinear relationship with voter turnout. A similar relationship was discovered between political participation on the one hand and media exposure, and geographical mobility on the other (see the next chapter for a summary of these and other major findings). In general, factors which can be considered as indicators of modernism or of social status have shown a curvilinear relationship with voter turnout.

In this chapter we will tie these factors together and examine their joint impact on political participation. In order to do this we have prepared an overall index of exposure to modernization influences; the variables which have gone into this index are : the place of residence, level of education, occupation, degree of exposure to mass communications, extent of physical travel, number of possessions, and the range of opinions on public issues.

All these factors have been presumed to be related to the development of modernizing attitudes. Recent literature in political science is full of references to a traditional-modern dichotomy, and to the characteristics of each political state;[2] we therefore do not think that a detailed justification for the inclusion of above factors is necessary. Urbanism is obviously related to modernism for cities alone have developed the complex of skills and know-how that characterize the modern industrial economy; further, cities alone provide extensive contact with many components of our modern civilization—railways, buses, telephones, movie theatres, etc.

Education, media exposure and physical travel are also obvious correlates of modernism. These factors, the first two through vicarious experiences and the third through actual physical experience, reinforce "empathic" predispositions—the hall-mark of the modern man. Similarly, certain occupations are more likely to inculcate modern attitudes than others. White-collar workers, professionals, and factory workers are more influenced by modern instruments than, for instance, farmers, unskilled labourers or the unemployed.

We have also included possession of things in our modernism index. The 1964 national poll asked its respondents whether they owned any of the following things : watch or clock, calendar, sewing machine, bicycle, book(s), radio, electric light, piped water. The more things that a person owned, the higher the score that he received on our modernism index. The number of possessions must be distinguished from the economic status of a person. Although the two are obviously related, many traditionally oriented persons may be wealthy (money-lenders in the Indian villages, for example) and not own the kind of things named above. Persons who are more likely to buy these things are the ones who have come under the influence of modern culture, either via frequent visits to the city or via some education. Therefore, possession of things is a better indicator of modern influences than the economic status of a person.

The last factor that has gone into our modernism index is the range of opinions on public issues that a person has. In both the 1967 and the 1964 national polls, respondents were asked whether the government should be doing anything about the following problems: uneducated children, high interest rates, bad housing conditions, illegitimate children, unemployment, over-population, social inequalities, and arranged marriages. If the person gave an opinion that the government should be or should not be doing something about each of these issues, he was given a positive score, but if he gave no opinion or said "don't know" he was given a score of 0. These scores were then added and incorporated in our modernism scale. We regarded the opinion range of a person as a very good indicator of his modernity.[3] Recent literature in political science has demonstrated that having opinions on a wide range of issues is characteristic only of modern man. Traditionals have few opinions, to the extent of extreme parochialism where an individual has little perception even of his own self, not to speak of wider public questions.[4]

Details of the modernism index are available in the Appendix, but it may be briefly mentioned here that different dimensions on each of the above factors were arbitrarily assigned equal weights. For example, no education was given a weight of 0, a little education that of 1, and higher education that of 2. Similarly, no com-

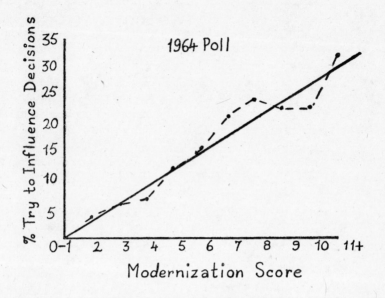

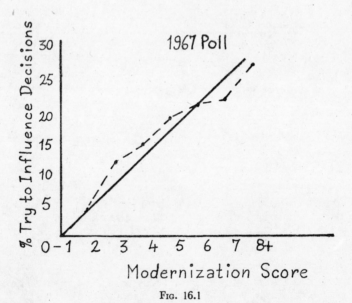

Fig. 16.1

Modernization and Attempted Political Influence.

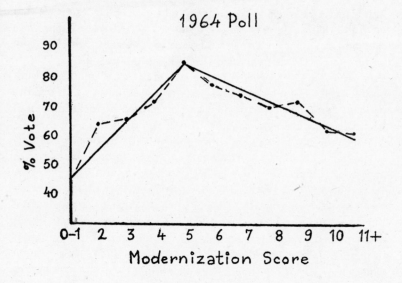

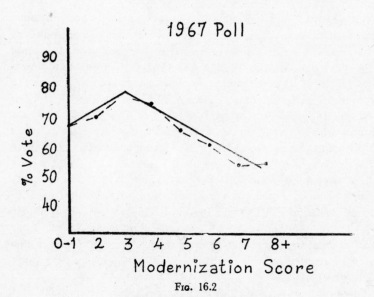

Fig. 16.2

Modernization and Voter Turnout.

munications exposure was given a weight of 0, some exposure that of 1, and high exposure that of 2, and so on. These weights were then added, giving us a rough measure of modernism ranging from 0 (no factors conducive to modernism) to 14 (all factors highly conducive to modernism). The modernism scale could be built only for the 1967 and the 1964 national polls; only two of our dependent variables (voter turnout and attempted political influence) have therefore been examined in this chapter.

When we plot the relationship between modernism and attempted political influence on the one hand, and between modernism and voter turnout on the other, we discover two different patterns. In the former case (FIG. 16.1), we discover that the level of exposure to modernization influences is directly related to the level of attempted political influence—each rise on the modernism scale is accompanied by a corresponding rise in the level of participation in political influence activities. For example, in 1964, among those who scored 0-1 on the modernism index, not even a single person had participated in any of the political influence activities; in contrast, among those who received the highest score, as many as 33 per cent tried to influence decisions.

But when we plot the modernism score against voter turnout, the relationship changes. We find (FIG. 16.2) that voting frequency is curvilinearly related to the degree of modernism. That is, voting frequency rises with the rise in the level of exposure to modernization influences, but a point is reached when any further rise in exposure to modernization is accompanied not by further rise but a consistent decline in voting turnout. For example, 53 per cent of those who scored 10 on the scale voted in the last election while 85 per cent of those who scored only 5 went to the polls. Another comparison is that people who score 0-1 on the scale voted less by only 8 percentage points (45 per cent as opposed to 53 per cent) than those who scored 10. Data from the 1967 poll show roughly the same pattern. Differences are an increase in voting (to 65 per cent) among the most parochial and a decrease in voting (to 53 per cent) among the most highly modernized. Also, the peak of the curve occurs at a lower modernization level than in the 1964 study —at a score of 3 in 1967.

These findings suggest that voter participation at the polls and participation in other kinds of activities should be treated separately. Such a view of political participation is of course contrary to the usual treatment of the subject in political science literature, where various political activities have been regarded as an expression of the same phenomenon. The evidence from India presented in this study indicates that voting is a special kind of an act; some people, especially the educated and modernized elite, are likely to engage in more demanding forms of participation but at the same time they are less likely to exercise their franchise.

The finding with respect to voter turnout is indeed very puzzling and contrary to expected results. Most political behavioural research indicates that turnout increases linearly as the level of such factors as education and mass media exposure (two of the cleanest measures of modernism) rises. How can we account for the fact that the more modernized, unlike their counterparts in the developed countries, do not exercise their franchise to the same extent as do the less modernized, or in some cases, as do even the most traditional persons?

We have raised this question in several different places in this study. We have speculated that voting frequency is related to the political attitudes of a person, especially attitudes toward the political system and its legitimacy. We hypothesized that non-voting among the upper classes and the more modernized may be a consequence of their political unhappiness, alienation and disgruntlement. This political unhappiness in turn may be a result of the rise in the level of demands which accompany the modernization process, deterioration suffered in the economic and political spheres, and negative appraisal of the emerging political culture. We think that these factors are responsible for the dissatisfaction among the Indian elite, and we will discuss them in the following few pages.

First, contrary to common belief, the process of modernization breeds instability and unhappiness, at least in the short run. This is because modernization creates demands at a faster rate than the rate at which they are satisfied. It is a well-known fact now that the so-called "revolution of rising expectations" has not found fulfilment. The struggle for freedom from colonial rule created hopes of a new and a better world. Further, those who are exposed to mass media or receive education come to believe that traditional institutions are not God-given and that alternate and better arrangements are possible. Thus, a great flood of expectancy and aspiration, of desire and demand, has been awakened during the past two decades. However, the growth of expectancy and aspirations is one thing, and their satisfaction quite another. Advantages of progress are hard to attain, and desires are more easily aroused than gratified. Thus, in much of the under-developed world, needs are growing much more rapidly than the technology which will fulfil these needs. The result is frustrations and alienation. Persons who have received some education, or who are exposed to other modernizing influences, are the most frustrated because it is they who are most aware of the gaps between what they seek and what they can get. There is a fear that we may witness a radical counter revolution, "a revolution of rising frustrations."[5]

Thus, one reason for alienation and frustration among the upper classes in India may be a direct result of the new awareness which accompanies modernization; the second reason may be the emergence of a new parochial political culture in the country. Before we turn to a discussion of this latter phenomenon, it should be noted that many educated persons blame the present political framework for both these developments.

INDIA's TWO POLITICAL CULTURES

Myron Weiner has written that in post-Independence India, two political cultures—one "the mass political culture," and the other "the elite political culture"—have emerged. Our data on political participation patterns in India support this interpretation.[6]

According to Weiner, the elite political culture, once the ruling culture, is now a "defensive" political culture. It is predominant at the national level of government—in the parliament, in the bureaucracy, in the army, and in many of the prominent universities and colleges. It declines as one moves to the state capitals, and it is almost non-existent in the small towns and villages. Its members are the Western educated intelligentsia and the urban middle classes, and it usually expresses itself in the English idiom. One of the characteristics of this culture, as indicated by our data, is that its members do not vote in heavy numbers on the polling day.

The mass political culture, on the other hand, is an "expanding" political culture. It is predominant at the local levels of government—in the town municipalities and in the village Panchayats. It is beginning to reach out to the state legislatures and even to the national parliament. The mass political culture is composed of people who are less educated, more traditional, less national minded and more imbedded in caste and communal ties. It expresses itself in the local idiom, and one if its characteristics is that (and this is indicated by our data) its members are more likely to turn out at the polls than members of the elite culture.

The increased political participation among the masses is the direct result of democratization and decentralization of power, which the elite themselves have created. India is one of the few countries where power was deliberately decentralized. This decentralization was instituted with the promulgation of the 1950 Constitution (a work of lawyers, constitutional experts and other intellectuals), which conferred considerable powers on state governments over such subjects as education, agriculture and development programmes. The single most important provision of the Constitution, however, related to universal adult suffrage. In one stroke, millions of people who for centuries had been inert subjects were given control over the choice of their governors.

In 1959, steps were taken to further decentralize power, and the local government system called the Panchayati Raj was instituted in the villages. Under this system, popularly elected assemblies came to control many of the village affairs which had been under state jurisdiction. These assemblies are becoming depositories of real power as they gain more control over finances for education, rural electrification, road building, street paving and many other such projects under the government's rural development proprammes.[7]

One important consequence of this democratization of power has been that more and more people have entered the political arena; this is documented by many writers, and is also indicated by our own data. Participation rates have consistently risen among rural, illiterate and the depressed masses. Another consequence has been the introduction of parochial issues into political competition. Campaigns are now being increasingly conducted on the basis of appeals to ethnic ties of the electorate. Karl Deutsch once wrote: "Men discover sooner or later that they can advance their interests in the competitive game of politics and economics by forming coalitions—coalitions which will depend to a significant degree on social communication and on the culture patterns and personality structure of the participants."[8] It can be said that politicians in post-

Independence India have discovered that the natural bases of forming coalitions are the caste and ethnic ties of the populace. Thus, caste, language and communal groups have sprung up which seek concessions from the government in the interests of their members. And, during election campaigns, ethnic origins of the candidates are emphasized, and political parties place more importance on communal associations of the candidates than on individual merits.

Given the existence of parochial ties in the populace, and given the system under which each adult person, irrespective of his education and social status, has one vote, the rise of the mass political culture is almost a certainty. The elected politician, unlike the colonial administrator who preceded him, must elicit public support; he cannot impose allegiance. And, so long as the bulk of the population is moved by appeals to local and traditional ties, there is no surer way of winning the election than by emphasizing these ties. The introduction of a popularly elected representative system based on universal adult suffrage has therefore led not to national integration, but to the reverse—increased linguistic, racial, regional and religious divisions.

From the point of view of winning the allegiance of illiterate masses to the system, the process of democratization of power may have good effects. The speed with which the common people have won concessions from the government makes it unlikely that they would defect from the present political system, or even perhaps from the Congress party which has spearheaded this democratization. But from the point of view of the urban, educated and modernizing middle classes, and especially the intellectuals, the whole system seems to have gone astray. Economic development has not come about as they expected and theirs is still the backward country of which they are ashamed. But the urban, educated, modernized elite is particularly unhappy about the character of the emerging mass political culture. The most serious defect of this culture is that political competition seems to be heavily based on loyalty to caste, religion, language and place of residence rather than loyalty to one India. Thus, instead of heightened national unity, the process of electoral competition has led to increasing national disunity. As Weiner says, "Castes and religious groups oppose one another. States quarrel over their boundaries and over the distribution of water from rivers which cut across state lines and compete for public investments by the central government. Castes demand representation in state cabinets and in state assemblies. And some states even try to discriminate against the investors and workers from other states."[9] It is felt by the educated that many of these loyalties are exploited by politicians for the pursuance of their selfish power aims.

The failure of the rapid economic programmes and the emergence of the mass political culture are two of the factors which contribute to dissatisfaction among the educated class. To these should be added two other factors: economic stagnation among the salaried employees, and the shift of power from urban centres to rural areas.

ECONOMIC AND POLITICAL LOSSES

A very disquieting element in the position of the middle classes is that their economic position has improved only a little since Independence. The group that has suffered the most are the salaried employees in the government and private business and teachers. According to a 1957-58 government survey, 70 per cent of 36,000 full-time university teachers were earning incomes below Rs. 301 per month, and less than 10 per cent were receiving incomes above Rs. 450 per month. Compared with government administrative employees at higher levels, or those in managerial positions, or those in commerce and trade, the salaries of teachers and other white-collar employees have declined substantially.[10] We have earlier referred to high unemployment rates among the educated (see chapter on Income). It is estimated that about 50 per cent of those who graduate from colleges do not find employment for extended periods of time.

Since Independence, the locus of power has also been shifting from urban intellectual groups to rural masses. Before 1947, one of the main centres of Congress power was in urban educated groups, frequently western educated, and generally high caste. Nehru was the leader of this element in the Congress party. After Independence, the intellectual groups have gradually lost power within the Congress party. Although Nehru remained the prime minister from 1947 to 1964, the composition of the national parliament changed. If members of the "law, press, and the professions" are considered to include urban intellectuals, then there was a decline in the representation of this group from 55 per cent in 1947 to 44 per cent in 1952 and to about 35 per cent in 1962. Rural representation, on the other hand, increased from 15 per cent in 1947 to 40 per cent in 1962.[11] Another research indicates that the percentage of lawyers declined from 35 per cent to 17.5 per cent from the First to the Fourth Lok Sabha, while agrarian interests increased from 22.4 per cent to 31.1 per cent.[12] This shift in power is more perceptible at the state level. In Madras, for example, Rajagopalachari, a Brahmin intellectual who knew English and Sanskrit well, and who authored a number of books, was followed by Kamaraj, a villager with very little formal schooling. In West Bengal, for another example, the leadership passed from the hands of B. C. Roy, a doctor, to lesser intellectual elements in the Congress party.[13]

There is thus strong evidence which points to the fact that the urban middle classes, especially the intellectuals among them, are dissatisfied with the Congress rule. We have discussed four factors that have contributed to this disillusionment: heightening of demand level under modernization influences, emergence of parochial political culture with its emphasis on particularistic loyalties, economic deterioration, and the loss of political power.

IMPLICATIONS FOR THE FUTURE OF DEMOCRACY

The disillusionment and frustration among the educated classes is real. A recent study of the Delhi state found that, in general, the upper, more educated classes were much more negatively disposed toward political authority than were the lower classes. For example, 56 per cent of the highly educated (high school and above) as opposed to 30 per cent of the illiterate, believed that public officials were doing a "poor" job. The authors of the study concluded: "The suggestion implicit in these findings is that improvement in social status is accompanied by increased hostility toward the administrative system, that there is a greater tendency to criticize public authority as a person moves from his traditional and depress-ed social status toward more enlightenment, higher income, and more exposure to modernization influences."[14] Similarly, Alex Inkeles' research led him to conclude that in India persons who were informed, knowledgeable and rational were also less satisfied and more critical of government and politics.[15]

The unhappiness and disillusionment among the educated classes find expression in several aspects of their political behaviour. Some intellectuals have left the Congress party and have joined the opposition parties, particularly the leftist and the socialist parties. Some others have withdrawn from partisan loyalties, and one often hears in some intellectual circles the argument for a "partyless" democracy for India. The argument for partyless democracy draws its sustenance from the view that a large number of political parties and splinter groups, which have emerged on the Indian scene, have intensified conflict at all levels of Indian society, aggravated caste and communal tensions, and encouraged men to seek power for its own sake. The advocates of partyless democracy believe that it is possible to organize political life democratically and yet eliminate political parties.[16]

Of greater concern to the government are perhaps those groups who have taken to extremist politics as active supporters of the leftist or the rightist parties. These extremist groups are particularly strong among the Bengali middle classes in Calcutta. There is thus some truth in Myron Weiner's observation, that

> In the new nations it is often those who fought for freedom and created the new political order who have become most alienated from the political system. Military take-overs are almost always carried out with the blessing of many important political groups and often almost the entire intelligentsia. The shift from democratic to authoritarian political frameworks has come about not because of mass upheavals, but because of attitudes and behaviour of sections of the ruling elite—in political parties, the bureaucracy, and the military. [17]

The process of disillusionment among the educated middle classes may not have gone as far as it did in some new nations which witnessed the emergence of military regimes. The probability of a military coup is somewhat more remote in India if for the simple reason that India is a very complex country, and even if the military officers were inclined to stage a coup, it would require perfect rapport and coordination among the four widely scattered Commands—a difficult feat to bring about. Effective civilian control over the armed forces in India has been unchallenged since Independence. We must also consider the role of the states and the masses in this calculus. States have gained real power and they would be inclined to maintain the present democratic framework which has facilitated this distribution of power. Furthermore, the masses are increasingly becoming part of the political process, and it is not too far-fetched to conceive that they would oppose any groups that might want to destroy the system, at least by not cooperating with them. In the final analysis, however, the stability of the regime depends on what takes place in the national parliament; whether one party or a coalition of parties can provide direction and unity to the country or whether the nation will witness a series of weak and shaky governments.

NOTE ON FUTURE RESEARCH

We have attempted in this study to explore political participation patterns in India and how they vary among different social and psychological groups. The kinds of variables that we could examine were limited by the questions originally asked in the Indian Gallup polls. While we have discovered some very interesting leads, we are also aware of the limitations of our study. Our data offer little evidence concerning "the meaning of the vote," i.e. what value do Indians attach to the act of voting. Do people view voting to be an effective instrument of popular control of government ? Or, do they view it with cynicism? Further, do they consider voting to be among the significant civic obligations that citizens are supposed to perform? Or do they lack such citizenship duty feelings?

The question that clearly needs further investigation is lower voting rates found among the educated populace of India. We have offered several suggestive hypotheses in this regard, but we need a stronger empirical base. Here, we may speculate that nonvoting among the elite is the outcome of one or more of the following factors: (a) apathy, i.e. complete lack of interest in political matters; (b) disgust with the party system, candidates or issues at hand; (c) disaffection and alienation from the existing political system; (d) lack of voting duty, i.e. failure to perceive voting to be an important civic obligation; (e) perceived meaninglessness of the voting act, i.e. a belief that voting does not significantly affect quality of leadership and hence is meaningless. Our study shows that non-voting among the elite is not a consequence of political apathy or lack of interest in political matters. The members of the elite score high on political information, knowledge and concern. If this is so, then non-voting must be related to alienation or unhappiness of the elite, i.e. factors (*b*) to (*e*) listed above.

Though factors (*b*) to (*e*) may all be viewed as being indicative of alienation or unhappiness among the elite, the very differentiation of these factors suggests that it is important to distinguish *what* individuals are alienated from or are unhappy with. Thus it might be expected that individuals who perceive the voting act as meaningless—factor (*e*)—are less likely to vote than individuals who are characterized by other factors. Of course, it is expected that non-voting among the elite who cannot be characterized by any of these factors will be higher than among those elite members who can be so identified. The crucial thing here, however, is to seek to determine the *meaning* of voting and non-voting. The consequences for the political system and society generally may be vastly different, depending on the reasons for which citizens either vote or do not vote. For example, factor (*b*) may be a meaning that is less serious for the stability of the political system than are the other meanings. Disgust with parties, candidates or issues rise and fall over time with particular candidates and programmes. In this sense, factor (*b*) is more temporal than are other factors, and hence more easily rectified by changes in candidates and/or policies and not in constitutions.

Further, if studies of voting behaviour are to be meaningful from the perspective of the overall functioning of the political system, it is necessary to determine the extent to which the political leadership in the country recognizes voting as the communication of demands from the populace. We suggest, in other words, that future research should examine whether the Indian leadership holds a democratic and representational view or an elitist and a manipulative view of elections.

NOTES

[1]The method used has been one of simple and partial correlations. Most of

the time, we sought to determine the relationship between two variables after the effect of a third or a fourth variable was controlled. A better method would have been multiple correlations, where the effect of a given variable is measured after all other factors are controlled. We used the variance analysis techniques of A.I.D. for a related objective. The A.I.D. device, developed by John Sonquist and James Morgan (see their *The Detection of Interaction Effects*, ISR, University of Michigan, 1964), is concerned with the problem of determining which variables, or a set of variables, are related to a particular phenomenon, under what conditions and through what intervening variables. It attempts to determine which independent variables will give a maximum improvement in ability to predict values of the dependent variable. The preliminary analysis, using this technique, indicates that the variable most strongly associated with voter turnout is age (above 26), followed by party identification (Congress or non-Congress as against none). "Some" education and "moderate" media exposure were also related. On attempted political influence, the factor that explains most of the variance in the dependent variable is the feeling of civic competence, followed by income and education.

The data analysis through this technique is incomplete at this stage. Most unhappily, we could not examine the 1967 poll, for the A.I.D. programme as presently available to us, did not allow manipulation of such a large sample as that of the 1967 study (10,000 respondents).

[2]Note especially the works of Alex Inkeles: "Making Men Modern," *American Journal of Sociology*, 75:2 (Sept. 1969); "The OM Scale: A Comparative Socio-Psychological Measure of Individual Modernity," *Sociometry*, 29:4 (Dec. 1966); and "The Modernization of Man," in M. Weiner, ed., *Modernization* (N.Y.: Basic Books, 1966), pp. 138-50.

[3]It may be noted here that the direction of opinion on these issues was not significantly related to political participation. That is, persons who were consistently in favour of government intervention were not significantly different from those who were consistently against such intervention. The only major difference was between those who had no opinions on any issues, those who had opinions on some, and those who had opinions on most.

[4]Note, for instance the works of Daniel Lerner and Almond and Verba, respectively, these are: *The Passing of Traditional Society* (N.Y.: Free Press, 1958), and *The Civic Culture* (Boston: Little, Brown, 1965). In this context, Lerner observes, "Especially important, for the Participant Style, is the enormous proportion of people who are expected to 'have opinions' on public matters — and the corollary expectation of these people that their opinions will matter. It is this subtly complicated structure of reciprocal expectations which sustains widespread empathy. Only in the lowest reaches of America's social hierarchy, for example, is it still discussed whether people *ought* to have opinions." p. 51.

[5]See Daniel Lerner, "Toward a Communications Theory of Modernization," in Lucian W. Pye, ed., *Communications and Political Development* (Princeton: Princeton University Press, 1963), pp. 330-31.

[6]Much of the discussion here on the emergence of two political cultures is derived from Myron Weiner's "India's Two Political Cultures," in his *Political Change in South Asia* (Calcutta: F.K.L. Mukhopadhyay, 1963), pp. 115-52. Our readers may be reminded that our use of the term "elite" is a broad one, and

includes members of the middle class.

[7]See Adi H. Doctor, "India's Experiment in Democratic Decentralisation: Study in the Problems of Leadership & Mass Participation," in S.P. Aiyar and R. Srinivasan, eds., *Studies in Indian Democracy* (Bombay: Allied Publishers, 1965), pp. 373-89.

[8]Karl Deutsch, "Growth of Nations," *World Politics*, 5:2 (Jan. 1953), p. 183.

[9]Weiner, *op. cit.*, p. 138.

[10]George Rosen has excellent material on economic gains and losses since Independence among major social groups·in India. See his *Democracy and Economic Change in India* (Berkeley: University of California Press, 1967), Chapters 8 and 9. See also Rajni Kothari, *Politics in India* (Boston: Little, Brown, 1170).

[11]Rosen, *op. cit.*, pp. 72-73.

[12]Ratna Dutta, "The Party Representative in Fourth Lok Sabha," *Economic and Political Weekly*, 4 (Jan. 1969), p. 179.

[13]The shift in power from urban to rural areas has been documented by a number of writers. For documentary evidence, see Chap. 3 above, footnotes 11 to 16.

[14]Samuel J. Eldersveld, *et al.*, *The Citizen and the Administrator in a Developing Democracy* (Glenview, Ill.: Scott, Foresman, 1968), p. 58 and passim.

[15]Alex Inkeles, "Participant Citizenship in Six Developing Countries," *American Political Science Review*, 63:4 (Dec. 1969), pp. 1120-41.

[16]The argument for a partyless democracy has been boosted by Jayaprakash Narayan, one of the few public figures who retains the respect of the intelligentsia. Jayaprakash Narayan has advocated that India should adopt a "Communitarian" system under which party politics would be eliminated and there would be a system of indirect elections from village councils up to the national legislature. The *Indian Political Science Review*, 2:1 (Oct. 1967-Mar. 1968), published a forum on "Partyless Government." Some 14 political scientists and public figures argued for and against the idea of partyless democracy. It may also be noted that the disillusionment with political parties is not unique to India. When Ayub Khan took over in Pakistan in 1958, the first thing he did was to ban all political parties.

[17]M. Weiner, *op. cit.*, p. 137.

CHAPTER SEVENTEEN

Summary of Major
Findings

URBAN-RURAL RESIDENCE

As compared with rural residents, residents of urban communities are *more* likely to be interested in politics, to discuss political matters, and to try to influence decisions.

Surprisingly, however, urban residents are somewhat *less* likely to turn out at the polls than rural residents. This relationship holds true independent of the effect of education, income, or mass media exposure.

Our data also indicate that over the past decade, the rural residents have become more involved in politics.

EDUCATION

The more educated (those with at least a high school education) are *more* likely to be interested in political matters.

The more educated are *more* likely to discuss politics with friends, neighbours and colleagues.

The more educated are *more* likely to participate in activities which seek to influence decisions.

At the same time, however, the more educated are *less* likely to turn out at the polls or to attend public meetings and rallies than the less educated. The lower voting frequency among the highly educated may be a result of the following factors:

(*a*) Length of time required to cast one's ballot. Since balloting may take several hours, the more educated may not want to spend this amount of time.

(b) Group pressures. Group and factional pressures to vote are perhaps heavier on the less educated than on the highly educated.

(c) Dissatisfaction. The more educated seem to be dissatisfied with the performance of the Congress government. For instance, they are more likely to say that the government is doing a "poor" job, and that an opposition party rule would "help" the country.

(d) Alienation. The more educated may even be alienated from the political system. For instance, they are more likely to believe that the present democratic framework in India, based as it is on universal adult suffrage, has accentuated caste, communal and linguistic divisions in the country.

OCCUPATION

In general, people in the professions, in government employment, in business and trade, and in farming are more active in politics than manual workers, farm tenants, and those not in the labour force (students, the unemployed, and the retired).

Persons in the professions are about the most active on all measures of participation discussed in this book except on voting. The farmers, on the other hand, turn out at the polls in higher numbers than any other group. The most apathetic group is composed of the unemployed and the retired.

INCOME

The economic threshold of political involvement occurs around Rs. 50 per month. Very few people below this income level participate in any political activity.

The more affluent are more likely to take interest in politics, to discuss politics, and to do something to affect laws.

At the same time, the less affluent are *as* likely to turn out at the polls as the more affluent.

Among all income groups, turnout tends to decrease as the level of education increases.

Age and Marital Status

Persons below the age of 30 are markedly less likely to vote than those above 31.

Voting frequency declines among those in their sixties and seventies, but even these people are more likely to vote than those under 30.

At the same time, however, the young are more likely to engage in political discussions with friends and colleagues.

In addition to advancing age, marital status and family-size are also positively related to voter turnout. Married persons are more likely to vote than those who are single; and those who have larger families are still more likely to vote than those who have smaller families.

Sex

As compared with men, women are significantly less involved in politics. They are less likely to take interest in politics, to talk politics, to attend meetings, and to do anything to change laws. Their voting rate is about 12 per cent lower than that of men.

Sex differences on political participation tend to be sharper in the rural areas than in the cities.

The lower the level of education, the greater the difference between male and female participation rates.

Women belonging to the Muslim faith are markedly less likely to exercise their franchise than those belonging to the Hindu religion.

When data are examined by states, sex differences on voting are much sharper in the less literate and the less modernized states (Bihar, M.P., Orissa and Assam) than in the more literate and modernized states (Kerala, Madras, Panjab, Maharashtra, etc.).

Religion and Caste

The turnout rates do not vary significantly among major religious groups in India. Muslims, Christians, and Sikhs are as likely to vote as members of the Hindu community.

Concerning caste, members of the lower castes are as likely to vote as those of the upper castes. At the same time, however, members of the lower castes (Shudras and Untouchables) are less likely to try to influence decisions than members of the upper castes (Brahmins, Kshatriyas and Vaishyas).

Mass Media Exposure

Consumption of mass communications is confined primarily to the upper status persons. Persons with lower educational or income levels have little or no exposure, and if they consume media at all, these are more likely to be radio and films—the media which do not require skills of literacy.

Persons who are exposed to more media are more likely to attend meetings, to discuss politics, and to do something to affect laws.

Mass media exposure is curvilinearly related to voter turnout; that is, persons who are sometimes exposed to media are more likely to vote than those who are never exposed to media or those who are frequently exposed to media.

Mass media exposure has greater impact on the behaviour of the less educated persons than on the behaviour of the highly educated persons.

Geographical Mobility

Geographical mobility is part of the SES or the modernization syndrome. Persons who live in cities, who have received some education, who are relatively well-off, and who are exposed to mass communications, are also more likely to have travelled extensively.

Persons with higher mobility are more likely to participate in activities which seek to affect laws. This relationship is stronger at lower levels of education than at higher levels.

Geographical mobility is curvilinearly related to voter turnout.

Political Information

The acquisition of information on political objects goes along with urban residence, higher education, higher income and frequent exposure to mass communications.

Among the less educated (illiterates or a little education), rising level of information is accompanied by a rise in the level of voting and participation in political influence activities.

Among the highly educated, an increase in the level of information makes relatively little difference whether or not they would vote or do something to affect laws.

POLITICIZATION

On the basis of electoral and survey data, it was found that political offices are highly sought after positions in India. On the average, from 4 to 5 persons contest each legislative seat.

In Delhi, government employment is accorded higher prestige than employment with a private firm.

Twice the percentage of persons in Delhi as in Detroit would "encourage" their sons to go into politics as a career.

Persons with medium status—those with some education and with medium incomes—are more favourably disposed toward political recruitment of their sons than persons with low or very high education and income.

The more politicized (those with favourable attitudes toward political recruitment) are more likely to vote, to attend meetings, and more likely to give money to parties than the less politicized.

Feelings of politicization tend to have greater impact on the political behaviour of the less educated than on the behaviour of the highly educated.

PARTY IDENTIFICATION

Regarding social bases of party support, it was found that Congress is popular among all social groups, although it is somewhat more popular among the elderly (those socialized during India's freedom struggle), the less educated, the religious and ethnic minorities, and those living in the rural areas. The opposition parties, in general, are proportionately stronger among the youth, the educated, the Hindus, and those living in the cities.

Persons who support the Congress party are more likely to vote than those who support one of the opposition parties. At the same time, the opposition supporters are somewhat more likely to take interest in political matters, to attend meetings, to discuss politics, and to try to affect laws.

Attitudes toward parties (party evaluations) were also significantly related to voter turnout. Those who have positive attitudes toward the Congress, and who favourably evaluate Congress performance, are much more likely to vote than those who have positive attitudes toward the opposition parties.

CIVIC COMPETENCE

About 50 per cent of the Indian respondents were found to exhibit feelings of civic competence or of subjective effectiveness.

Feelings of civic competence are more prevalent vis-a-vis the Local government (village, town, city government or council) than the National government.

Feelings of efficacy increase as the level of formal schooling increases.

Concerning strategy of influence, from one-fourth to one-third of the Indian respondents indicated that they would work with local groups of friends and neighbours to counteract legislation that they did not like.

Indian respondents indicated higher confidence on working with appointed officials than with elected representatives.

The higher the level of efficacy feelings, the greater the degree of participation in activities which seek to affect laws.

Citizen competence feelings and voter turnout are not significantly related.

MODERNIZATION

The Index of Modernization Influences was constructed on the basis of the following variables: place of residence, education, occupation, geographical mobility, mass media exposure, number of possessions, and the range of opinions on public issues.

It was seen that participation in political influence activities rises directly as the modernization score rises.

Voting turnout, however, rises and then declines as the level of modernization influences increases. Among those who have a medium score on the modernism scale, as many as 85 per cent vote; this contrasts with about 50 per cent voting rate among those who have the very least or the very highest score on the scale.

Scales and Indexes

WE HAVE USED a few indexes as a measure of the political attitudes and demographic characteristics of the respondents; here we discuss the construction of each of these indexes, in the order in which they appear in the text.

MASS MEDIA EXPOSURE INDEX

This index was built using the following three questions in the 1964 national poll.

(1) "Have you ever listened to a radio?" If yes, "How often do you listen to a radio?"

(2) "Do you read a newspaper?" If no, "Do other people read the newspapers to you?" If yes to either of these two questions, "How often do you read a newspaper (or are newspapers read to you)?"

(3) "Have you ever seen a movie?" If yes, "How often do you go to a movie?"

The frequency of exposure to different media were given the following weights:

Frequency of exposure to Newspapers or to Radio	Weights Assigned	Frequency of exposure to Movies
Never	0	Never
Less than once a month	1	Less than once a year
At least once a month	3	At least once a year
Almost every day	7	Almost every week

The maximum possible score for a person is 21—the one who reads a newspaper and listens to a radio almost daily and in addition goes to a movie almost every week. The minimum possible score is 0—for a person who has never been exposed to any of these media. The addition of different weights were given the following meaning:

No exposure:	Score of 0 or 1;
Low exposure:	Score of 2 to 9;
Medium exposure:	Score of 10 to 16;
High exposure:	Score of 17 and above.

GEOGRAPHICAL MOBILITY INDEX

The index is based on the following four questions in the 1964 national survey.

(1) "How about travelling? Have you ever been on a train or a bus?"
(2) If yes, "When was the last time you travelled on a train or a bus?"
(3) "Have you ever been to another State?"
(4) "Have you ever been to another country?"

The answers to these questions allowed us to arrange our respondents on a 4-step scale, ranging from "no" to "high" mobility. The meaning of each category is roughly as follows:

No mobility: A person who has never been on a train or a bus.
Low mobility: Has been on a train or a bus, but has not travelled within the last one year.
Medium mobility: Has travelled within a month and has been to another state or country, or has travelled within a week but has not been to another state or country.
High mobility: Has travelled within a week and in addition been to another state or another country.

POLITICAL INFORMATION INDEX

The Political Information Index was constructed on the basis of the following two questions, asked in both the 1967 and the 1964 national studies.

(1) "Now, will you please name three important or well-known leading men in the Congress party today?"
(2) "And, who are two important national leaders outside the Congress party?"

The answers to these questions were coded 0,1,2,3,4 for the Congress leaders and 0,1,2 for Opposition leaders—each numerical symbol representing the number of leaders that the respondent would identify. These scores were added and given the following meaning:

No information:	Score of 0;
Low information:	Score of 1 or 2;
Medium information	Score of 3 or 4;
High information	Score of 5 or 6.

CIVIC COMPETENCE INDEX

The Civic Competence Index was devised from the following questions; asked in both the 1967 and the 1964 national polls:

(1) "Suppose that some action or policy or law were being considered by the (specify local unit: town, village, city government or council) which you disagreed with, because it was unjust or harmful, or something like that. What are possible things you think you could do about it?"
(2) "If you made such an effort, how likely is it that anything good would come of it?"
(3) "If such a case arose, how likely is it that you would actually do something about it?"

The same set of three questions was asked about an unjust law or policy being considered by a national government unit.

The answers to these three questions were dichotomised into positive and negative responses. If a person said that he could do something to affect decisions, he was considered to have answered positively, no matter what he said he could do. The same dichotomy was used about the likelihood of action—if an individual said that it was "very likely" or "moderately likely" that something good would come of his efforts (question 2) or that he would actually do something (question 3), he was given a positive score; on the other hand, if he said "slightly likely" or "not at all likely" or "don't know, etc." he was given a negative score.

Using this dichotomous method, the following meanings were given to various scores:

No Competence: The respondent could not imagine anything that he could do to affect local or national decisions; that is, the person answered negatively to question 1, both at the local and the national level (in which case questions 2 and 3 were not asked). Total positive score: 0.

Low Competence: The respondent answered positively to question 1 (either at the local or the national level or at both levels), but negatively to questions 2 and 3. Total positive score: 1 or 2.

Medium Competence: Answered positively to question 1 and in addition also answered positively to either 2 or 3. Total positive score: 3 or 4.

High Competence: Answered positively to all the three questions at both levels of government. Total positive score: 5 or 6.

INDEX OF EXPOSURE TO MODERNIZATION INFLUENCES

In order to measure the joint impact of several interrelated characteristics on political participation, an Index of Exposure to Modernization Influences was constructed. The variables included in this index were: the place of residence, level of education, occupational characteristics, degree of exposure to mass communications, extent of physical travel, number of things owned, and the range of opinions on public problems. The rationale for the inclusion of each of these variables has been discussed in Chapter 16.

Different dimensions on each of these variables were assigned arbitrary weights as follows:

	0	1	2
Place of residence	Rural	Urban	
Education	None	A little	High school and above
Occupation	Unemployed, Retired, Domestic servants	Unskilled-workers, Farmers, Businessmen	Professionals, White-collar workers, Students
Mass media exposure	None	Low or medium	High
Geographical Mobility	None	Low or medium	High
Number of things owned	0-1	2-3	4 or more
Number of public issues on which opinion offered	0-1	2-4	5 or more

These weights were added giving us a measure of modernism ranging from 0 (no factors conducive to modernism) to 14 (all factors highly conducive to modernism). The actual range of the scale for the 1964 poll was from a score of 0 to 11. The 1967 national poll did not have information on media exposure, geographical mobility, or the number of things owned by the respondent. The Modernism Index for this poll could therefore be built only on the basis of the remaining four questions. The range of the scale for the 1967 study varied from a score of 0 to 8.

Bibliography

AIYAR, S. P., ed., *The Politics of Mass Violence in India,* Bombay: Manaktalas, 1967.

ALMOND, GABRIEL A. and POWELL, G. B. JR., *Comparative Politics: A Developmental Approach,* Boston: Little, Brown & Co., 1966.

ALMOND, GABRIEL A. and VERBA, SIDNEY, *The Civic Culture,* Boston: Little, Brown & Co., 1965.

APTER, DAVID, *The Politics of Modernization,* Chicago: University of Chicago Press, 1965.

ARORA, SATISH K. and LASSWELL, HAROLD D., *Political Communications: The Public Language of Political Elites in India and The United States,* New York: Holt, Rinehart and Winston, 1969.

BAILEY, F. G., *Politics and Social Change: Orissa in 1959,* Berkeley: University of California Press, 1963.

BANERJI, ANJAN KUMAR, ed., *The Fourth General Election in India: An Analysis,* Calcutta: Benson's, 1967.

BARNABAS, A. P. and MEHTA, SUBHASH C., *Caste in Changing India,* New Delhi: Indian Institute of Public Administration, 1965.

BAUER, RAYMOND, ed., *Social Indicators,* Cambridge: The M.I.T. Press, 1966.

BAXTER, CRAIG, *District Voting Trends in India: A Research Tool,* New York: Columbia University Press, 1969.

——, *The Jana Sangh: A Biography of an Indian Political Party,* Philadelphia: University of Pennsylvania Press, 1969.

BAYLEY, DAVID H., *The Police and Political Development in India,* Princeton, New Jersey: Princeton University Press, 1969.

BERELSON, BERNARD; LAZARSFELD, PAUL and MCPHEE, WILLIAM, *Voting,* Chicago: University of Chicago Press, 1954.

BHAGAT, K. P., *The Kerala Mid-Term Election of 1960,* Bombay: Popular Book Depot, 1962.

BISCO, RALPH L., "Social Science Data Archives: A Review of Developments," *American Political Science Review,* 60:1 (March, 1966), pp, 93-109.

BLAIR, HARRY W., "Caste, Politics and Democracy in Bihar State, India: The Elections of 1967," Ph. D. Thesis, Duke University, 1969.

BRASS, PAUL R., *Factional Politics in an Indian State: the Congress Party in Uttar Pradesh,* Berkeley: University of California Press, 1965.

——, "Political Participation, Institutionalization and Stability in India," *Government and Opposition,* Vol. 4 (Winter, 1969), pp. 32-53.

BRECHER, MICHAEL, *Political Leadership in India: An Analysis of Elite Attitudes,* New York: Praeger, 1969.

BURGER, ANGELA S., *Opposition in a Dominant Party System*, Berkeley: University of California Press, 1969.

CAMPBELL, ANGUS; CONVERSE, PHILIP E.; MILLER, WARREN E. and STOKES, DONALD E., *The American Voter*, New York: John Wiley, 1960.

CANTRIL, HADLEY, *The Pattern of Human Concerns*, New Brunswick, New Jersey: Rutgers University Press, 1966.

CENTRE FOR THE STUDY OF DEVELOPING SOCIETIES, OCCASIONAL PAPERS: No. 1, *Party System and Election Studies*, Bombay: Allied Publishers, 1967.

CHANDIDAS, R.; MOREHOUSE, WARD; CLARK, LEON and FONTERA, RICHARD, *India Votes: A Source Book on Indian Elections*, New York: Humanities Press, 1968.

DASTUR, ALOO J., *Menon vs. Kripalani: North Bombay Election, 1962*, Bombay: University of Bombay, 1967.

DENNIS, JACK, "Support for the Institution of Elections by the Mass Public," *American Political Science Review*, 64-3 (September, 1970), pp. 819-35.

DEUTSCH, KARL W., *Nationalism and Social Communications*, Cambridge: The M.I.T. Press, 1953.

DIPALMA, GIUSEPPE, *Apathy and Participation: Mass Politics in Western Societies*, New York: Free Press, 1970.

ELDER, JOSEPH W., "Religious Beliefs and Political Attitudes," in Smith, Donald E., ed., *South Asian Politics and Religion*, Princeton: Princeton University Press, 1966, pp. 249-76.

ELDERSVELD, SAMUEL J.; JAGANNADHAM, V., and BARNABAS, A. P., *The Citizen and the Administrator in a Developing Democracy, an Empirical Study in Delhi State, India*, Glenview, Ill.: Scott, Foresman & Co., 1968.

"Elections and Party Politics in India: A Symposium," *Asian Survey*, 10:11 (Nov. 1970); a special issue on Indian party politics; articles by Rajni Kothari, Dwaine Marvick, Ram Joshi, Bashiruddin Ahmed, Robert Hardgrave, Douglas Madsen, and Samuel J. Eldersveld.

ERDMAN, HOWARD L., *The Swatantra Party and Indian Conservatism*, London: Cambridge University Press, 1967.

FINIFTER, ADA W. "Dimensions of Political Alienation," *American Political Science Review*, 64:2 (June, 1970), pp. 389-410.

FORRESTER, DUNCAN B., "Electoral Politics and Social Change," *Economic and Political Weekly*, 111 (1968), pp. 1075-94.

FRANDA, MARCUS F., *West Bengal and the Federalizing Process in India*, Princeton: Princeton University Press, 1968.

GEERTZ, CLIFFORD, ed., *Old Societies and New States*, New York: The Free Press, 1963.

GOULD, HAROLD A., "Changing Political Behaviour in Rural Indian Society," *Economic and Political Weekly*, 11 (1967), pp. 1515-24.

GOYAL, O. P., and HAHN, HARLAN, "The Nature of Party Competition in Five Indian States," *Asian Survey*, 6:10 (Oct., 1966), pp. 580-88.

HARDGRAVE, ROBERT L., Jr., *The Dravidian Movement*, Bombay: Popular Prakashan, 1965.

——, *India: Government and Politics in a Developing Nation*, New York: Harcourt, Brace & World, 1970.

HARRISON, SELIG S., *India, the Most Dangerous Decades*, Princeton: Princeton University Press, 1960.

HUNTINGTON, SAMUEL P., *Political Order in Changing Societies*, New Haven: Yale University Press, 1968.

INDIAN INSTITUTE OF PUBLIC OPINION, *Monthly Public Opinion Surveys*, New Delhi: Vol. 1—onward.

INKELES, ALEX, "Participant Citizenship in Six Developing Countries," *American Political Science Review*, 63:4 (Dec. 1969), pp. 1120-41.

JHANGIANI, MOTILAL A., *Jana Sangh and Swatantra: A Profile of the Rightist Parties in India*, Bombay: Manaktalas, 1967.

KARNIK, V. B., *Fourth General Election*, Bombay: Lalvani Publishing House, 1967.

KASHYAP, SUBHASH C., *The Politics of Defection*, Delhi: National Publishing House, 1969.

KEY, V. O., *The Responsible Electorate, Rationality in Presidential Voting 1936-1960*, New York: Vintage Books, 1968.

KOCHANEK, STANLEY A., *The Congress Party of India: The Dynamics of a one-Party Democracy*, Princeton: Princeton University Press, 1968.

KOGEKAR, S. V. and PARK, RICHARD, L. eds., *Reports on the Indian General Elections, 1951-52*, Bombay: Popular Book Depot, 1956.

KOTHARI, RAJNI, ed., *Caste in Indian Politics*, New Delhi: Orient, Longman Ltd., 1970.

——, *Politics in India*, New Delhi: Orient Longman Ltd., 1970, and Boston: Little, Brown & Co., 1970.

KRISHNA, GOPAL, "One Party Dominance—Developments and Trends," *Perspectives*, a supplement to *Indian Journal of Public Administration*, XII: 1 (January-March, 1966), pp. 1-65.

KRISHNA MURTHY, K. G., and Lakshmana Rao, G., *Political Preferences in Kerala: An Electoral Analysis of the Kerala General Elections, 1957, 1960, 1965 and 1967*, Delhi: Radha Krishna, 1968.

LAPALOMBARA, JOSEPH G., and WEINER, MYRON, ed., *Political Parties and Political Development*, Princeton: Princeton University Press, 1966.

LANE, ROBERT E., *Political Life: Why and How People Get Involved in Politics*, New York: Free Press, 1959.

LERNER, DANIEL, *The Passing of Traditional Society*, New York: The Free Press, 1958.

LEWIS, OSCAR, *Village Life in Northern India*, New York: Vintage Books, 1958.

LIPSET, SEYMOUR M., *Political Man: The Social Bases of Politics*, New York: Doubleday, 1960.

——— ROKKAN, STEIN, ed., *Party Systems and Voter Alignment: Cross*

National Perspectives, New York: The Free Press, 1967.

McCall, Charles H., "Paths to Political Participation," Ph. D. Thesis, Yale University, 1965.

McDonough, Peter, "Electoral Competition and Participation in India: A Test of Huntington's Hypothesis," *Comparative Politics*, 4:1 (Oct. 1971), pp. 77-87.

Masani, M. R., *The Communist Party of India, a Short History*, New York: Macmillan, 1954.

Matthews, Donald R., and Prothro, James W., *Negroes and the New Southern Politics*, New York: Harcourt, Brace, & World, 1966.

Mayer, Adrian C., *Caste and Kinship in Central India*, London: Routledge & K. Paul, 1960.

Merritt, Richard L., and Rokkan, Stein, ed., *Comparing Nations: the Use of Quantitative Data in Cross-national Research*, New Haven: Yale University Press, 1966.

Milbrath, Lester W., *Political Participation: How and Why Do People Get Involved in Politics?* Chicago: Rand McNally, 1965.

Milnor, A. J., *Elections and Political Stability*, Boston: Little, Brown & Co., 1959.

Morris-Jones, W. H., and Gupta, B. Das, "India's Political Areas: Interim Report on an Ecological Electoral Investigation," *Asian Survey*, 9:6 (June, 1969), pp. 399-424.

Myrdal, Gunnar, *Asian Drama: An Inquiry into the Poverty of Nations*, 3 Vols., New York: Pantheon, 1968.

Narain, Iqbal, ed., *State Politics in India*, Meerut: Meenakshi Prakashan, 1967.

Nayar, Baldev Raj, *Minority Politics in the Punjab*, Princeton: Princeton University Press, 1966.

Nettl, J. P., *Political Mobilization, A Sociological Analysis of Methods and Concepts*, New York: Basic Books, 1967.

Nie, Norman H.; Powell, G. Bingham, Jr. and Prewitt, Kenneth, "Social Structure and Political Participation: Developmental Relationships," Parts 1 & 11, *American Political Science Review*, 63: 2-3 (1969), pp. 361-78, 808-32.

Overstreet, Gene E., and Windmiller, Marshall, *Communism in India*, Berkeley: University of California Press, 1960.

Park, Richard L., *India's Political System*, New York: Prentice-Hall, 1967.

——, and Tinker, Irene, *Leadership and Political Institutions in India*, Princeton: Princeton University Press, 1959.

Pattabhiram, M., *General Election in India*, Bombay: Allied Publishers, 1967.

Philips, Cyril H., *Politics and Society in India*, New York: Praeger, 1962.

Poplai, Sunder Lal, ed., *1962 General Elections in India*, New Delhi: Allied Publishers, 1962.

Pye, Lucian W., *Aspects of Political Development*, Boston: Little, Brown, & Co., 1966.

——— ed., *Communications and Political Development*, Princeton: Princeton University Press, 1963.

—— *Politics, Personality and Nation Building: Burma's Search For Identity*, New Haven: Yale University Press, 1962.

RABUSHKA, ALVIN, "A Note on Overseas Chinese Political Participation in Urban Malaya," *American Political Science Review*, 64:1 (Mar. 1970), pp. 177-78.

RAM, MOHAN, *Indian Communism: Split Within a Split*, Delhi: Vikas, 1969.

RAO, V.K.R.V. and DESAI, P.B., *Greater Delhi: A Study in Urbanization, 1940-1957*, New York: Asia Publishing House, 1965.

RICHARDSON, BRADELY M., "Urbanization and Political Participation: The Case of Japan," *American Political Science Review*, 67:2 (June 1973), 433-52.

ROKKAN, STEIN, *Citizens, Elections and Parties*, New York: David McKay, 1970.

ROSEN, GEORGE, *Democracy and Economic Change in India*, Berkeley: University of California Press, 1967.

ROSENTHAL DONALD B., *The Limited Elite: Politics and Government in Two Indian Cities*, Chicago: Chicago University Press, 1970.

—— "Deurbanization, Elite Displacement and Political Change in India," *Comparative Politics*, 2:2 (Jan. 1970), pp. 169-202.

RUSSETT BRUCE M., "Social Change and Attitudes on Development and the Political System in India," *Journal of Politics*, 29 (1967), pp. 483-504.

SHASTRI, K. N. R., *Analytical Study of 1967 General Elections in India*, Agra: Vishva Bharati Prakashan, no date.

SHETH, D. L., "Political Development of Indian Electorate," *Economic and Political Weekly*, 5 (January 1970), p. 1-16.

SHILS, EDWARD, "Influence and Withdrawal: The Intellectuals in Indian Political Development," In Marvick, Dwaine, ed., *Political Decision Makers*, New York: The Free Press, 1961.

SINGER, MILTON, and COHN, BERNARD S., eds., *Structure and Change in Indian Society*, Chicago: Aldine Publishing Company, 1968.

SIRSIKAR, V. M., *Political Behaviour in India: A Case Study of the 1962 General Elections*, Bombay: Manaktalas, 1965.

SMITH, DONALD E., ed., *South Asian Politics and Religion*, Princeton: Princeton University Press, 1966.

SOMJEE, A. H., *Democracy and Political Change in Village India: A Case Study*, New Delhi: Orient Longman, 1972.

—— "Caste and Decline of Political Homogeneity," *American Political Science Review*, 67:3 (Sept. 1973), pp. 799-816.

SRINIVAS, M. N., *Caste in Modern India and Other Essays*, Bombay: Asia Publishing House, 1962.

—— *Social Change in Modern India*, Bombay: Allied Publishers, 1966.

STEINER, JURG, *Burger and Politik*, Meisenheim am Glan, Verlag Anton Hain, 1969.

STERN ROBERT W., *The Process of Opposition in India: Two Studies of How Policy Shapes Politics*, Chicago: University of Chicago Press, 1970.

SURI SURINDAR, *1962 Elections—A Political Analysis*, New Delhi: Sudha Publications, 1962.

TALBOT PHILLIPS, *The Second General Elections*, New York: American University Field Staff, 1957.

TINGSTEN HERBERT, *Political Behaviour*, London: P. S. King, 1937.

TURNER, ROY, ed., *India's Urban Future*, Berkeley: University of California Press, 1962.

VERBA, S., AHMAD, B., and BHATT, A., *Race, Caste and Politics: A Comparative Study of India and the United States*, Sage, 1971.

―― NIE, NORMAN, and KIM, JAE-ON, *The Modes of Democratic Participation*, Sage, 1971.

VERMA, S. P., and BHAMBHARI, C. P., *Election and Political Consciousness in India*, Delhi: Meenakshi Prakashan, 1967.

WEINER, MYRON, ed., *Modernization: The Dynamics of Growth*, New York: Basic Books, 1966.

―― *Party Building in a New Nation: The Indian National Congress*, Chicago: Chicago University Press, 1967.

―― *Party Politics in India*, Princeton: Princeton University Press, 1957.

―― ed., *Political Change in South Asia*, Calcutta: F. K. L. Mukhopadhyay, 1963.

―― *The Politics of Scarcity: Public Pressure and Political Response in India*, Chicago: University of Chicago Press, 1962.

―― *State Politics in India*, Princeton: Princeton University Press, 1968.

―― and Rajni Kothari, ed., *Indian Voting Behaviour*, Calcutta: F. K. L. Mukhopadhyay, 1965.

WIEBE, PAUL, "Elections in Peddur: Democracy At Work in An Indian Town," *Human Organization*, 28:2 (Summer 1969), pp. 140-47.

ZAGORIA, DONALD S., "The Ecology of Peasant Communism in India," *American Political Science Review*, 65:1 (March 1971), 144-60.

GOVERNMENT OF INDIA DOCUMENTS

India: A Reference Annual, New Delhi: Ministry of Information and Broadcasting.

Manual of Election Law, Delhi: Ministry of Laws, 1966 (5th ed.).

Report on the First General Elections in India, 1951-52, 2 vols., Delhi: Election Commission, 1955.

Report on the Second General Elections in India, 1957, 2 vols., Delhi: Election Commission, 1959.

Report on the Third General Elections in India, 1962, 2 vols., Delhi: Election Commission, 1962.

Report on the Fourth General Elections in India, 1967, Delhi: Election Commission, 1967.

Index